COMPUTERS AND EDUCATION

Computers and Education

Towards a Lifelong Learning Society

Edited by

Martín Llamas-Nistal
University of Vigo,
Vigo, Spain

Manuel J. Fernández-Iglesias
University of Vigo,
Vigo, Spain

and

Luis E. Anido-Rifon
University of Vigo,
Vigo, Spain

KLUWER ACADEMIC PUBLISHERS
DORDRECHT / BOSTON / LONDON

A C.I.P. Catalogue record for this book is available from the Library of Congress.

ISBN 1-4020-1599-2

Published by Kluwer Academic Publishers,
P.O. Box 17, 3300 AA Dordrecht, The Netherlands.

Sold and distributed in North, Central and South America
by Kluwer Academic Publishers,
101 Philip Drive, Norwell, MA 02061, U.S.A.

In all other countries, sold and distributed
by Kluwer Academic Publishers,
P.O. Box 322, 3300 AH Dordrecht, The Netherlands.

Printed on acid-free paper

Contents

IE 2002 Organisation

Programme Committee

Alvaro Galvis, Universidad de los Andes, Colombia.
Angel Velázquez, Universidad Rey Juan Carlos, Spain.
António José Mendes, Universidade de Coimbra, Portugal.
António Moreira, Universidade de Aveiro, Portugal.
Antonio Vaquero, Universidad Complutense de Madrid, Spain.
Carlos González, Instituto Tecnológico de Costa Rica, Costa Rica.
Carlos Delgado, Universidad Carlos III, Spain.
Cristina Gomes, Escola Superior de Educação de Viseu, Portugal.
Geraldo Ayala, Universidad de las Américas, Puebla, Mexico.
Gustavo Rossi, Universidad Nacional de La Plata, Argentina.
Isabel Fernández De Castro, Universidad del País Vasco, Spain.
Jaime Sanchez, Universidad de Chile, Chile.
José Raúl Pérez, ITESM, Mexico.
Juan Quemada, Universidad Politecnica de Madrid, Spain.
Lucila Santarosa, Universidad Federal de Rio Grande do Sul, Brazil.
Luis Maldonado, Universidad Pedagogica Nacional, Colombia.
Manuel Ortega, Universidad de Castilla-La Mancha, Spain.
Marisela Quintana, Universidad Nacional de Ingeniería, Nicaragua.
Martín Llamas, Universidad de Vigo, Spain.
Natalia Castanon, Universidad Metropolitana, Venezuela.
Paulo Cysneiros, Universidad de Pernambuco, Brasil.
Paulo Dias, Universidade do Minho, Portugal.
Pedro Hepp, Universidad de La Frontera, Chile.
Raul Wazlawick, Universidade Federal de Santa Catarina, Brasil.

M. Llamas-Nistal et al. (eds.), Computers and Education. Towards a Lifelong Learning Society, ix–xii.

Roberto Moriyón, Universidad Autónoma de Madrid, Spain.
Rosa Vicari, Universidad Federal de Rio Grande do Sul, Brasil.
Vitor Giraldo, Universidad Central de las Villas, Cuba.
Vitor Teodoro, Universidad Nova de Lisboa, Portugal.

Organizing Committee

Martín Llamas Nistal, Universidad de Vigo, Spain. (Co-President)
Manuel J. Fernández Iglesias, Universidad Vigo, Spain (Co-President)
Manuel Caeiro Rodríguez, Universidad de Vigo, Spain.
Manuel Ortega Cantero, Universidad de Castilla-La Mancha, Spain.
Judith Soledad Rodríguez Estévez, Universidad de Vigo, Spain.
Luis E. Anido Rifón, Universidad de Vigo, Spain.
José Bravo Rodríguez, Universidad de Castilla-La Mancha, Spain
José María Pousada Carballo, Universidad de Vigo- Spain.
María José Marcelino, Universidade de Coimbra, Portugal.
Juan Carlos Burguillo Rial, Universidad de Vigo, Spain.
Juan Manuel Santos Gago, Universidad de Vigo, Spain.

Collaborating Students

Eugenio Francisco Martínez Pacheco (Coordinator)
Paula Fernández Sanjuán (Coordinator)
Yolanda Rodríguez Márquez
Jesús González Barrajón
Raquel Santaolalla Bejarano
David Martínez Álvarez
David Serrano Amarelle
Francisco Javier Rodríquez del Campo
Ángela Mondragón Viñas
Enrique García Ramos
Pablo Sendín Raña

The GIST Team – Grupo de Ingeniería de Sistemas Telemáticos

http://www.gist.uvigo.es

Additional Referees

José Bravo
Miguel Redondo
Crescencio Bravo
Maria José Marcelino
Isabel Pereira
Arnaldo Santos
Luis R. Salgado
Ana Carla Amaro
Luis Francisco Pedro
Fernando M. Ramos
Isabel Cabrita
Pedro Cravo Pimenta
Bento Duarte Silva
Olga Mariño
Luz Adriana Osorio
Diego Ernesto Leal
Lileya Manrique
Patricia Escobar
María Mónica Carlier
Jorge Trench
Mara Carneiro
Marlise Geller
Liliana Passerino
Margarita Martínez Santamarta
Carlos Lázaro Carrascosa
Víctor Fresno
Francisco Nava
Tomás Pérez
Ana Arruarte Lasa
Maite Urretavizcaya
A. Díaz de Ilarraza
Jose A. Vadillo Zorita
Nerey Ortega
David Macías
Luis Bayardo
María Eugenia Bello
María A. Aguilar
Amelia Tovar
Ana Díaz
Ana Isabel Gonzalez
María E. Garassini
Elena Martínez.
Phillip Schalx
Raquel Crespo García
Luis Sánchez Fdez
Abelardo Pardo
Andrés Marín López
Mª C. Fdez Panadero
Vicente Luque
José J. García Rueda
Lauro Nakayama
Ricardo Silveira
Filipo Perotto
Louise Seixas
Viviane Possamai
Maria Aparecida Livi
Rosa M. Carro
Alvaro Ortigosa
A. Fdez-Valmayor
Antonio Navarro
Antonio Sarasa
Juan C. Burgillo Rial
Luis Anido Rifón
Manuel Fdez. Iglesias
Manuel Caeiro
Judith S. Rodríguez
Juan M. Santos Gago

Acknowledgments

We would like to thank the Regional Government of Galicia's *Secretaría Xeral de I+D* and *Dirección Xeral de Universidades*, and the Spanish Ministry of Science and Technology (Grant TIC2002-10338-E) for their financial contribution.

We would also like to thank the Universidade de Vigo's Vice-rectorate of Research and Caixanova for their unconditional support to the organization of IE 2002.

Our special thanks to Rose Marra, David H. Jonassen, Albert Sangrá and Ignacio Jara, invited speakers, for their high quality contributions to the success of the conference.

Other institutions and organizations also contributed to the success of IE2002. Among them, we would like to express our most sincere gratefulness to ADIE (Asociación para el Desarrollo de la Informática Educativa – Association for the Development of Informatics & Education), RIBIE (Red Iberoamericana de Informática Educativa – Latinamerican Network of Informatics & Education), the University of Castilla-La Mancha's School of Informatics, and the Vigo City Council.

And last, but not least, thanks to all the people that contributed to make IE2002 a most remarkable event: paper referees, scientific and organizing committee members, session chairs, and all the students that collaborated in the organization of IE2002.

Martín Llamas Nistal
Manuel J. Fernández Iglesias
Co-Presidents of the Organizing Committee IE 2002

M. Llamas-Nistal et al. (eds.), Computers and Education. Towards a Lifelong Learning Society, xiii–xiv.

Preface

This post-conference volume contains a selection of the best papers presented at IE 2002, which took place in Vigo, Spain in November, 2002. IE 2002 was a joint conference on Computers & Education for the Spanish speaking community: the RIBIE Latin-American Congress on Informatics & Education (6th edition), the International Symposium on Computers & Education (4th edition), and the International Workshop on Educational Software (7th edition). These events have become a reference for Latin-American research and development groups, institutions and final users. Additionally, this conference hosted the 1st Galecia Workshop, organized by the Group for Advanced Learning Environments using Communication and Information Aids, a European Union MINERVA/SOCRATES thematic network on Computers & Education.

This joint conference brought together international groups of researchers and practitioners to share experiences, making it possible to establish international relations to enable future collaborations in future initiatives at all levels. 130 papers were accepted for presentation from more than 300 submitted.

Computers and Education. Towards a Lifelong Learning Society includes 23 re-revised papers selected among the presented papers. The selection was made according to the initial ranking provided by the reviewers, and an additional on-conference ranking process provided by session chairs. Invited authors were requested to revise their accepted contributions to IE2002 to include on-conference and post-conference reviewers/session chairs remarks, and to provide an English version of their papers.

This volume collects the most relevant work from outstanding researchers in the field of Computers & Education in Latin countries at both

M. Llamas-Nistal et al. (eds.), Computers and Education. Towards a Lifelong Learning Society, xv–xvi.

sides of the Atlantic Ocean. It deals with the topics established for discussion at the conference, namely web-based courseware systems and tools; computer networks and education; distributed systems and e-learning; human-computer interaction; collaborative learning; e-learning; artificial intelligence, multimedia and hypermedia in educational software; design, development and evaluation of educational software; teachers' education and training for e-learning; and methodological approaches to information and communication technologies in education.

The primary audience of this book includes, but it is not limited to, researchers and practitioners in e-learning, computer-based education, educational software, distributed learning, lifelong learning, and open and distance learning; teaching staff at all educational levels; developers and users of educational software and computer-mediated educational tools; and institutions involved in the development and standardization of learning technologies.

Martín Llamas
Manuel J. Fernández
Luis Anido
Co-editors

Chapter 1

TOOLS FOR CREATION AND MANAGEMENT OF DIDACTIC RESOURCES IN EIE

Félix Buendía[°], Juan.C. Burguillo*, José. V. Benlloch[°], Daniel Rodriguez*, José M. Gómez[°], Juan J. Vidal*

°E.T.S. de Informática Aplicada. Dpto. de Informática de Sistemas y Computadores. Universidad Politécnica de Valencia. P.O. Box 22012, 46071 Valencia (SPAIN). E-mail: {jbenlloc,fbuendia}@disca.upv.es

**E.T.S.I. de Telecomunicación. Dpto. de Tecnologías de las Comunicaciones. Universidade de Vigo. Lagoas-Marcosend. 36200-VIGO (SPAIN). E-mail: jrial@det.uvigo.es*

Abstract: Nowadays, the creation and design of didactic resources and tools in the technological context is becoming a challenging task, because of the diversity and complexity of new standards, services and applications. Therefore, collaboration among different working groups from different institutions is needed. This collaboration requires to create conventions and to use standardised formats to allow interoperability and to simplify the tasks to be performed by such groups. In this paper we describe several tools oriented to the management of didactic resources, which have been obtained as a result of the cooperation between two groups, one from the University of Vigo, and another one from the Polytechnic University of Valencia. The first contribution of the paper describes the use of structures, denoted as "Packages" following IMS specifications. These packages are combined with metadata to characterise those resources using a standard format denoted by LOM and proposed by IEEE LSTC. As a complement to those packages, we use LMML (Learning Material Mark-up Language) documents and X-Quest questionnaires to define the contents linked to our courses. The second contribution describes the architecture and features of new tools (Xedu and X-Learn) designed for the creation, edition, management and visualisation of didactic resources. Our final aim is to use both contributions in the European Network THEIERE (Thematic Harmonisation in Electrical and Information Engineering in Europe) oriented to the harmonisation of resources and curricula in the EIE (Electronic and Information Engineering) field.

M. Llamas-Nistal et al. (eds.), Computers and Education. Towards a Lifelong Learning Society, 1–12.

Keywords: educational standards, interoperability, didactic resources

1. INTRODUCTION

Nowadays, the creation and design of didactic resources and tools in the technological context is becoming a challenging task, because of the diversity and complexity of new standards, services and applications. There is a need for notations that allow the specification of didactic resources in a standard format, simple to process and to achieve interoperability among scattered working groups.

In the European context, there are several projects as Ariadne 1 or GEM 2 working on these topics. The Ariadne project has developed a big amount of tools to generate different types of didactic resources as simulators, questionnaires, examples and systems for managing them (Knowledge Pool Systems). The GEM (Global Educational Multimedia) system works as a server for products, information and services related to e-learning. Both cases are big scale projects that use database technology due to the enormous amount of information exchanged.

The context described in this paper is rather different and is focused on the management of didactic resources in the EIE (Electronic and Information Engineering) field. Therefore, we have developed tools for a specific context using the notations proposed by IMS 3 or IEEE LSTC 4. Besides, we will introduce some flexible formats for describing several type of resources such as the X-Quest 5 questionnaires and the LMML (Learning Material Mark-up Language) 6 7. This feature provides a bigger flexibility and simplifies the management of specific contents in a reduced framework. The tools developed are the outcome of the cooperation between two working groups, one from the University of Vigo and the other one from the Polytechnic University of Valencia.

The rest of the paper is organised as follows. Section 2 describes an approach for the organisation of didactic resources and the Xedu environment for managing and accessing LMML contents and X-Quest questionnaires. Section 3 describes the X-Learn environment used to create, to manage and to display multimedia courses. Section 4 presents an example of application inside the THEIERE network. Finally, section 5 presents the conclusions and further works.

2. MANAGEMENT OF DIDACTIC RESOURCES

In this section, we introduce a framework to organise and to manage didactic resources based on the use of structures denoted as "Packages" following IMS specifications. We also use metadata to fully characterise the resources using the LOM standard proposed by IEEE LTSC. The main problem about these notations is their inherent difficulty to specify the resource contents. For this reason, and because we define our own type of resources, we also introduce new content formats as the LMML documents and the X-Quest questionnaires.

2.1 Resource Packages

The IMS Content Packaging is a standard that provides interoperability among objects included inside the packages. The most important concept of the IMS Content Packaging is the criterion to organise such resources under some type of scheme, e.g., a sequence or a hierarchy. For instance, we can insert in a "Content Package" all the contents of a topic and then, present those contents in a hierarchical tree to allow users the access to any section in any order, or using a predetermined sequence. Figure 1 shows an example of XML code included in a "package". Such package specifies several <item> elements inside a <organization> entity identified as "WEBTHEIERE". In this context, a hierarchical structure is selected for the <organization> entity. Every <item> is characterized by an identifier and a reference to a resource.

```
<manifest identifier="Manifiest1" version="1.0">
<metadata>
  <schema>IMS Content</schema>
  <schemaversion>1.0.0</schemaversion>
</metadata>
<organizations default="WEBTHEIERE">
  <organizationidentifier="WEBTHEIERE" structure="hierarchical">
     <item identifier="ITEM1" identifierref="RESOURCE1"/>
     <item identifier="ITEM2" identifierref="RESOURCE2">
        <item identifier="ITEM6" identifierref="RESOURCE6">
           <item identifier="ITEM8" identifierref="RESOURCE8">
            <item identifier="ITEM9" identifierref="RESOURCE9"/>
           </item> ...
```

Figure 1-1. Package example

```
<resources>
<resource identifier="RESOURCE2" type="webcontent"  href="RES2.xml">
  <metadata>
     <lom>
        <general>
      <lomtitle>
```

```
            <langstring xml:lang="en">Computers</langstring>
            <langstring xml:lang="es">Ordenadores</langstring>
        </lomtitle>
          </general>
      </lom>
    </metadata>
  </resource>...
```

Figure 1-2. Resource area of the package

Figure 2 shows part of the code that defines one of the resource items, previously specified. Each resource has a type to specify the format (e.g. *webcontent* used for publication in a Web environment) and a location (href stores the resource file). It also has a <metadata> item that describes information about the resource, in this case, related with a "Computer" topic. This metadata information is based on the Learning Object Model (LOM) that describes the resource following the IEEE LSTC standard. In this example, the description is limited to the title of the topic that can be specified in two different languages: English (en) and Spanish (es) using the LOM "LangString" attribute.

The use of standards is very important to achieve interoperability in the management of resources through tools designed by different manufacturers. Another problem is the resource management in order to edit or display them. In our case, we have developed an environment to select, edit and display the resources using the IMS notation. Figure 3 shows part of the environment that allows instructors accessing to any didactic resource from the information contained in the IMS Package.

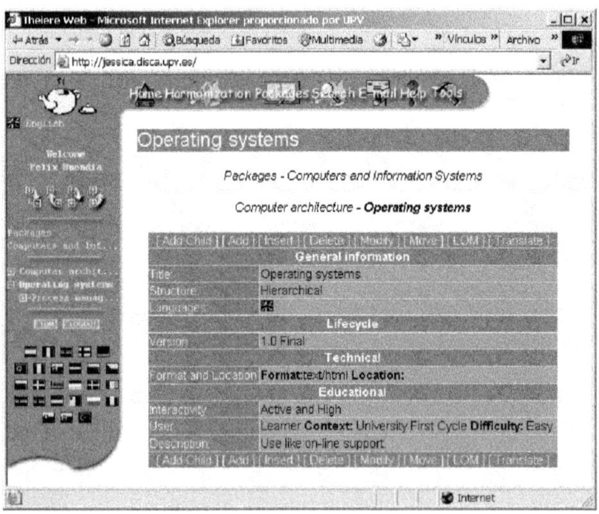

Figure 1-3. Tool for managing didactic resources

This environment organises the information about EIE resources in units called Packages. Each EIE Package has assigned its own IMS Content Package that structures the resource information and enables its edition control by the person in charge of the topic. Therefore, it is possible to delegate the maintenance of the different didactic resources in their respective sites, obtaining a more efficient management. Furthermore, the environment has been designed to consider different native languages. This option is selected using the flag icons on the left frame as shown on Figure 3. Figure 4 presents part of a course description about Electronics using the LOM specification. Since the information that describes the didactic resources is stored using the LOM notation, its contents can be searched by any particular feature (difficulty, interoperability level, language, target description, etc.).

```
<?xml version="1.0" encoding="UTF-8"?>
<!DOCTYPE lom SYSTEM "imsmd_rootv1p2.dtd">
<lom>
    <general>
        <identifier>_1</identifier>
        <title>
            <langstring xml:lang="es">El diodo</langstring>
            <langstring xml:lang="en">The diode</langstring>
        </title>
        <description>
            <langstring xml:lang="es">En este sección se explica el
funcionamiento de un diodo.</langstring>
            <langstring xml:lang="en">In this section, the diode working is
explained</langstring>
        </description>
        <keyword>
            <langstring xml:lang="es">diodo</langstring>
            <langstring xml:lang="en">diode</langstring>
        </keyword>
```

Figure 1-4. Example of LOM specification

2.2 Resource contents

As it has been described in the previous section, the IMS packages organize and store the resource information. Resources can have associated metadata information using the LOM notation to permit reusing and to simplify searching. After that, we will focus on the resource contents. In this sense, the IMS specification provides a questionnaire format denoted by QTI. This notation is very rich and powerful but it is also quite complex to be used. In our reduced framework we have chosen more flexible notations such as LMML documents or X-Quest questionnaires.

LMML (Learning Material Mark-up Language) is a language based on XML to represent different types of contents. For this reason, it uses a Document Type Definition (DTD) that can be particularized for different contexts: CS (Computer Science), OR (Operation Research), etc. The LMML contents are based in entities named <ContentModules> as definitions, examples and exercises. These entities can contain multimedia objects (images, animations, text, etc.) named <MediaObjects>.

We have developed the Xedu environment 8 that provides several tools to display LMML documents in different formats, e.g. HTML or PDF. It is also possible to use the LMML notation to specify forms to interact with the user. Figure 6 shows a form example that allows the learner to solve an exercise.

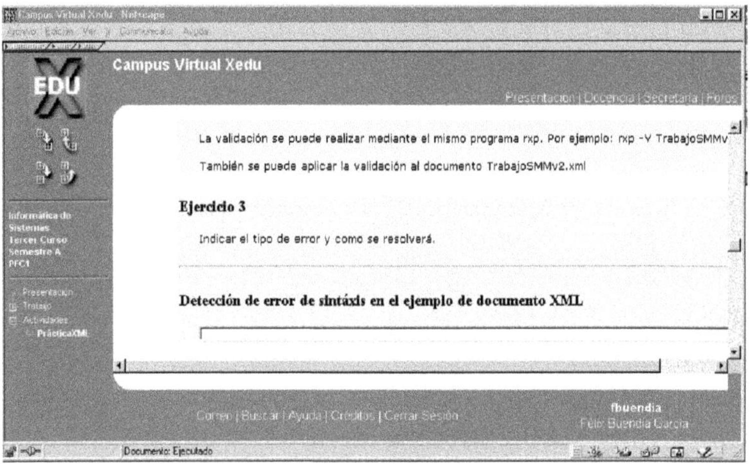

Figure 1-5. Example of form obtained from a LMML document

3. X-LEARN: CREATION, MANAGEMENT AND DISPLAY OF MULTIMEDIA COURSES

In this section, we introduce X-Learn, a learning environment that has been designed for the creation, management and display of multimedia courses. X-Learn system architecture implements a client/server model using the Java programming language to achieve platform independence. Teachers and students access X-Learn through any commercial browser. On the server side it is necessary to use a Web server with Java servlet support.

We consider a course as a unit in this context. The course components and their contents will be managed by the X-Learn tool.

3.1 Authoring Tool

As it was described in section 2, the course structure follows the "Package" model, in such a way that courses have a tree structure. This format allows the instructor to include any course into thematic units of higher level. It is possible to specify for any course learning paths depending on the chosen difficulty level. Every resource in a course is described with metadata using the LOM notation, which lets to reuse, classify and maintain the resources already created.

In the client side, the instructor accesses to the environment using a web browser following a login/password scheme. After authentication, an applet is loaded to edit and manage the course contents. The tree scheme allows instructors to include branches and leafs (the course contents) whenever it is needed. Before adding any content, the general course description must be filled: title, author, description, deadlines, dates, etc. This information is used later to generate the LOM description. It is also possible to specify access requirements for any resource (for instance, to visit other resources or to achieve a minimum mark in a questionnaire). Several learning paths can be defined at this stage, depending on the skill level of the student. After the resources have been included, their contents can be defined using a simple HTML editor for text and images. The contents can be stored in several formats as HTML or LMML.

On the server side, there is a Java servlet (see Figure 7) that is in charge of authentication. Moreover, this servlet sends to the client and stores in the XML database, the course structures and its contents. When the contents are saved, the servlet checks their correctness as XML documents to verify the integrity of the database. All the system information is stored in the database in XML format.

3.2 The Course Viewer

On the client side, students access to the environment using any commercial browser to select one among the set of enabled courses. After the authentication phase, an applet is loaded to show the course structure in a tree representation with all its resources and contents. The student can navigate freely through the course, except when he/she tries to view parts with access requirements. In this case, first it is checked that the student fulfils the specified requirements.

In the server side, a Java servlet manages all this process. Besides, this servlet supervises the student progress through the course and stores the traces generated by him. The student traces are composed by the resources already accessed to, as well as results of the questionnaires realised. Those traces are stored also in XML format. Moreover, the student traces provide additional information to the teacher. This information can be used later for tutoring, assessment and to check those parts of the course that need to be improved.

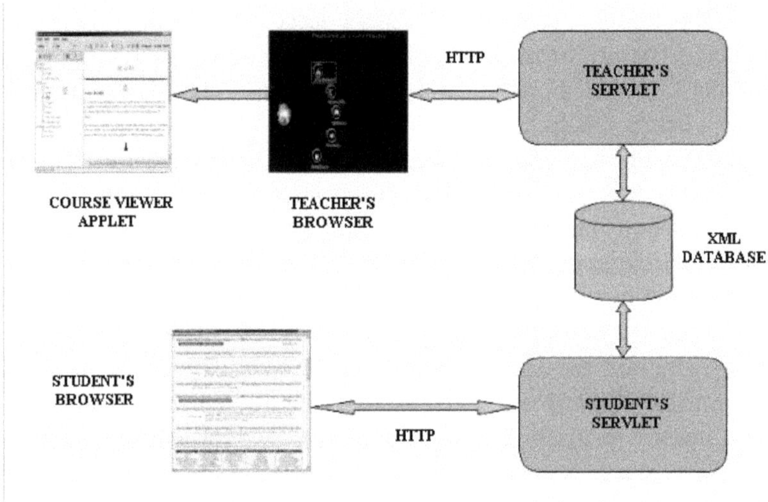

Figure 1-6. System architecture

3.3 Questionnaire Evaluation: X-Quest

Questionnaires are another category of didactic resources that was not considered in the original LMML specification. We have developed a questionnaire tool named X-Quest that provides the next features:

- Typical questionnaire classes: true/false, multiple choice, multiple answers, fill in blanks and any heterogeneous combination of the basic types.
- Questionnaires may include multimedia resources: text, images, audio, video, etc.
- It is possible to define several feedback messages for any evaluation.

Figure 8 shows the friendly and intuitive X-Quest interface. It is very simple to create basic questionnaires using X-Quest, but it also includes advanced options such as the possibility to divide the questions in groups, or to provide requirements for a group of questions, etc. All these features provide great flexibility in the evaluation process. Furthermore, the tool allows the instructor to follow the student progress using a statistical module where the information referred to previous questionnaires is presented.

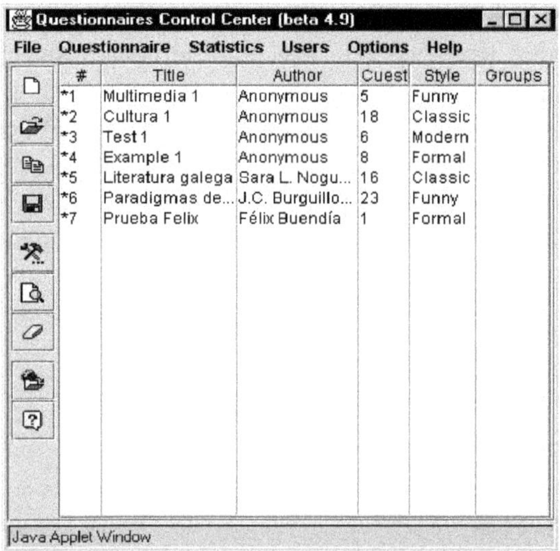

Figure 1-7. Main interface module of X-Quest

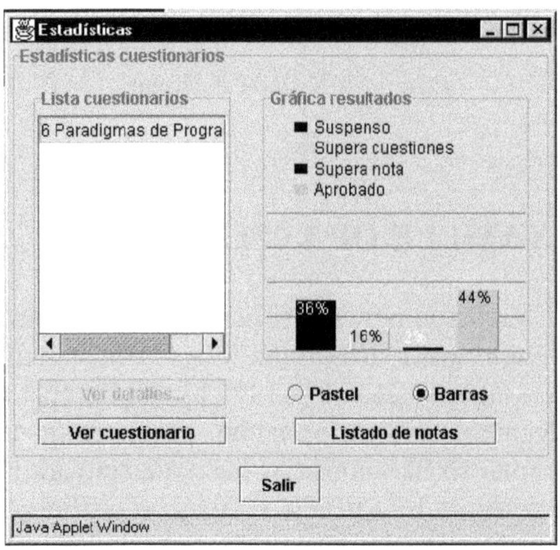

Figure 1-8. Statistical module of X-Quest

Figure 8 shows an example of the statistics interface. All the information managed by the X-Quest is stored in the XML database and it can be imported/exported in a format compliant with the IMS standard. The two modules that compose X-Quest appear in Figure 9. The first one is a graphical interface that manages the creation and edition of questionnaires. This model produces as output, an XML resource compliant with the IMS

QTI specification. The second module uses the XML properties to provide a presentation format that fits into any environment. Presentation examples can be, for instance, HTML pages displayed by a browser, a PDF file or any other format that can be automatically processed. When a student is evaluated, his/her answers to the questions are sent to the server where they are processed and stored, together with the generated traces. Afterwards, the results are sent back to the student and a feedback message appears if it was configured so.

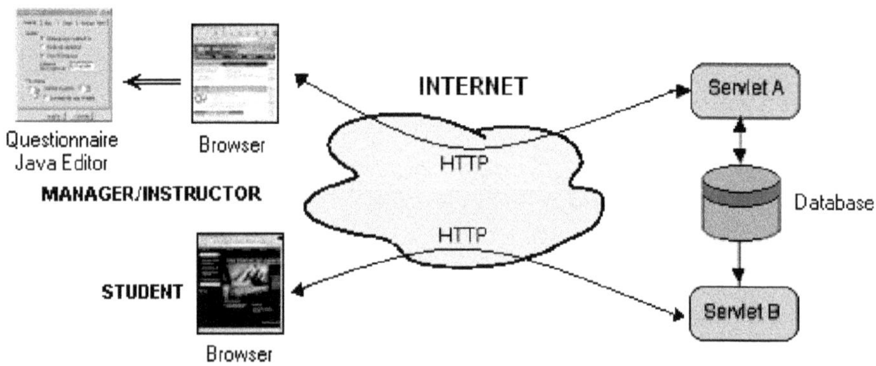

Figure 1-9. X-Quest architecture

4. AN EXAMPLE OF APPLICATION

The THEIERE thematic network (Thematic Harmonisation in Electrical and Information Engineering in Europe) 9 has been started with the aim of continuing the working line started in 1996 by the European Association for Education in Electrical and Information Engineering (E.A.E.E.I.E.) as promoter of the former INEIT-MUCON thematic network (1996-2000). One of the main objectives of EAEEIE is to achieve common curricula and to define a minimum knowledge basis for an engineer in Electronics / Informatics / Telecommunications in the European context. One advantage of the THEIERE framework is its big flexibility at the time to define courses from a repository of didactic resources.

For example, suppose that we want to define a course on electronics and that we already have an important pool of material for this discipline developed by several working groups and stored in different web sites. It is evident that the design of the course is a difficulty inherent to the process and independent from the authoring and management tools. Therefore, this difficulty has to be solved by a group of experts in the discipline using criteria as: the previous knowledge about the subject the student has, the duration of the course (in hours or credits), professional profiles, competencies achieved after finishing the course, pedagogic focus, etc.

Once the course has been designed, the fact that every didactic resource has a link to a LOM specification will simplify the searching of material to create the course. Think, for instance, in a basic course about electronics (e.g. for computer engineers), where three big blocks have been included: semiconductors (diode, bipolar transistor, field-effect transistor), digital circuit technologies and the operational amplifier. As they are elemental concepts, there can be a big amount of resources containing such topics. For every selected content, the authors can search resources with different degrees of difficulty. For instance, they could select basic resources for first year students or more advanced resources for students of second cycle, or even resources for postgraduate students.

As a function of the proposed pedagogical focus, the didactic resources that conform with the designed course will be different. For example, there can be much more theoretical modules or, on the other side, emphasize on contents related with practical applications. Typical already solved exercises can be included or it can be bounded to unsolved questions. In this second case, there can be exercises about circuit analysis with closed answers, or design exercises, with solutions contained in several ranges to be corrected by the teacher. On the other hand, a more ambitious practical approach could use interactive simulation tools or even, the access to remote laboratories, where the students can control real processes.

5. CONCLUSIONS

In this paper we have described several contributions that have been obtained from the collaboration between two working groups, one from the University of Vigo and the other from the Polytechnic University of Valencia, both in Spain.

The first contribution describes the use of structures denoted as "Packages" following IMS specifications, which combined with LOM metadata, can characterise the resources in EIE topics. In this context, several experiences conducted by teachers from the EIE field have been started to evaluate their utility. Additionally, we use LMML (Learning Material Mark-up Language) documents and X-Quest questionnaires to define the resource contents. The experience of applying these new formats is rather positive, especially those ones concerned with questionnaire evaluation. A remaining aspect is the need for tools to simplify the authoring of LMML documents.

The second contribution describes the architecture and functionality of X-Learn, an environment for creation, management and display of multimedia courses accessible via WWW. As future works in this environment, the authors consider the possibility to include new features in X-Learn as intelligent agents and adaptive schemes to personalise the learning contents and their presentation to any student.

The final aim of the work presented in this paper is to support the THEIERE thematic network, which is oriented to the harmonisation of didactic resources and curricula in the EIE field.

REFERENCES

1. ARIADNE. http://www.ariadne-eu.org
2. GEM. http://gem.jrc.it/
3. IMS Global Learning Consortium. http://www.imsproject.org/
4. IEEE LSTC. http://ltsc.ieee.org/
5. BURGUILLO, J.C; SANTOS, J.M.; RODRÍGUEZ, D.A.; BUENDÍA, F.; BENLLOCH, J.V. AND RODRÍGUEZ, J. A. Questionnaire-Authoring Tool to Support Computer Based Training through Distance Evaluation. EAEEIE' 01 Annual Conference on Education in Electrical and Information Engineering. Nancy. May 2001.
6. Learning Material Markup Language 1.1. http://daisy.fmi.uni-passau.de/pakmas/lmml/11/
7. BUENDÍA, F.; BENLLOCH, J.V; GOMEZ, J.M.; BURGUILLO, J.C. AND RODRÍGUEZ, D. Introducing LMML into the development of didactic resources on IEE. 12th Annual Conference of the EAEEIE, York (UK) 2002.
8. AGUSTÍ, M; BUENDÍA, F.; BENLLOCH, J.V. XEDU, an Implementation of an Open Learning Management System. ITHET 2002. Proceedings of the 3rd International Conference on Information Technology Based Higher Education and Training (ITHET 2002), UNESCO. Budapest, Hungary, 4-6 July 2002.
9. THEIERE, Thematic Harmonisation in Electrical and Information EngineeRing in Europe. http://www.eaeeie.org/theiere/

Chapter 2

TESTING AND EVALUATION OF AN ON-LINE COLLABORATIVE ENVIRONMENT TO SUPPORT THE REHABILITATION OF CHILDREN WITH TRISOMY 21

Almeida A.[1], Ramos F.[1], Cotrim L.[2], Ferreira T.[2]
[1]*Department of Communication and Arts, University of Aveiro;* [2]Portuguese Association of Trisomy 21 Carriers, Portugal

Abstract: This paper describes the test and evaluation of a multi-user distributed communication environment (ANCORA) designed to help the rehabilitation of children with Down's Syndrome. The main contribution of this environment is, more then just to correct individual or generic deficits, to promote the interaction between children providing tools enabling the establishment of the participation strategies most suited to each individual child according to his/her own specific characteristics. The platform also includes collaboration devices and data collection mechanisms to provide management information for system and effectiveness evaluation.

Key words: collaborative learning, multimedia in educational software, evaluation of educational software, e-learning, down's syndrome

1. INTRODUCTION

This paper describes the testing and evaluation of a distributed on-line environment to support rehabilitation, participation and inclusion of children with Trisomy 21 (ANCORA).

In the present context of fast global development and dissemination of communication technologies, it is important to study models of access, participation and social integration of all. It is therefore important to study the mechanisms that stimulate the transversal use of theses new tools, namely as they concern pedagogical proposals for specific audiences.

M. Llamas-Nistal et al. (eds.), Computers and Education. Towards a Lifelong Learning Society, 13–24.

The aim of this work is therefore to widen the scope of opportunities offered to persons who do not follow the typical trends of development, by proposing a rich learning environment, which is context driven and adapted to the specific needs of its users. Following this line of thinking, we stress the importance of contexts and situated cognition [1] in the processes of learning and rehabilitation and also explore the social dimension of rehabilitation. This approach is based on the assumption that interactions between subjects occur in shared situated environments, in social interfaces that act as mediation and communication: disability is, undoubtedly, more than a mental or motor dysfunctional phenomenon; it is a multidimensional dynamic that includes educational, behavioural and social aspects [2].

2. PARTICULARITIES OF THE TARGET AUDIENCE: TRISOMY 21

Considering that it is fundamental to make a detailed diagnosis and characterisation of the target audience [3], a survey of the main characteristics of this specific group of subjects was undertaken with a view to creating a conceptual model adapted to the specifics of Trisomy 21.

Trisomy 21 is caused by the presence of an extra copy of chromosome 21 and is considered the most frequent genetic cause of mental disability. Recent studies covered 99.7% of the DNA sequence of this chromosome which represents 1 to 1.5% of the human genome [4]. It is a chromosome abnormality with multiple implications and it is estimated that there are one million people in the world with Trisomy 21. This chromosome change can be accidental, circumstantial or hereditary, becoming the most common cause of psychomotor development delay (1/3 of cases).

As to cognitive impairment, these individuals depict a few problems at the level of language. This deficit results from auditory difficulties as well as from problems at the level of simultaneous and sequential processing, namely concerning comprehension of chronology, synthesis of successive events, sequential auditory memory and the construction of recently acquired knowledge [5]. Furthermore, children with Trisomy 21 exhibit visual performance that is superior to their auditory counterpart, requiring the exercise of their memory by means other than the auditory [5]. And although these limitations can be considered at the level of language as the ones responsible for the difficulties encountered in the social and symbolic spheres, studies by Sigman [6] demonstrate that Trisomic children, when compared with other groups with mental disability, are socially communicative and capable of imaginary play. It is within this context that Sigman underlines the importance of early intervention in the areas of communication and play, highlighting its benefits for the development of competencies in the social and language areas. On the other hand, children with Trisomy 21 like to learn by themselves through experience, not taking advantage of human mediation processes. Studies on this particularity show the benefit, in the case of Trisomy 21, of distal communication processes (mediated by tools and artefacts that can be freely manipulated) and not the ones typical of proximal communication (human mediation) [5]. This phenomenon seems also to be related to social avoidance manifestations during learning situations that have been observed in children with Trisomy 21 [5].

As to the play behaviour of these children, Curado, Neto and Kooij performed a study and observed a tendency towards exploration and manipulation of toys associated with difficulties in evolving towards the stages of imitation, combination and construction: "they spend most of the time in the situation of exploring and experimenting the materials, involving themselves longer in activities of holding, inspecting and manipulating, not evolving towards more elaborate stages of play." [7]. The authors also state that the deficits at the level of social and emotional communicative capabilities, together with the deficits at the level of fine psychomotor skills, affect the development of play activity. [7] It is therefore important to select strategies that promote constructive play activities that provide effective tools for the construction of adapted and familiar environments and contexts. As stated by Johnson, Welteroth and Corl, "the play quality of children with special needs is related to general and specific aspects of the environment of their education in infancy" [8].

The aspects described above serve, therefore, to strengthen and frame the development model for a distributed communication technological platform for the promotion of rehabilitation of children with Trisomy 21 that allows them to perform collaborative work, within a distal approach to minimise proximal contact during the moments of learning.

3. FOUNDATIONS AND CONCEPTUAL MODEL

ANCORA's conceptual model was developed from the particularities and needs of its target audience. The key concept is the proposal of a distributed collaboration environment capable of integrating the different user profiles within a global dynamic promoting transfer of knowledge and full social integration. The model explores, therefore, the potential of the use of narrative discourses as platforms for structuring and contextualising learning, allowing also for work on the afore mentioned deficit of chronological comprehension, typical of Trisomy 21. According to Schank

[9], narratives favour the contextualisation, generalisation and consolidation of knowledge as well as the processes of participation and integration: thus, ANCORA's conceptual model is based on narrative construction schemes, allowing children to participate in specific activities in terms of manipulation of entities (objects, actions and characters) and the construction of scenarios. This approach of modular and dynamic construction supports the construction of visual environments, narratives and activities that are always adapted and situated in terms of the interactions of the group of children on-line. On the other hand, the developed model explores the processes of cognitive construction and learning in open environments, stemming from the constructivist and post-constructivist paradigm that suggest that social development occurs in parallel with cognitive development, in a process in which dialogue and inter-relating assume a role of special importance in the construction of knowledge and in educational processes [10].

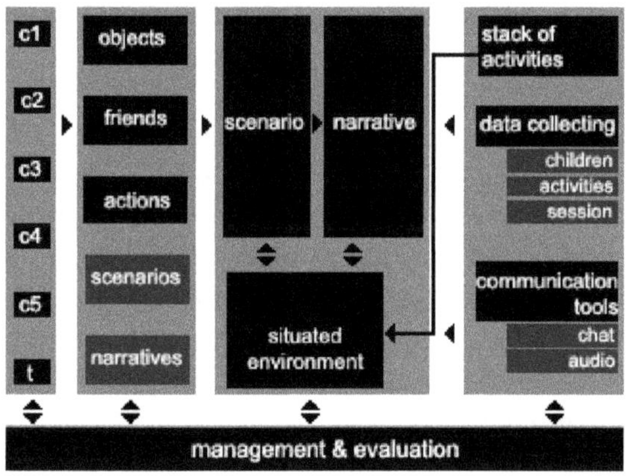

Figure 2-1. ANCORA's conceptual model

The model also derives from the formal theoretical assumptions of situated cognition, given that it stresses the importance of learning phenomena as situated processes, inserted in specific contexts and ecologically mediated by means of tools and artefacts [1]. The model is based, therefore, on schemes of "role-play" that allow the children to participate in the proposed tasks by the manipulation of entities, scenarios and narratives that support the shared and contextualised construction of the learning environment.

Figure 1 shows the model described: the different users (on-line children and therapist) share a synchronous visual environment of shared construction of scenarios. To interact and participate they have different archives of objects, actions and characters that they manipulate so as to build a scenario that shows, automatically, a narrative in which activities proposed by the therapist on-line are dynamically integrated. It also has two communication tools (voice and chat). There is also a layer of evaluation and monitoring of interactions that allow for the collection of relevant information for the therapist on-line.

4. PROTOTYPE

So as to test and validate the conceptual model described above, a prototype was developed based on a TCP/IP network distributed platform that allows access to geographically disperse users. Bearing in mind the main modules defined in the conceptual model, the prototype supports different functionalities:

- Interaction in graphic environment (simple and intuitive interface that allows for direct manipulation of entities as well as the integration of pictures, sounds and animations);
- Management and control of users (login and password validation and register of new users);
- Collaboration in a distributed environment (network collaboration tools for geographically disperse users);
- Control of communications (information transfer between users and with the server);
- Management of databases (access to data bases, both of users and entities, and dynamic evaluation of these);
- Sharing of a *white-board*/construction of scenarios (direct manipulation (*drag and drop*) of entities that constitute the data base (objects, characters, actions) and shared visualisation of these by the children and therapist on-line);
- Retrieval of the time sequence/narrative (possibility, according to the order in which the *drag and drop* of entities was performed, of retrieving a narrative, that is, a short text in which the sequence of events corresponds to those of the entities in the scenario; the narrative is constructed according to text *labels* that are associated to the entities that constitute the scenario and by resorting to pre-defined elements of textual linking that ensure the construction of a coherent text);
- Embedding of activities (possibility, according to the entities (present either in the scenario or in the narrative), of triggering rehabilitation activities that are contextualised in relation to the interactions performed by the group of children on-line; the prototype developed contains 12 different activities (such as selecting words, counting, making groups of 5, etc.) which enable the therapist on-line to collect data pertaining to the

performances of children, permitting in this way a dynamic evaluation of the children);

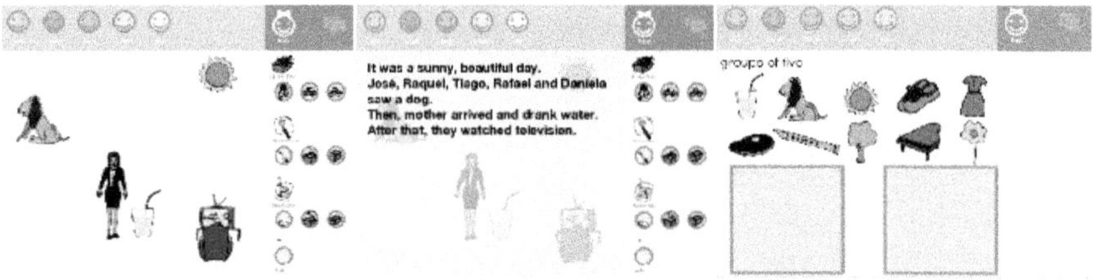

Figure 2-2. Scenario, narrative and activity

- Transmission of voice (possibility of real time transmission of voice so as to ensure synchronous communication between therapists and children on-line);
- Transmission of text (possibility of real time transmission of text, so as to ensure the sharing of opinions between the therapist on-line and the child's carer (adult) on-line).

5. EVALUATION

As a way of validating the model, an open evaluation of the prototype was undertaken so as to ensure the understanding of the complexity of natural environment phenomena and following a methodological process that privileged the analysis of behaviours according to the perspective of the subjects under investigation [11]. Therefore it was considered fundamental to collect the data in the field, in contact with the children, in their natural context, using comparative case study methodologies and field experimentation. Two groups of five children with Trisomy 21 from two institutions (APPT21 - Associação Portuguesa de Portadores de Trissomia 21, and Capuchinho - Centro de Apoio Psicológico de Espinho participated in these tests and field evaluations.

The evaluation of ANCORA, as an open and multi-disciplinary process, was structured according to two main moments: a first moment of formative evaluation and a second one, wider in scope, of final/global evaluation.

5.1 Formative evaluation

The formative evaluation had as its objective the gathering of information during the development of the prototype, as a way of seeking constant adaptation of implemented solutions to the particularities of the target audience. Therefore, diagnosis and characterisation of the test groups was performed to develop a careful and accurate characterisation of their profiles. Furthermore, during the development of the prototype, evaluations were performed as to usability and accessibility as well as different simulations and tests of the system with the goal of assessing its robustness [12] [13].

Therefore, besides a socio-economic characterisation of the families of the various children that composed the two groups and a characterisation of the institutions where the tests took place, a diagnosis of initial IT skills of the subjects in the two groups was performed. This diagnosis contemplated three main moments: initial characterisation of IT experience, an interaction test with different peripherals/input devices and an interface solutions test.

Initial characterisation of IT experience was performed by means of a questionnaire addressed to the parents and technicians who look after the children in the institutions. Data was collected under the following parameters: duration of experience, peripherals used, peripherals preferred, contexts of use, applications used, success/lack of success of the experience. Collected data showed that, contrary to Capuchinho, the majority of children from APPT21 had greater duration of IT experience, a wider familiarity with different peripherals, as well as with different contexts of use and applications, revealing a higher degree of success in the use of technologies. It is important to mention that the IT experience of the Capuchinho group was reported as non-systematic, taking place, on average, only once every three months. As to variety of peripherals in general, and between the mouse and the keyboard, the mouse was the one that the majority of children seem to prefer.

As to the tests of interaction with different peripherals/input devices, and with the aim of assessing competencies of interaction with different devices and trying to determine which peripheral is more adequate for the test groups, five sessions with four devices were performed: mouse, track-ball, touch-screen and keyboard. For this purpose, and in an application developed for the purpose, six interaction situations were created and proposed, corresponding to six functions taken as fundamental in the interaction with these devices: to place the hand/finger on the device, to move, to move to object, to select object, to drag object and to drag object to a limited area [14]. For the keyboard, the six interaction situations were: to insert letters, to insert numbers, to copy words, to copy numbers, to write the name and to do *backspace*.

For the evaluation of the interaction with the four devices, four categories of register were used that correspond to four behaviors of execution: without aid, with verbal aid, with physical aid, with incapacity of execution [14]. The results of these tests demonstrated that the majority of the children are capable of using the proposed paradigms of interaction since the value of the tasks executed without aid, in the various devices, reached 48% while the percentage of incapacity did not exceed 14%. As far as each of the tested devices is concerned, *touch-screen* was the one that was globally used with more effectiveness (80% of the tasks proposed without aid), followed by the mouse (48% without aid). *The Track-ball* presented the highest values of incapacity.

As to the evolution of the sessions, it can be concluded that the majority of the children showed progress at the level of learning so as to interact with the devices, the mouse being the device where this evolution was more significant. Only with the keyboard was such strong evolution not found since learning in the interaction with this device did not depend on the learning of the motor dexterity to interact, but on the abilities of character recognition. Thus, and despite *touch-screen* having presented indicators that it is the most efficient solution, we considered that the mouse would be the most balanced solution in the context of this work. In fact, the learning curve in the interaction with the mouse, allied with the results obtained in the execution of the majority of the functions, allowed us to decide that this would be the device to favor in this experiment (also in the sense of facilitating other interactions with other interactive multimedia applications which these subjects would encounter in the future). On the other hand, the mouse was also considered the most appropriate device since it already presented good results at a low cost, and this cost/benefit concern is also the transversal concern of this study in order to allow it to propose realistic solutions for the largest possible number of institutions and families. Nevertheless, and keeping in mind that some of the children needed some help in the work with the mouse, training with this device was recommended, namely as to the functions of selecting and dragging objects. By the same token, in the case of the keyboard, recommendations were made so as to train character recognition. In both cases, a small application was developed that included different screens, with different situations, aiming at training the functions mentioned.

Finally and in order to verify the adequacy of the interface solutions that were being developed, some of the graphic solutions that were being developed at the level of the conception of the interface were also tested. For this purpose, 4 situations were defined: *font size*, figure-background contrast, colors and graphics used for the entities (objects, actions and characters). These tests demonstrated that the majority of the children opted for the largest *font* and for the stronger figure-background contrast. The identification of the entities of the archives was equally performed with success, demonstrating the effectiveness of the interface schemes that were being implemented.

5.2 Final evaluation

The evaluation of the prototype was carried out in ten test sessions with the two groups of five children from APPT21 and CAPUCHINHO, in the presence of an accompanying adult and an observer per child and also a therapist on-line in each group.

The data was collected through the mechanisms of automatic data retrieval offered by the interface of the therapist on-line and through the observation and video recording of the sessions. The data retrieved from the system on the interface of the therapist on-line contemplate the number of children on-line, the number of children with effective participation, the created narratives, the children who had participated in the scenes that had retrieved narratives, the number of entities placed in the scene, the average time of execution of the activities, the successes and failures in the activities (per activity and child). Complementary data, inserted by the therapists on-line in previously defined open fields, were also collected. Apart from the visualization of these data, the therapist on-line could also print or save them.

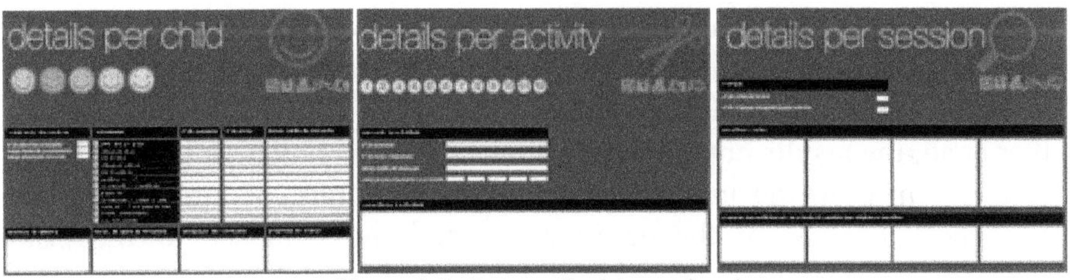

Figure 2-3. Automatic data retrieval

As to the observation of the interactions of the children on-line, and so as to make an evaluation of the interactions in a controlled and rigorous way, a form was used that included a systematization of the previously defined parameters to be evaluated. Five independent observers, with previous training for this effect, observed the ten test sessions, writing down and registering all the interactions of the children. This form ensured the register of nine main groups of data: execution of the tasks, motivation and satisfaction, distraction and fatigue, peripherals/*input devices*, system errors, interruptions, abandonment, voice communications, text communications (*chat*). A final open field was also included in which observers jotted down additional and complementary information in the registers.

As to the register of the execution of the tasks as well as of the use of the peripherals, the form offered four categories of register [14]: without help, with ease and total autonomy; without help, with some ease and autonomy; with verbal help; with physical help; with execution incapacity. As to the register of motivation and fatigue, four categories of register were defined: a lot, some, a few, none. As to the register of system errors, interruptions, abandonment, voice and text communications, a scale of occurrences (yes/no) was used, together with an open field for the description of the occurrence.

At the end of the ten sessions the children were interviewed in order to collect subjective data [14] and also to carry out an evaluation of the gains at the level of the sequential processing and chronological understanding (by means of presenting the scenes constructed during the sessions and requests for the retelling of the narrative in question). Final interviews with the technicians of the two institutions were also carried out (both those who acted as accompanying adults and the therapists on-line).

Overall, the results of these test sessions show, as to the execution of the tasks proposed, that the values of incapacity did not exceed 10% in both groups (although they were slightly higher for CAPUCHINHO). Greater autonomy occurred in APPT21 while in CAPUCHINHO help predominated. Considering the evolution in the execution of the tasks, from the first to the tenth, a very positive learning trend was observed, with incapacities and help decreasing and autonomy increasing.

As for motivation and fatigue, the data collected illustrate that, in the majority of the tasks, the children from both groups were globally very motivated (although slightly more in the CAPUCHINHO group). On the other hand, the results obtained also show a positive evolution on the part of the children as to the understanding of the dynamics of turn taking, the collaborative nature of the environment and the sequence of the tasks proposed.

In short, this moment of evaluation was of the utmost importance not only to provide the validation of the tested prototype, but also to identify details to be modified and improved, as well as to understand better the particularities of the target audience.

5.3 EVALUATION EXPERIENCE IN THE FIELD

Relatively to the experience of evaluation in the field, it is important to mention some relevant subjective data that were collected at the end of this study. At the interpersonal level, we could witness the establishment of relationships between pairs that shared the same difficulties and the same motivations to overcome them, both as they pertain to the joint construction of something, or even considering the sharing of successes and failures. Generally speaking, these interpersonal relationships between pairs of "equals" are typically not promoted either in APPT21 or in CAPUCHINHO, taking into account the normal structure of work carried out at these institutions. An increase of communicative initiatives and contributions through voice communication was also observed. In the area of cognitive abilities, and considering the development of the activities proposed, there is evidence of a gradual increase in the speed and success in the performances of the children. This performance success was also observed in the long-term memory summary evaluation.

The children who participated in this experiment confirmed our belief: the computer seems to be, in fact, a powerful alternative tool for the acquisition of conceptual information on the part of children carrying Trisomy 21.

6. FUTURE WORK

The study we present here has so far proven that communication technologies, like the Internet, can become privileged platforms of intervention and rehabilitation of children with special needs. On the other hand, one can also observe that technologically mediated learning environments are appropriate for work with children with Trisomy 21, providing not only the development of specific abilities but also their social interaction. This study also confirms the importance of multidisciplinary work for the development of solutions for citizens with special needs, in a process of mutual influence between the particularities of the target audience, formal conceptualization of the proposed model, integration of available technological solutions and adaptation of the models of graphical interface.

As a follow up of this work, we are currently developing a study around the conception of a site to support this community of shared interests in Trisomy 21: it is an on-line tool for the exchange of information, experiences and sharing of opinions that we believe will be able to act as a catalyst of the interdisciplinary and distributed processes of intervention and participation we referred to above.

ACKNOWLEDGEMENTS

The authors thank the financial support of the Calouste Gulbenkian Foundation that allowed for the tests and field evaluations to take place. A word of thanks also to all technicians, parents and children of APPT21 and CAPUCHINHO, and to the dedicated team who developed the prototype (Ricardo Marques, Ricardo Gonçalves and Álvaro Sousa). Finally, a special thank to António and Gillian Moreira for their help in translating this paper.

REFERENCES

1. Clancey, William J., Situated Cognition: On Human Knowledge and Computer Representations. Cambridge University Press, Cambridge: 1997.
2. ICIDH-2, International Classification of Functioning and Disability, Beta-2 Draft, Short Version. Geneve: World Health Organisation, 1999.
3. Redmond-Pyle D., Moore A., Graphical User Interface Design and Evaluation, a practical process. Prentice Hall: 1995.
4. Roger H. Reeves. Recounting a Genetic Story. Nature magazine, vol. 405, 18 May 2000.
5. Condeço T., Cotrim L., Palha M., Buckley S.. Ensino da leitura para o desenvolvimento da linguagem. Revista Integrar nº. 17, Setembro/Janeiro 1999, Secretariado Nacional para a Reabilitação das Pessoas com Deficiência.
6. Sigman M., Rusjin E., Continuity and Change in the Social Competence of Children with Autism, Down syndrome and Development Delays. Monographs of the Society for research in Child Development, Oxford: 1999.
7. Curado, M. A.; Neto, C.; Kooij, R. V. Comportamento Lúdico da Criança Portadora de Trissomia 21 in: NETO, C. (Ed.). Jogo e Desenvolvimento da Criança. Lisboa: Faculdade de Motricidade Humana, Universidade Técnica de Lisboa, 1997.
8. Johnson, J. E.; Welteroth, S.; Cori, S. Jogo Sociodramático, Avaliação na Intervenção Precoce in: NETO, C. (Ed.). Jogo e Desenvolvimento da Criança. Lisboa: Faculdade de Motricidade Humana, Universidade Técnica de Lisboa, 1997.
9. Schank, Roger C., Tell me a Story, Narrative and Intelligence, Northwestern University Press. Illinois: 1998.
10. Anastasia Tryphon, Jacques Vonèche (editors), Piaget – Vygotsky, The Social Genesis of Thought, Psychology Press, East Sussex, 1996.
11. Bodgan R., Bilken S., Investigação Qualitativa em Educação, uma introdução à teoria e aos métodos. Porto Editora, Porto:1994.
12. Nielsen, J. How to conduct a heurist evaluation.
13. http://www.useit.com/papers/heuristic/heuristic_evaluation.html
14. Checklist of Checkpoints for Web Content Accessibility Guidelines 1.0 http://www.w3.org/TR/WCAG10/full-checklist.html
15. Pereira, L. M., Serviços Multimédia para Pessoas com Deficiência ou Idosas. Faculdade de Motricidade Humana, Universidade Técnica de Lisboa, Lisboa: 1995.

Chapter 3

A STUDY OF INTERFACE FOR ROODA ENVIRONMENT

Cooperative Learning Web

Patricia Alejandra Behar, Juliano de Vargas Bittencourt, Silvia de Oliveira Kist, Aluisio Pinheiro
NUTED/FACED/UFRGS

Abstract: In this paper, a study developed for the construction of a new interface in the last version of ROODA will be presented. The investigation project ROODA – Cooperative Learning Web (in Spanish: Red Cooperativa de Aprendizaje) deals with interdisciplinary knowledge integrating Digital Technology with Education. It is an innovative way of creating virtual learning environments whose objective is the construction of an interface over which research and studies about the effectiveness of such technologies in undergraduate and graduate courses can be made. The aim is cognitive, socio-affective and professional development among students and teachers. Telematic resources and different ways of producing material through the web were used to promote communication/interaction/cooperation within the environment.

Key words: virtual learning, cooperative/collaborative learning, man-machine interaction, interface centered on learner.

1. INTRODUCTION

The investigation project **ROODA**[1] – **R**ede c**OO**perativa **D**e **A**prendizagem – (in Portuguese RODA means wheel, circle, the notion that all is connected with all, no departing or arrival point; in Spanish, Red Cooperativa de Aprendizaje) deals with interdisciplinary knowledge that integrates Digital Technology with Education as an innovative way to create distance learning platforms.

[1] Available in http://rooda.edu.ufrgs.br

M. Llamas-Nistal et al. (eds.), Computers and Education. Towards a Lifelong Learning Society, 25–36.

This article presents one part of the project which is a study to develop its interface in the last version of ROODA environment. As it is, the importance of the interface project in distance learning in general is discussed. Thus, ROODA will be presented, its philosophy and functions, the study developed about interfaces, the interface in use today, future work and, last, final considerations. It is important to emphasize that this project is part of the studies being developed at NUTED – Nucleus of Digital Technology applied to Education of the Education College (FACED), at Universidade Federal do Rio Grande do Sul, Porto Alegre, RS, Brasil.

2. THE ROODA ENVIRONMENT

ROODA is a virtual learning environment whose objective is to change the transmissive educational paradigm and the concepts of interaction, cooperation and communication are key issues in the process. For this matter, a virtual environment whose objective is to eliminate distance among participants has been developed, promoting virtual meetings and constituting places where sociocognitive interactions and conflicts are possible. This way, when two or more students work together, conflicts may occur which may cause imbalance to be followed by equilibrium again in an endless dialectical spiral [1]. The learner has synchronous and asynchronous tools which aim to promote cooperative work in the ROODA platform. Besides, he/she has some tools for personal reflections and areas where teachers make course materials available. These resources are grouped according to a paradigm centered on the learner, not on the course. In the first case, the user enters the environment and accesses information referring to courses he/she is enrolled in. In the second, there is a compartmentalization according to course where the student should be part of the virtual space of a class.

It is important to highlight that ROODA is software licensed upon GPL, based on the free software proposal. The development of the system as Free Software came up from its own philosophies which, somehow, resemble the ideas defended by some educacional notions.

Currently, ROODA's layout has been remodeled. After a study about the interface was carried out, that very interface was all redrawn. The new version aims to become more intuitive for the user, so that people with little experience in the use of computers can do it more naturally. The change was due to observation and experiences done with students in interaction in the environment, in different disciplines taught at the College of Education at the Federal University of Rio Grande do Sul, Porto Alegre, Brazil. The reports pointed to the difficulties to deal with the environment and, especially with the interface. The information has been collected since the first quarter of 2000 up to the present class period. In this paper, the data collected will not be detailed but it is important to mention, for the sake of information, that there was such procedure for the decision to redraw the object of this present study, its interface. ROODA is now being used at its third version, since its first implementation in January 2000 and it is used at this university and in other states of the country.

3. AN INTERFACE STUDY

Inicially ROODA was concerned with issues that regarded the implementation of tools that made interaction and cooperation possible in virtual environments. Moreover, it should be compatible with pedagogical methodologies that involve the students in active and participative learning with their colleagues and with the new role of the teacher. However, as practice in the environment was going on, questions came up about whether the previous prerrogatives were, in fact, enough to guarantee the effectiveness of distance learning. Through interaction of users (students and teachers) with the environment, a gap was felt between the intention of the group developing the project (project people and ROODA programmers) and the real use of the environment. In many occasions, it was observed that the user created "false ideas" about the way a determined tool worked and this prevented him/her from doing what he/she desired. Such fact excluded them from the group formed by their colleagues and generated among learners and/or teachers a feeling of powerlessness and/or incompetence over technological artifacts. From these experiences, it was realized that the interface bridging communication between men and computer was the critical issue in the ROODA environment. This interface failure jeopardized other factors in the environment such as pedagogical planning and interaction tools that had to be re-structured, as they will be presented in section 4.

According to Norman [3] the interface is a medium that is placed between user and tasks to be carried out. In this author's view, the interface of a software must be invisible, allowing the user to focus his attention solely on the work to be done. Thus, the studies made about interface led to the belief that fundamental concepts, conditions and images must be taken into consideration so the object of interaction can be easily understood. This is the idea that we call interface metaphor. The creation of interaction objects which generate an image that is presented to the user and with which he may interact is the important thing in an interface. These objects fill the screen of the interface and can be based on the metaphor mentioned above, through their representation, be it by buttons, windows, menus, switches, among others. Therefore, the idea is that the learner should not have to think about the environment itself, focusing on the object of the study, in this case, on the content of a specific subject matter. In other words, the interface of the environment cannot constitute a problem for the student/teacher, but it has to be a "transparent" resource for them. A good interface needs to have elements that simplify the realization of tasks so the learner does not have to learn new commands or navigation types [5]. It is also important that the icons that appear on the screen be known and intuitive to the great public, so the user may feel comfortable and may associate them in the real world as they are based on existing objects of daily life.

What led to the study of a new interface was the empirical analysis about issues that referred to aspects of the interface and the environment as a whole, carried out through interviews and observations in undergraduate and graduate courses.

As a result, we went on to the construction and study of an idea based on metaphors for the development of a new interface of ROODA. The objective, from then on, was to facilitate interaction and learning of students, so no training to use the environment should be necessary allowing them to work rapidly and efficiently.

When an interface is being built, it is also very important to define the guidelines for the graphic planning that take into account concerns related to students'visual perceptions of aesthetics. Apart from a light and harmonious design that does not overload the page , it is possible to create icons that represent several moments and pedagogical worries which are part of classes in the environment, as well as charts and illustrations. This way, a closer bond is formed with the student, aiming at the visual and thematic enrichment that facilitates interlocution of material with learners. Pedagogical mediation, then, goes beyond visual satisfaction to the appropriation and identification of the product with its interlocutor.

Ergonomy and design must be taken into account as the student will be for hours in front of the screen of a computer, seeing colours, shapes and information. Aesthetics is an attractive feature. The interface of an environment has to be well presented, with attractive resources that stimulate navigation, discoveries of new possibilities that should be intriguing and be in a language that calls the attention [4].

Norman [7] presents several examples of frustrations faced by people who cannot carry out simple, daily activities. It is possible to include the use of a computer as one of these activities and one that may cause strong emotional reactions for the subject. This kind of experience determines the relationship the person will develop with technological artifacts. Similarly, it is possible to say that distance learning interface platforms are key in determining how a student will relate to his/her course, the contents, the other subjects in the environment and how learning in such course will take place. We transcribe, henceforth, some experiences that illustrate our point.

In the second version of ROODA platform there was a bug in the software that exhibited the following message on the desktop: "No message for you". In reality, this system should exhibit the choices of the environment (forum, chat, diary) since the last time the user logged out of the system, but for lack of time in that moment, the exit was not well implemented and there was a wrong idea of what had taken place.

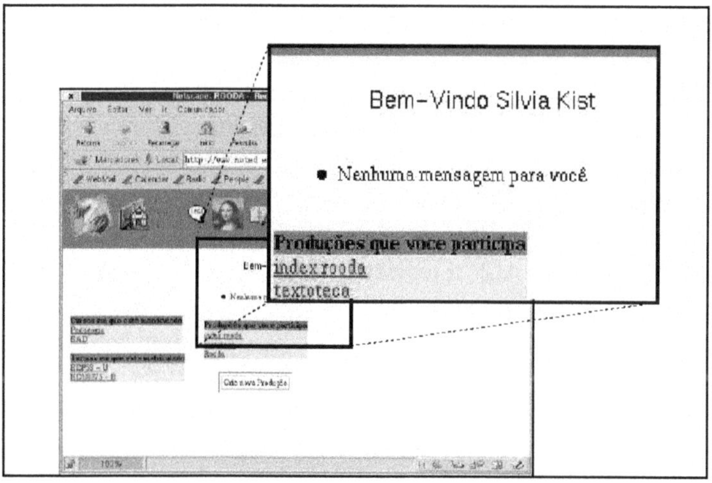

Figure 3- 1. Detail of existing bug on the desktop.

During the use of ROODA environment, several users reported their frustration because they had never received a message. In truth, they felt excluded from the group, as the following transcription shows:

"You see, as soon as I type my user and password, it opens saying there is no message for me. Why doesn't anybody send me a message? :- (message from Finder captured from the Data Base).

This feeling of insecurity caused the user to think he/she was being excluded from the group, without receiving any attention and totally isolated. To illustrate further, we will present some other examples that show this kind of sensation when facing the environment. In any case, it is important to emphasize that, gathering from users' manifestations, the interface could not be any longer seen as exempt as we used to think it was.

Clearly, the interface determines the way learners are going to interact within the system and, consequently, with their peers. Thus, it is impossible to underestimate the importance of building an interface especially for long distance learning platforms.

4. THE CURRENT INTERFACE

The interface was restructured and, as a consequence, the whole environment, from a need detected in the studies made about it. Interaction between learner and environment was being harmed to the point that some tools were being underused due to an interface that was little intuitive and not illustrative at all.

ROODA's third version was used in four disciplines with students from undergraduate and graduate courses from UFRGS. They raised issues of environment interface through notes in the forum and diary. These data checking served to ground the construction of a new interface, as it has already been said. Next, we go on to describe some functions that were changed as a result of the study about the interface.

4.1 Navigating in the environment

After observations and interviews with ROODA users, the idea to improve the visual and interactive part of it came up. Organizational aspects of the environment were the first to be tackled starting with the upper bar where communication tools were made available (forums, chat and e-mail). This is beneficial to the interface and prevents the user from getting lost within the environment, remaining visible throughout the navigation period.

The initial page of ROODA, called Webfolio, allows the learner to access productions, and contributions in the environment. Inside the Webfolio, there is a work area that facilitates the e-mail box checking, forums, messages, published pages, personal data, diary, classes and productions. Besides this, the user has information and access to what was carried out by the groups during his/her absence from the environment.

"S., don't know how to proceed because I have no access to the classes. Isn't it enough to enter ROODA's page to see the classes? I tried to talk to P. or SK but they are not there, what can I do?" (message from Finder). It is necessary to highlight that the names of the users were kept anonymous, for that reason, only initials were used.

Observing the message above, it is noticed that the student could not find the material of the classes inside the environment. That happened because, to access the page of the class, it was necessary, first, to enter the class, and later to choose the option of visualizing the page of this class. It was verified that it was a very simple action but it was a slightly long path that required several clicks and that the users got lost. Therefore, in the new version, a shortcut was included to allow users to go straight to the page.

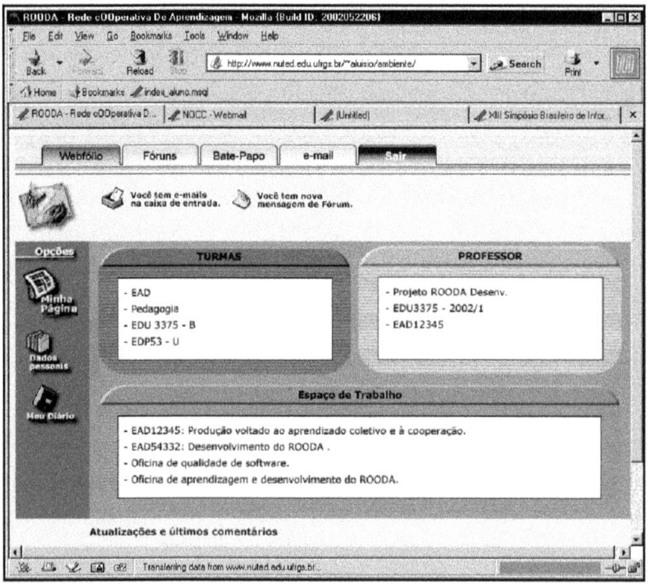

Figure 3- 2. ROODA's desktop with Webfolio.

4.2 Productions

It is a system that facilitates the cooperative work among the learners of a class. It allows students to share files (pages, html, text etc...) and make their work available so that it can be accessed by the work team, partners and the teacher. This allows teachers to follow up on the development of the work and intervene when they judge necessary. It also allows interested people to integrate the teams, besides contributing with comments and critics on the productions. The main difference in the current interface is the design and the direct presentation of messages of the team and of the system about production. The objective is to maintain the user and/or visitors updated on the modifications in their activities. The main problem found in the system was the lack of a mechanism where the learner could follow and negotiate the activities that his/her work group carries out in a shared production. Even though the tool has a diary of activities where the students should register the development of a production, they ended up articulating their project outside the environment, through email or telephone. This way the registration of the learning process through the environment was jeopardized, leaving, many times, for evaluation means, only the final published product.

"Hello SK., I'll do the work with D. and maybe Z. will come along. Yesterday, by phone we talked about the softwares we will analyze". (message from Finder). Therefore, the main alteration on the interface was to place the tool in a more visible place so as to highlight it. It is thought that cooperation among participants is favored if a summary of the last alterations made in the production and a space for negotiations is placed in the initial page allowing for an increase of interactions through the platform. Besides that, the development of a system that maintains a historical record of sent files favors the reconstruction of the pathway of learning.

4.3 Files Upload

In fact, the system of files upload does not constitute a tool by itself, but it is a function used in several other tools of the system to send files from the local machine where the learner works to the platform in the Internet. For example, the productions use the upload to send the pages worked by the group. Each learner's personal page is also sent using this system and, the sites of the disciplines are published in the same way.

When the upload system was built, the pattern followed was the same used by other sites that make spaces for page publications available like the YahooGeocites and the HP. In this model, the user visualizes the files that are in the server, and he/she can carry out operations on these as copying, pasting, erasing, moving, etc. When he/she wants to send an updated file, he has to choose "send files", select it and click on it.

However, having been built based in systems of publication of pages so largely used, ROODA's tool of upload presented serious interface problems. The users, mainly the beginners, had difficulties in understanding the need to send the files for the server and they presented errors coming from problems in the construction of the WEB pages, as referring an image like a local file.

"Today me and A. we tried to publish a page, but we didn't manage it. Teacher B. was the one who ended up publishing, we were attentive to learn, but, many times, I got lost with so much moving for publication. At the end, I think I understood but I need to do it alone to make sure I have learned how to publish a powerpoint presentation on Rooda". (message found in the diary). As it can be observed in the text described, the main problem is the users' incomprehension about how the upload system works. There is no clear guideline that tells the user how to initiate the process, let alone guidelines that will help him/her during the process. The current interface highlights the send button so as to make clear for the learner that that is the first step to be taken. Once started, an assistant guides the user throughout the task until it is finished.

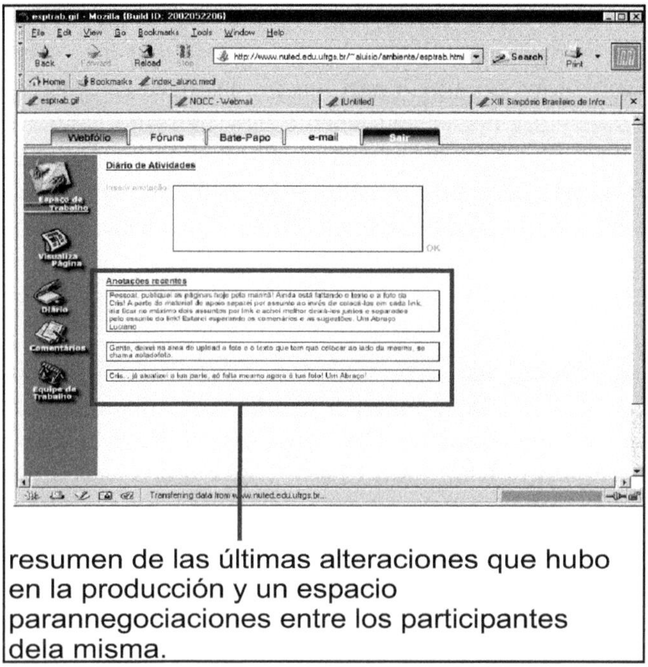

Figure 3- 3. Initial page of production.

4.4 Finder

It is a system of instantaneous messages that integrates all the connected learners to the environment as long as they are online. This tool allows classes to be given outside the classroom environment. The Finder is a window apart from the environment that lists all the users connected to ROODA and facilitates real time communication with each member (one-to-one). Statistics on the database of ROODA's environment shows that this tool was the most used one by the users. However, the interface also presented serious problems, some of which are presented below:

"I lost the last message. Repeat". (message of the Finder); " – Good evening, S.! Good work. - fala SK. Hi... good evening... but who has sent this message? ? ? :) - S. answers" (dialogue in the finder)

The messages presented were recorded in the database of the finder and they point to the error found in the pattern of sending and receiving messages - whenever the learner received a new message, a dialogue box would open warning him about the sender's name, and asking him if he wanted to read the message. In case the answer was affirmative, the message was exhibited. But some problems came up such as that of losing messages, as there were no registers of previous dialogues. One of the modifications carried out in the environment was that the conversations in the current version works like a chat where messages are posted in order of emission and they are not erased when a new message is received or sent. Another modification was the inclusion of status options (normal, invisible and busy). That was necessary to allow users to use the environment without being bothered and to allow them to alter their status when they desired.

4.5 "Bate-Papo"

ROODA's "bate-papo" appeared in the first version of the environment with the name of Chat, denomination that has accompanied it until the last remodeling of the environment. This was the first interface error in relation to this tool - the use of the term Chat. This word is very meaningful for people who use Internet, but it is not very representative for the unexperienced user. Therefore, a usual term in Portuguese has replaced it that refers to an informal conversation, the "bate-papo".

5. FUTURE ASSIGNMENTS

Besides the tools presented previously, ROODA's platform possesses others that were not approached in this paper as they were not the central focus of it, and because no significant alterations were made in its interface. A more detailed description of all the functionalities can be seen in [10] and [12]. It is necessary to highlight that an interface should not be restricted to the likes of its authors, because it is projected for its users. Therefore, if it has a low-quality project, or a design that does not take into account their mental representation, the environment will be sub-used in their functionalities or, it will simply stop being used. Within this perspective it is clear that the best path for the maturity of an interface is to test it with its users. Thus, the next step of this study and, consequently restructuring ROODA's interface is to carry out empiric tests, specifically interaction rehearsals [11], with the objective of validating the alterations described during this paper, and to detect which are the points that demand a deeper study.

6. FINAL CONSIDERATIONS

It is possible to conclude that the direct observations of the users with the environment were good to call the attention of the design and programming group of ROODA that the moment of making a restructuring in the interface had arrived. As a result, it was necessary to make a deep investigation on interfaces of distance learning education to adapt these ideas to the referred platform.

Therefore, through this work is highlighted the importance of the study of interfaces in platforms for distance learning that are, usually, dealt with in the aesthetic level only, ignoring important aspects such as the emotional impact that they cause in learners and, consequently in their learning. Through this study it was shown that the interface cannot be seen as an exempt object in the teaching and learning process, and that this should be consistent with the methodological design chosen for the environment.

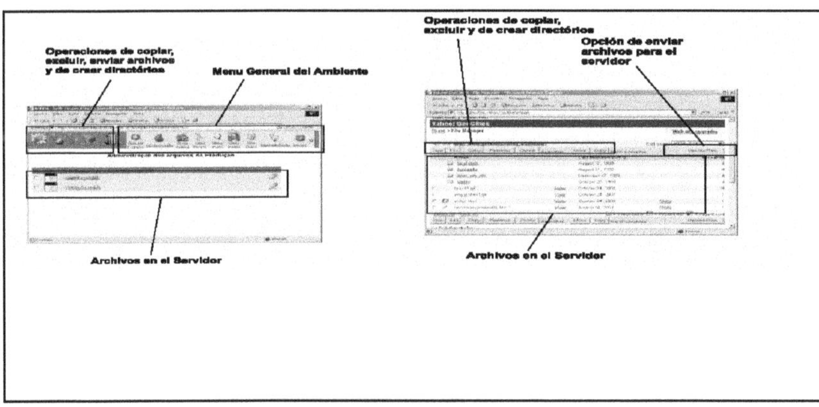

Figure 3-4. Comparison among the system of upload of ROODA (left) and of the YahooGeocities (right).

Therefore, the current interface is the result of an investigation carried out by ROODA's team on the data registered by the users in the environment. It can be gathered that the interface can hardly be faced as an icon and/or window group of a software or page; it has to be projected and analyzed in relation to the interaction between man and machine.

In sum, a new interface was developed in the third version of ROODA which encompasses a series of prerogatives described in this approach that were taken in consideration to make it more intuitive, friendlier and of easier access and navigation for its users.

Finally, it is important to highlight the investigation work, creation, implementation and application of an entire environment of distance learning in a series of courses of the university and their great acceptability on the part of students and professors.

REFERENCES

1. Jean Piaget, Psychology and Pedagogy: the answer of the great psychologist to teaching problems, Editora Forense, Rio de Janeiro, 1970.
2. Debora Laurino Maçada, Rede virtual de aprendizagem: interação em uma ecologia digital, Ph.D. thesis, Universidade Federal do Rio Grande do Sul - PGIE, Porto Alegre - RS - Brasil, 2001.
3. Donald A. Norman, The Art of Human-Computer Interface Design, chapter Why Interfaces don't work, pp. 209-219, Addison-Wesley Publisher, first edition, 1990.
4. Donald A. Norman, The Invisible Computer, MIT Press, first edition, August 1999.
5. Marcelo dos Santos, Educação e Arte no Mundo Digital, chapter Criar meu Website, UFMS/CEAD, 2000.
6. Robin Jeffries, James R. Miller, Cathleen Warton, and Kathy Uyeda, User interface evaluation in the real world: a comparison of four techniques, in Human factors in computing systems conference proceedings on Reaching through technology. 1991, pp. 119-124, ACM PRESS.
7. Donald A. Norman, The Design of Everyday Things, Currency/Doubleday, March 1990.
8. Marco Winkler, Avaliação de usabilidade de sites web, 2001, Minicurso ministrado non IHC'2001 – Workshop sobre Fatores Humanos em Sistems Computacionais - Florianópolis, SC.
9. Jakob Nielsen, Projetando Websites, Editora Campus, first edition, 8 2000.
10. Patricia Alejandra Behar, Silvia de Oliveira Kist, Juliano de Vargas Bittencourt, "A caminho de um ambiente para educação a distância - rooda rede cooperativa de aprendizagem, in Anais XII do Simpósio Brasileiro de Informática na Educação. 2001, pp. 89-95, Sociedade Brasileira de Computação.
11. Jeffrey Rubin, Handbook of Usability Testing: How to Plan, Design, and Conduct Effective Tests, Wiley & Sons, New York, first edition, 1994.
12. Patricia Alejandra Behar et al. Un estudio de interface para el ambiente ROODA – Rede cOOperativa De Aprendizagem, in Memórias del VI Congreso Iberoamericano de Informática Educativa, Vigo, Espanha, nov. 2002.

Chapter 4

ORGANIZING ACTIVITIES OF PROBLEM-BASED COLLABORATIVE LEARNING WITH THE DOMOSIM-TPC SYSTEM

M. A. Redondo, C. Bravo, J. Bravo, M. Ortega
Universidad de Castilla – La Mancha – Spain
{Miguel.Redondo,Crescencio.Bravo,Jose.Bravo,Manuel.Ortega}@ uclm.es

Abstract: The collaborative learning activities with telematic environments promote the development of shared knowledge among the participants. In these environments the technology can provide mechanisms to the access and management of the generated knowledge as well as the organization, structuring, and monitoring of the activities. In this paper we describe the design decisions adopted and the support included in the DomoSim-TPC system to organize and negotiate activities of collaborative learning of design techniques by problem solving.

Key words: CSCL, eLearning, design learning, Domotics

1. I. INTRODUCTION

Collaborative learning environments engage learners in the realization of cognitive and meta-cognitive activities promoting the development of shared knowledge by the members of a group. In these environments technology provides mechanisms for the use of hypermedia information, for remote access to the information, and for distance realization of activities, the organization and structuring of these activities, etc. The CSILE [1] and Notebook [2] systems are representative examples demonstrating the previous assertion.

When the subjects to learn are highly experimental, instructional models like the Problem Based Learning [3] or the Project Based Learning [4]

M. Llamas-Nistal et al. (eds.), Computers and Education. Towards a Lifelong Learning Society, 37–49.

reinforce the engagement among the students and the activity they carry out. Koschmann [5] proposed an approach relating the advantages of the Problem Based Learning and the use of technology to support learning processes. Other researchers like Jonnassen [6] think about identifying and modeling different types of problems in order to systematize the cognitive activity developed while a problem is solved. Later, they will try to determine the way in which the technology could support these activities.

For example, [7] remarks that one of the most important characteristics that technology should provide is to facilitate the structuring, representation, storage, and recovery of collaborative learning activities for their analysis and reuse.

In this paper we describe the support that has been included in the DomoSim-TPC system [8] to organize activities of collaborative learning for design techniques by problem solving. Mainly, we focus in presenting the decisions taken to organize work groups, to structure the learning activities, and to monitor the problem resolution that the students carry out. This is possible because the learning domain in which our system is applied allows us to exploit these characteristics.

The following section gives an overview of the Domosim-TPC system. Section 3 describes the model adopted to organize and manage the learning activities. Finally, we will draw some conclusions of this work.

2. THE DOMOSIM-TPC ENVIRONMENT

We base on the principles of Computer Supported Collaborative Learning (CSCL) [9] as an instructional paradigm to situate the social and technological aspects related with this investigation. We interpret the learning like a social and distributed process, where we consider in a special way the dialogue between the participants in a cooperative way when building the solution to a problem. With this position we have developed DomoSim-TPC: a distribute environment with support to distance learning of domotic design.

The term Domotics (Home Automation) is associated to the set of elements that, installed, interconnected and automatically controlled at home, release the user from the routine of intervening in everyday actions and, at the same time, they provide optimized control over comfort, energetic consumption, security and communications.

To carry out the learning activities the concept of workspace is used. A workspace is a virtual structured area containing resources and tools to solve tasks (in our case design problems).

In particular, in addition to the available tools in the workspaces, an activity of domotic design learning is defined by: the problem formulation properly structured, the constraints and possibilities to exchange information among the members of the workgroup and with the teachers, the definition and assignment of roles, the establishment of general constraints, and the help level defining the degree of difficulty of the problem and the level that the system offers to the students. Thus, the activities the students carry out are organized in three stages:

1. Planning a design strategy. In this stage the students, in an individual way, plan the steps to build a model satisfying the requirements specified in the problem formulation. This is, they define the solution and the procedure to achieve it. In this process the user's actions to create a plan are monitored and analyzed by the system using pattern-matching techniques. The plan created by the user is compared to an optimal plan of design for this problem. This optimal plan is built in an automatic way from a generic plan (see section 3.3). Using the result of this matching, the tool [10] adapts to the student's actions displaying messages in order to advise them to choose the most appropriate action in each moment.
2. Discussion, argumentation, and search of agreement in the characteristics of the design plans individually built. In this stage, two cognitive exercises are developed: designing and collaborating. The participants discuss with arguments about the models, their elements, and the steps to carry out in order to build them. From this process a common proposal is obtained reflecting the viewpoint of each participant.
3. Detailed design and simulation in group. Before verifying the validity of the proposed solution the learners should detail and to organize the attributes associated to the objects constituting the model built. This is carried out using a collaborative tool based on direct manipulation of domain objects [11]. Next, the students reflect about hypotheses and study cases contrasted by means of the simulation of the model. In this simulation all the participants can interact in real time contributing to the detection of operation mistakes and to discover inconsistencies in the model.

3. ORGANIZING ACTIVIES

We define the activities using the structural model proposed by Engeström [12] to model social activities with the Activity Theory. Analysing and studying this model with the final users that would have to organize and to plan the realization of activities, we observed the necessity of tools to define the components of an activity. Next, the foundations and details of these tools are described.

3.1 Users and work groups administration

The users of DomoSim-TPC are classified in two general categories: teachers and students. This classification requires of a first level of role administration in which access rights are defined in the context of the system. Other systems consider other categories of users [13], but in the domain in which our system is applied we have observed that only these two are necessary.

The environment includes a tool dedicated to the maintenance of the information relative to the users and their characteristics [14]. This maintenance can only be carried out by participants with access rights to it (generally teachers). The users are organized in work groups for the realization of the design activities. These groups are constituted by one or more students and they can be coordinated by one or more teachers (generally by only one).

3.2 Design problems

The learning activities consist in solving design problems. The objective of a design problem is to create situations in where the learners face the characteristic tasks of the domain to study, with the purpose of satisfying a set of requirements and necessities, and using some resources. Next, we highlight some elements that characterize the specification of a design problem in Domotics:

- Identification and summarized formulation of the problem.
- Characteristics of the house in which the problem is situated.
- Information of the environment or context in which the house is situated.
- Requirements and necessities of the services and the management areas to automate as well as their general characteristics.
- Tasks that are necessary to carry out and in which the problem can be structured. A mechanism or general strategy of resolution will be associated to each of these tasks.
- Hypothesis and study cases to verify the built model. This verification will be carried out by simulating the model, once its properties have been defined correctly.

DomoSim-TPC offers the functionality needed for experts and teachers to define new problems and study cases. These problems are stored in an organizational memory maintained by the system. Thus, the reuse of information in different situations and contexts is pursued. In the same way, we make the responsibility of the problems definition and of their educational objectives fall on the professionals in the teaching, with the aim of fostering a realistic process and effective learning.

We have developed several utilities in an iterative process in which we have actively participated with final users. This way, a flexible method has been reached for the problem specification by means of the definition of their elements.

The method structures the solving of the problems in tasks. For each task, the experts express a general strategy of resolution that the system registers and uses to guide the learners in their work.

We highlight the possibility to define different help levels that the system will be able to offer to the particular users as well as to the group during the resolution of the tasks associated to the activity. With this possibility we seek to offer enough functionality for the teachers to use scaffolding techniques [15, 16]. Thus, the resolution of problems with different levels of reinforcement help can be considered, depending on the previous knowledge of the participants. This is achieved by means of a process of successive integration of knowledge. For example, at initial stages simple problems with high help level can be proposed. However, when the learners demonstrate an intermediate skill, more complex problems with low help can be proposed.

In particular, three categories or levels have been considered: High, Medium, and Low. Associated to each one of these levels the system will make verifications contrasting the model and strategy proposed by the student with the experts' knowledge for the task being solved. We name this knowledge *General Plan of Design* and *Optimal Plan of Design* (these concepts are explained in section 3.3).

Next, we describe the developments carried out with the aim of maintaining the organizational memory and their general structures of resolution.

3.2.1 Problem identification

The problem identification into the system is carried out by means of an alphanumeric code and some data constituting general information of this problem. Next, we summarize this information:

- Complexity level. This information is obtained from the experts and teachers and is used to classify the problems in three categories: high, medium, and low. Also, this information can be used to articulate scaffolding mechanisms.

- Problem formulation. A summary outlining the objective to achieve with this problem.
- Plan of the house. As a representation of the scenario in which the specifications of the problem are required.
- Design in the solution. This data is used to indicate if the problem is experimental and is outlined so that the students can carry out free-practice. That is, to enable the participants to design and to make simulations in order to observe the behaviour of the elements, but they are not forced to propose a solution satisfying the problem specifications.
- Observations. An additional field allows writing down another type of reviews.

3.2.2 House characteristics

In this section, characteristics relative to the house are included. Their own plan and those data describing physical aspects are taken into consideration. These data have a special effect in the problem to be solved.

The definition and administration of plans is carried out by means of authoring tools. Although the plan is defined as a 2D-object, it includes information relative to the height of each room. This way, calculations relative to the house considered as a volume can be carried out. We also consider the coefficient of loss of temperature for the construction materials used. This coefficient is used to simulate the behavior and evolution of the temperature.

Other information is considered in order to describe values of power, distribution of the energy in load lines, calories of the radiators, intensity of the points of light, etc. [14]. The information relative to each parameter of the house can be defined by different non-excluding ways:

- Undefined. It should be defined in the solution to the problem.
- Defined. The teacher set default values.
- Modifiable. The users can modify the values while solving the problem.
- Non-modifiable. The users should only work with the values proposed by the teacher, considering them part of the problem specification.

3.2.3 Context in which the house is situated

This category includes the characteristics relative to the environmental setting where the house is situated. We can mention some examples of parameters: evolution of the external temperature, evolution of the illumination during the day, incidence of the temperature inside the house, season of the year to optimize the design, etc.

3.2.4 Parameters, constraints and necessities of the problem

The design objectives of the model are defined by means of parameters that we organize in three categories: (1) Thermal comfort, (2) Luminosity comfort, and (3) Security.

The parameters belonging to these categories can have default values, which can be considered as a starting point when a simulation process of the model is carried out. We have developed an authoring tool to specify the parameters, constraints, and necessities [14].

To reach the objectives some constraints can be set. For example, for the thermal comfort, we have considered the number of radiators and the number of conditioned air equipments.

The necessities to satisfy in order to solve the problem are defined by means of the specification of requirements which refers to the obligatory condition of the elements or particular operators.

3.2.5 Simulation cases and work hypotheses

With the aim of focusing the simulation, each model built by the students is associated with different cases of simulation (study cases) and work hypothesis. A simulation case is a situation in which the behaviour of the model should be verified. In the developed tool it is possible to define up to three different simulation cases [14]. In the simulation process the users can reflect and discuss about the behaviour of the designed model. The mechanism of hypotheses definition helps to focus the topic of the discussion, since the simulation will be guided to decide if the model verifies what is expressed by a hypothesis. When the problem is defined, the teacher can fix up to two example hypotheses to guide the discussion between the students.

3.3 Structuring in tasks and general strategies of resolution

Considering the previously described data, the resolution of a problem is structured in diverse tasks or sections. In a first position we could consider that each task could contain the actions to solve the necessities outlined for a management area. However, the tasks that would be generated would be of a great span and their size would complicate the discussion around the actions that characterize them. This is emphasized in houses composed by a great number of rooms. We think it is a better approach to consider the solving of the automation of the services of each administration area on each defined section (room) as individual tasks. We have adopted this position. In each task we observe enough generality to abstract some rules or guides to follow for its resolution. For example, the automation of the services relative to the thermal comfort maintains a general outline for all the bedrooms, although it will be directly dependent of the constraints, necessities, and specific context where the problem is located.

We use a double entrance table to determine the identification of the design strategy or *General Plan of Design* (GPD) associated to each couple formed by a room and a management area. This plan includes information obtained from experts in the teaching of Domotics and it is made up of aspects belonging to the following categories:

- Elements. Referred to the operators that are part of the model or of the solution to the problem. The presence of these operators in the solution can be considered obligatory, recommended, or acceptable. Next, we define these terms:
  - An element is obligatory in a solution proposal if it is indispensable to solve the problem.
  - An element is recommended in a solution proposal if it is not obligatory but it improves the characteristics of the model built to solve the problem.
  - An element is acceptable in a solution proposal if it is not obligatory but it is possible, although it will not improve the characteristics of the outlined model.
- Relationships. Referred to the defined connections (links) among operators. The presence of each connection can be obligatory, recommend, or acceptable. To define these terms the previously mentioned definitions are applied.
- Constraints. They provide information relative to the order of the sequence of actions constituting the strategy to follow in order to build a good solution. That is, they establish an order among the actions to define the elements and the relationships that should be part of the model.
- Alterations. They define the influence that the parameters, constraints, and specific necessities of the problem have in the resolution strategy. These are classified in:
  - Modifications of the obligatory condition of one or several elements.
  - Modifications of the obligatory condition of one or several relationships.
  - Modification of one or several constraints.

We can formalize the information that is part of a General Plan of Design as it is indicated next. We define D as the set representing the domain of Domotics. A is the set of all the possible design actions in D. T is the task. It consists in building the domotical design model to automate the services of a management area in a room. We define $M_T \subset A$ as the set of the design actions constituting the model proposed to solve the task *T*.

Op is the set of all domotical operators and *Tip* = {*obligatory, recommend, acceptable*}. We define the *General Plan of Design* for a task *T* of a design problem (PGD_T) as $PGD_T = \{E_T, R_T, C_T, N_T\}$, where:

- E_T is the set of all elements that are part of PGD_T. The elements of E_T are couples (e, t), $e \in Op$ and $t \in Tip$.
- R_T is the set of all relationships that are part of PGD_T. The elements of E_T are couples (r, t), r is a relation among $e_1, e_2 \in Op$ and $t \in Tip$.
- C_T is the set of all constraints that are part of PGD_T. The elements of C_T are couples (c, a), $c \in (E_T \cup R_T)$ and $a \in A$,
- N_T is the set of all the possible and valid alterations registered in PGD_T.

We define the Optimal Plan of Design for a task (POD_T) of a problem using the parameters, requirements, and necessities that have registered as modifications in N_T. So that $POD_T = PGD_T \cup N_T$.

With the previously defined concepts, we can consider some operations like obtaining the set of the elements (operators) that make the minimum model that solves a task of a problem. The result of this operation is a set that we name ME_{min} and is defined as follows:

$$ME_{min} = e \in E_T \,/\, \exists (e,t) \in POD_T \wedge obligatorio(e)$$

The relationships that are part of the minimum model that solves a task are named MR_{min} and they are defined as follows:

$$MR_{\min} = r \in R_T \,/\, \exists (r,t) \in POD_T \wedge obligatorio(r)$$

An action $a \in A$ can be carried out if the design actions planned in a model M_T satisfies:

$$\forall (e,a) \in C_T, e \in E_{T,} a \in A \Rightarrow e \in M_T$$

Considering the previous formalization we can build an algorithm for the generation of the tasks that structure the resolution of a problem and for the inference of the Optimal Plan of Design associated to each task. The Optimal Plan of Design always is obtained from the General Plan of Design. The algorithm is shown in figure 1.

```
FOR each room R of the plan of the house DO
    FOR each management area A to study DO
        Create the task t(R,A) consistent of building the appropriate
        domotical design to guarantee the services relative to the
        area A in the room R
        Find the PGD_t(R,A) for the room H and the area A
        Calculate POD_t(R,A) considering PGD_t(R,A) and the parameters,
        necessities, and constraints defined in the problem.
        Associate POD_t(R,A) to the task t(R,A)
    END_FOR
END_FOR
```

Figure 4-1. Algorithm for the generation of tasks in which the resolution of a design problem is structured and obtaining the Optimal Plan of Design associated to each task.

3.4 Collaboration

Considering the reference model that we use, we need mechanisms to establish norms relative to the work in group. These norms make reference to the communication alternatives, to the criteria of work distribution, and to the way this becomes effective in order to verify the properties of the built models. Next, we describe the mechanisms and tools to establish these norms.

3.4.1 Communication constraints for the discussion

Among the norms that are defined for the participants in an activity and the involved community, we highlight those norms affecting the structures of conversation available during the negotiation process. In this process the design proposals that the learners outline to solve each of the tasks in which a problem is structured are justified and argued. In the process different types of contributions appear. The user can interact with contributions in different ways: replying, asking, etc. Contributions have been classified according to an object-action model. The types of contributions constitute the objects of the object-action model while the types of actions are considered as actions of the model. This model is applied in order to fix and restrict the action type (answer) that can be sent starting from an object (contribution). For example, we can restrict the communication possibilities determining that the answer type to a comment can only be an action generating an explanation. To represent these constraints we build a double entrance table in which we fix the types of objects and actions in each dimension. Each cell, $T(c, a)$, of this table contains a logical value indicating if an a-type answer can be sent to a c-type contribution. Thus, the way of discussing and arguing the individual proposal will depend on the configuration of this table. From the view point of the teachers, this functionality offers important possibilities to define the cognitive characteristics of the tasks to carry out. That is to say, besides varying the problem type it allows to settle down how the communication among participants should be to solve the problem.

3.4.2 Assignment and work distribution

Two possibilities have been considered to distribute the work among the members of a group: (1) Assignment of responsible or specialists in the realization of each task and (2) definition of roles enabling the realization of some tasks and restricting others.

The assignment of the responsibility to realize a task by a member of the group has an effect on this user. The user will have assigned the function of carrying out the design proposals that solve the problem outlined. The rest of the participants will only be able to request information, to send critical or to manifest their agreement or disagreement with reference to the positions of the responsible user. The constraints with respect to the communication established by the responsibilities assignment prevail over those defined in the previously described table.

From the view point of the analysis of the behavior of the work groups during the realization of different learning activities, it has been considered interesting to have enough flexibility to refine the general roles assigned to the users. Initially we have defined three types of roles: *Observer*, *Designer*, and *Critic*. Each role has some associate constraints about their behavior in the group. For example, an *Observer* will be able to see the process carried out by the rest and will not be able to outline proposals neither to send critics of the work of the other ones. A *Designer* will outline the initial designs and to comment them as answer to the critics of the rest. A *Critic* will request explanations about the work of the others and must determine possible errors in this work.

The roles supported by the system and the functions attributed to them are completely flexible to adapt to other situations and experiments with different objectives. As in the previous case, the constraints with respect to the communication established by the definition of roles prevail over those defined in the table described in the previous section, and also about the constraints generated by the responsibilities and specialists definition.

4. CONCLUSIONS

In this work we have used the possibilities offered by the technology to structure, represent, store, and recover activities of collaborative learning.

Thus, we have designed the organization of experiences for design learning in group. This organization is based on the model derived from the Activity Theory. Considering the necessities imposed by the domain in which the experiences are applied, we have developed a conceptual model. This model defines the relationships between the particular elements used for the representation of learning activities in DomoSim-TPC. The users are organized in groups made up of students and teachers. We use an organizational memory of design problems outlined by professionals in the teaching of the domain and automatically managed by the system. The experience of these professionals has been captured to determine the typical and general strategies to follow in order to solve these problems. Organizing and structuring the problems in different categories, we have been able to associate a strategy of general resolution for each category. We have called this strategy *General Plan of Design.* The general plans are modified depending on the objectives and specific requirements defined for a particular problem. These modifications generate an *Optimal Plan of Design* for each task in which a design problem can be structured. This allows us to propose the search of a solution to a problem and their construction mechanism as objective of the learning activities.

The activities relate work groups and the problems organized in tasks that should be carried out by such groups. The result of the realization of these tasks includes structured information which could facilitate the realization of an exhaustive analysis of the activity, in terms of the obtained solution, the building process followed, and its relationships. Even, this analysis could be carried out in a systematic way if the appropriate methods are outlined. This is an aspect in which we will study in deep in future works.

Currently, the system is being used experimentally in some schools of Technical Training (Professional Formation) of the province of Ciudad Real (Spain). In its organizational memory information of over 70 activities is stored, each one of them with different characteristics in its specification as well as in the norms established for their resolution.

ACKNOWLEDGEMENTS

This work was partially supported by the Junta de Comunidades de Castilla – La Mancha and the Ministerio de Ciencia y Tecnología in the projects PBI-02-026 and TIC2002-01387.

REFERENCES

1. Scardamalia, M., Bereiter, C., "Computer support for Knowledge-Building Communities". *Journal of the Learning Sciences*, 3 (3), pp. 265-283, 1994.
2. Edelson, D.C., Pea, R.D., Gómez, L.M.., "The collaboratory Notebook". *Communication of the ACM* 39 (4), pp. 32-33, 1996.
3. Barrows, H.S. , Tamblyn, (Eds.), *Problem-based learning: An approach to medical education.* New York: Srpinger, 1980.
4. Blumenfeld, P., Soloway, E., Marx, R., Krajcik, J., Guzdial, M., Palincsar, A., "Motivating project-based learning: Sustaining the doing, supporting the learning", *Educational Psychologist*, 26, pp. 369-398, 1980.
5. Koschmann, T., Kelson, A.C., Feltovich, P.J., Barrows, H.S., "Computer-Supported Problem-Based Learning: A principled approach to the use of computers in collaborative learning", in Koschmann (Ed.), *CSCL: Theory and Practice of an Emerging Paradigm*, NJ: Lawrence Erlbaum, Assoc. pp. 83-124, 1996.
6. Jonassen, D.H., "Toward a Meta-Theory of Problem Solving". *Educational Technology: Research & Development*, 48 (4), pp. 63-85, 2000.
7. Verdejo, M.F., Barros, B., "Creating an organisational learning memory for collaborative experiences in distance education", *Proc. of XV IFIP World Compueter Congress*, pp. 1035-1045, 1998.
8. Bravo, C., Redondo, M.A., Bravo, J., Ortega, M., "DOMOSIM-COL: A Simulation Collaborative Environment for the Learning of Domotic Design", *Reviewed paper in Inroads, The SIGCSE Bulletin of ACM*, 32 (2), pp.65-67, (2000).
9. Koschmann, T., "Paradigm shifts and instructional technology". In Koschmann (Ed.), *CSCL: Theory and Practice of an Emerging Paradigm*, NJ: Lawrence Erlbaum, Assoc. pp. 1-24, 1996.
10. Redondo, M.A., Bravo, C., Ortega, M., Verdejo, M.F., "PlanEdit: An adaptive tool for design learning by problem solving". In De Bra, Brusilovsky & Conejo (Eds.), *Adaptive Hypermedia and Adaptive Web Based-Systems (AH2002).* LNCS 2347, pp. 560-563. Springer-Verlag, 2002.
11. Bravo, C., Redondo, M.A., Ortega, M., Verdejo, M.F., "Collaborative Discovery Learning of Model Design", In Cerri, Gourdères & Paraguaçu (Eds.), *Intelligent Tutoring Systems* (*ITS2002*). LNCS 2363, pp. 671-680. Springer-Verlag, 2002.
12. Engeström, Y., "*Learning by Expanding: An activity-Theoretical Approach to Developmental Research"*. Helsinki: Orienta-Konsultit, 1987.
13. Anido, L., "*Contribución a la definición de arquitecturas distribuidas para sistemas de aprendizaje basados en ordenador utilizando CORBA"*. Doctoral Disertation: Departamento de Inteligencia Telemática. Universidad de Vigo, 2001.
14. Redondo, M.A., Bravo, C., Bravo, J., Ortega, M.., "Organización de actividades de aprendizaje colaborativo basado en problemas en el sistema DomoSim-TPC", *Proc. of IE2002, Llamas, Fernández y Anido (Eds.). Servicio de Publicaciones de la Universidad de Vigo, pp. 102.* 2002.
15. Rosson, M.B., Carroll, J.M., Scaffolded, J.M., "Examples for Learning Object-Oriented Design", *Communications of ACM*, 39 (4), 1996.
16. Ortega, M., Bravo, J., Bravo, C., Muñoz, J.J., Redondo, M.A., "Scaffolding and Planning Techniques in Distance Education: A case Study in Statistics", *Proc. of* Online Educa. Berlin, pp. 164-168, 1998.

Chapter 5

VIRTUAL LEARNING ENVIRONMENTS: THE CHALLENGE OF NEW OUTLINES IN THE CREATIVE PRODUCTION OF KNOWLEDGE

Marilú Fontoura de MEDEIROS; Gilberto Mucilo de MEDEIROS; Joyce Munarski PERNIGOTTI; Rubem Mário Figueiró VARGAS, Anamaria Lopes COLLA , Maria Bernadette Petersen HERRLEIN, Beatriz Tavares FRANCIOSI

Pontifícia Universidade Católica do Rio Grande do Sul/PUCRS VIRTUAL ead@pucrs.br

ABSTRACT: The actual paper is about the challenge of investigating how a large Brazilian University may set up virtual fields in its teaching-learning processes, seeking to spot its impact on socially constructed practices as they are built within *PUCRS VIRTUAL*. Analysis of such practice is carried out at two major levels i.e. (1) teacher skill development accounting for the epistemology of the actual-virtual in its singularity as well as (2) the networks operating passages in the construction of the paradigm that instigates our practice. In short, these endeavors promoted by teachers seek to install guarantee heterogenesis processes that are also multiple as learning spaces. These are autonomization processes, of difference, of creation.

Key words: DE Teacher Skill Development Courses (TSDC); Distance Education (DE); learning environments; paradigm transition; virtualities and heterogenesis.

1. INTRODUCTION

The Pontifícia Universidade Católica do Rio Grande do Sul/PUCRS, in its *PUCRS VIRTUAL* unit, dedicated to distance education, fits in as an *innovative project*, adding value to the teaching and the learning developed on a presence based modality, as it couples up dimensions linked to the

M. Llamas-Nistal et al. (eds.), Computers and Education. Towards a Lifelong Learning Society, 51–62.

advance of technologies of the digital era that allow for the enhancement and the socializing of knowledge. Upon such initiative, there´s the opening up not only of the challenge to face up to the practices that install new endeavors in the establishment of multiple processes in learning spaces but also the offering of multiple information access possibilities [1][2] to people who find themselves detached from the traditional information poles and available updated academic formation. *Knowledges and competences constructed on the basis of a new sensitivity, a remnant sensitivity, some power, the possibility of affecting and being affected* [3].

The process as it was installed at *PUCRS VIRTUAL* builds up a proposal and a pedagogical architecture that is made up by top human and technological actions within the multiple construction network of knowledge and action. Inherent to the conditions and paradigmatic processes, *PUCRS VIRTUAL* primes on the formation of competencies that aim at ensuring some kind of "*knowing*", some "*knowing how to be*" and some "*knowing how to live by*", beyond a mere "*knowing how to do*"[4].

The challenge set up by DE is the process making of the virtual. As such, above all, it is the search for *giving guarantees that this process comes to be the entry to some virtual culture that is, due to its own instigating and flexible nature, open to ongoing transformations and sure about the fact that the achieved plateau means nothing but a space for resting from the journey, just like links within the complex network that, day and night, open up and become enhanced in the practice of Distance Education* at *PUCRS VIRTUAL* [5][6][7][8][9][10].

2. A BRIEF MEANING OF *PUCRS VIRTUAL*

PUCRS VIRTUAL bears in its operational assumptions, *the constitution of some interdisciplinary staff* besides the required *setting up of a supporting platform* [11][12][13]. *A hybrid platform* [14] that adheres to social, political and philosophical presuppositions as well as to sociocommunicative and sociotechnical-methodological ones, are arranged: a techno-pedagogical structure featuring a system that relies upon a satellite (BRASIL INTELSAT/B3) for the generation of three bearers (2 x 256 Kbps) for videoconferences, one for tele conferences (digital-tvro with a 2,5 MHtz bandwidth) providing connexions for videoconferences through the Digidial system in 256 Kbps and the 24-hour daily support through the Internet using the RNP and, more recently, an exclusive 3 Mbits channel (Diveo provider) to provide access by *PUCRS VIRTUAL* students. Besides these facilities, tools and DE services, there is a free call 0800 line as well as conventional dialing lines. Along with the lessons there is also the possibility of accessing videotapes or CD-ROM by those students who are unable of sharing video/teleconferences and participating in actualial classes. There is also an open channel available, at given times, in order to provide faculty and tutorial assistance and monitoring. Figure 1 provides graphs depicting the use of both the platforms: mediations through video/teleconferences and mediations through the computer [15][16][17].

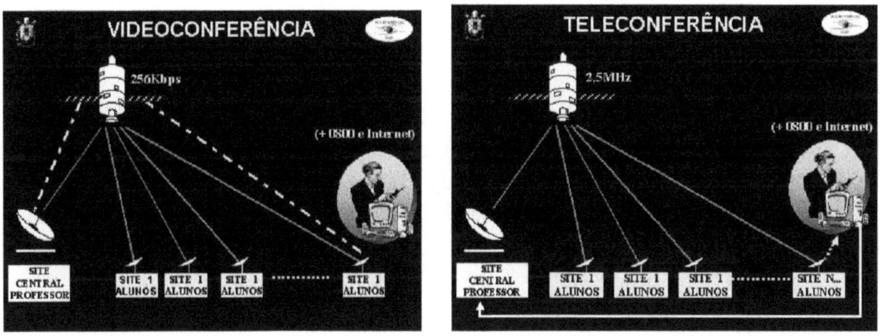

Figure 5-1: Platforms depicting technological mediations by PUCRS VIRTUAL

These challenging problems are permanently being managed. Just like a seeder, they are generating fields that call for answers and positions bringing about new inquiries. They are inherent conditions to the changes required by DE operations.

Each virtual course or project created at PUCRS VIRTUAL produces an own construction and brings about skill development, assistance and monitoring requirements by teachers, tutors and distance students themselves for it implies in the enabling of transit and construction of this hypermediatic paradigm as made virtual and hypertextualized. Such construction is not top down but, rather, a constructionist project [18][19] and also reconstructivist [20][21][22][23][24][25][26][27]. Proposals are actualed to the user/teacher in their multiple unfoldings according to an open, flexible and non-hierarchical architecture.

3. OUR STUDY IN FOCUS

In the actual study we have worked on the processes involved in the DE Teacher Skill Development Course at *PUCRS VIRTUAL*, a course that has already graduated about 400 faculty members in DE, around the University, on both intensive and extensive fashions. The early versions, each one involving 110 hours, were developed mostly as actualial courses, in their processes, hypertextualized, hypermediatic as well as rizomatic actions [28].

These images seek to translate the impact of the *effect* [29] that called for the making virtual the DE Teacher Skill Development Course as it generated uncomfortable inquiry about our own domains. It was in such ongoing search for thresholds and supporting points that we found ourselves faced with the updating of this TSDCs in DE.

More than this, in our perception we call this as assemblages. As point out by Deleuze [30], "these lines each have their own combinations, one cannot define them in an analogical [analogue] manner. In what we vaguely call a crystalline line, which has a whole history of its own, the determination of a crystalline line is not at all in relation to the material in the same situation (...); therefore, neither of these lines will have any general formula. Being a crystalline line does not imply that the matter of the instruments which trace it is crystal. (...) Actually they change in relation to each other."

4. THE ANALYSIS OF EVENTS

The *simultaneous presence of the old and the new*, not as a sequence over a time line, in an *inter-time*, *intermezzo*, in the updating that bears an extra dimension, by which it actuals both the old and itself. It is, thus, with a look into the actual that we turn our analysis without, however, neglecting the dimensions of ***founding*** and of ***foundation*** [31][32][33]. As for ***founding***, we highlight the *modus operandi* through which progressive occupation/reoccupation of spaces towards virtualization/updating (actualizing) takes place; and as for ***foundation***, we deal with the operational conditions of assumptions, the resolution potential at the dimensions of the possible and the real. So, the founding epistemology is updated upon action as a rhizome [34].

5. TEACHER SKILL DEVELOPMENT IN DE AS A STRATEGY FOR THE CREATION AND THE IMPLEMENTING OF A VIRTUAL CULTURE

In the sense of **foundation,** new approaches arise from the sociopolitical-philosophical, sociocommunicative, sociotechnical-methodological standpoint [35][36][37][38] that not only challenges and changes their own arrangement as Distance Education at *PUCRS VIRTUAL* but also contributes fundamentally to the redimensioning of the basis to the constitution of subjectivity towards its socioindividual condition. Enframed in the theoretical-practical ideas of Vygotsky [39], Habermas [40], Deleuze and Guattari [41] as well as Morin [42], besides the support provided by Lévy [43], by means of what we assume as communication gaps, our theory seeks to reflect on materiality in the creation of learning environments. In order to keep coherent with the supporting theories, actions in DE are made thematic, constructed and reconstructed in argumentative fashion, on an individual and collective basis.

Teachers are prepared in technological processes, mediated by the computer and by teleconference/videoconference processes, besides the investment in abilities linked to multimedia, finding the training itself, thus, faced up against the challenges of updating integrating media virtualities as regardful of the management of interaction processes, of cooperation and gains of autonomy.

Nevertheless, we keep in mind the fact that the use of computer resources, although they may be considered by some as a relatively simple learning experiences, according to the initial assumption that "they are just about transferring presential classes onto the technological apparatus of virtual education", such illusion is soon undone as the teacher perceives that the extent of the change imposed totally upsets the domain of teaching practice as it is traditionally carried out in the actualial modality.

6. THE EFFECT OF EVENTS ON TSDC IN DE

6.1 The updating, actualizing, of the virtual

The last release of the TSDC in DE accounts for nearly 70% of the virtual events as proposed by the installing of virtual learning environments. What seems to put up a paradox is evidence for the making actual of teacher training experiences that, to the day, are shown in this Web space, as an offer of teaching possibilities to construct other contexts besides those ones actualed. In this approach, the institution of intrinsic action plannings, of practices are a real invitation to the updating of the virtual and the new virtualizations of a possible actual. These actions assume the breaking up with the idea of model, of reactualization, of hierarchical exploration and are closed within their architecture [44]. Thus, as opposed to the idea of the model, the copy, the teacher constructs and updates his practice, creating other possibilities for the virtualities therein established.

Curious, in our case, as Deleuze said in Time-Image, as a crystal-image, the action we search is toward to an indivisible unity of the virtual image and the actual image. *"The virtual image is in the past, and to this space-time is recollected. It is always somewhere in the temporal past, but still alive and ready to be 'recalled' by in a actual image."*[45] This one of our challenge in terms of creates new concepts on DE.

6.2 The paradigm as a substrate of the willpower and the foundation

The DE at *PUCRS VIRTUAL* has its reality in a state of power that is constantly on the search for updating. These actions are supposedly instigated by the affecting power of skill developing courses. The creation of space-times for the problem does arise from usual educational practices by teachers, generated by DE, affecting the subject-teacher at the consciousness level. In this fashion, the willpower of these subjects unfolds into multiple directions, duplicating movements and migrations, creating maps in which the paradigm is made actual in its differences and intensities.

Situations managed in the TSDC in DE let show such potential. It is sometimes production, more than this, events that condensate singularities, generally for the creation of other plateaus, other maps, other fields. Even those ones in which teachers seek to "come to be as they were such", tending to deny them, this same is different, be it in intensity or in their mapping.

An image of the updating of such construction spaces is depicted, as follows, by the teaching practice of faculty who has gone through the training. For instance, in the field of teaching Chemistry, the updating of the paradigm carried out by the teacher has gone beyond the dimension of the applications to DE, of his own lessons, proposing actions designed for actualial class students, that strike all of the basic formation in Chemistry, spread over to the other units of the University. The organization of a Virtual Chemistry Laboratory and the 00100 project – with the motto, zero repetence, zero evasion and 100% approval [46], has creatively and innovatively updated the TICs actualed in the skill developing course, as well as the educational proposal of *PUCRS VIRTUAL*. Actions as such have an effect on the teaching environment and in the University itself, creating singular new movements that make up other knots, in a rizomatic construction that is polissemic and poliphasic.

In the field of learning management, yet in its administrative dimension of monitoring, about 3000 students from different courses have benefited from the full-time registry, follow up and interaction processes. Instead of operating according to fixed schedules, typical of the actualial modality, the positive *affecction* of the teachers with the webCT background gave rise to the *pathos* of sensitivity, of getting along with software created for the management of learning. As for the students, there is the chance offered of, far beyond the awareness of teachers, inviting the teacher to share ideas, to argue and counter-argue in chats, in forums [47].

6.3 The hypertext rizome as the possible come true

In the analysis of the practices in the TSDCs in DE, we search to bring into light the fact that "the virtual is not some degradation of the being – it is not the limitation or the copy of the ideal in the real [as opposed to Platonism] – but, on the contrary, in accordance to Bergson, it is the positive production of the reality and the multiplicity of the world (...) as an update along time (...) offering some adequate criticism to the notion of the possible" [48]. From such perspective, the virtual has the reality of some task to be carried out and from which existence there is produced at a given time and in a special space.

The construction of the notion of hypertext, in TSDC in DE development takes up the shape of a hypertextual tutorial that, besides placing the student in the center of the learning process, simultaneously triggers a reflection about its form and content. Each subject to learning reconstructs his path or his multiple paths, generating multiplicities. In such case, as well as in many experiences found at the TSDC, the *virtual goes by, just like that, from one region to the other, without ever wearing out, creating*, in each place, not only context novelties, but also novel things that repeat themselves and vary according to their relevance in other contexts or with other objects [49]. It is about *affecting and being affected*, as gone back to the ideas by Deleuze, departing from Nietzsche and Espinosa [50].

Despite the limitations that the printing on paper poses us, Figure 2 shows an image of the tutorial that stresses just one of the unfoldings proposed. The updating of the paradigm, not as a space of repetition, but of differentiation and creation is exposed from its front page[51], when the readdressing of the surfing proposition is organized in non-linear or hierarchical, but rather a rhizomatic fashion [52].

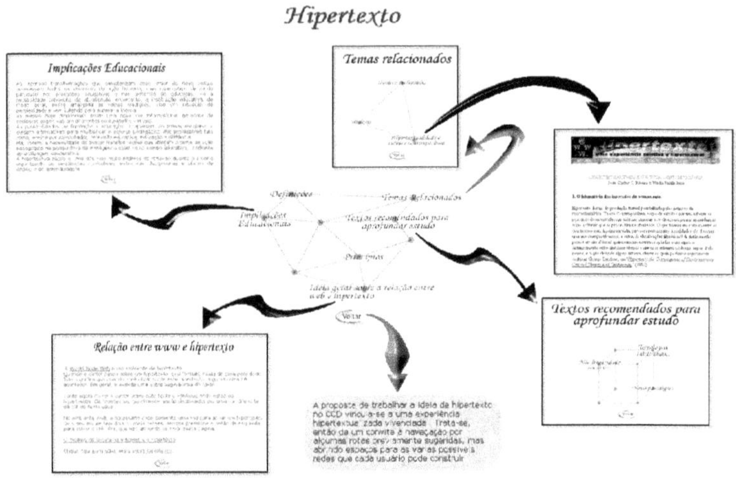

Figure 5-2: Expanded of the hypertext tutoria

6.4 Teacher Skill Development itself as a production of other managements

Our concretizing experience with TSDCs in DE and with the construction of *PUCRS VIRTUAL* is made up on creations. These creations do encompass events and bring about flows, updated actions. These flows are born into the function of virtualities, as they are created, and the way by which we create the possibilities to update these virtualities. In turn, this challenge, that is not only relative to the experiences developed in the long distance modality, but is also actual in the actualial modality, implies in either modality in order to deal with the condition of ***affecting and being affected*** [53].

In this respect, we have seeked to find in the reading-experience of Deleuze, in Nietzsche and Espinosa, the conditions, the events that would allow for our generation of flows, even within ourselves, flows that could generate new happenings to give evidence to our willpower, as well as our condition of being affected, as related to the power of acting, of updating [54]. We were not interested in operating solely on the idea of copy; we were rather interested in the dimension creation and recreation starting from ourselves, not only as the ones to give an aval to the process; rather for feeling and letting ourselves be affected in order to make valid what was constructed.

Moreover, that this effect as a means of willpower, as a power of being affected, defines that: *"The receptivity of a body not as a passive agent, but as a 'sense of affection, a kind of sensitivity, a sensation', an affection that is an assignment to the power of the body. Both in Nietszhe, as in Espinosa, thus, the the pathos does not involve a body that "suffers" from passion; on the contrary, the pathos involves affections that pinpoint the activity of a body, the creation as joy"*[55].

7. FOR THE SAKE OF A PROVISORY CONCLUSION

Here we are, at this point in time, about to provide an endpoint to something that is part of a process by its flexible and instigating nature, open to continuous transformations, sure about the fact that the achieved plateau means nothing but a space to rest after the journey, bonds that in a complex network, day and night, open up and spread over the practice of Distance Education at PUCRS VIRTUAL [56]. These assumptions prove the need and the timely occupation of this space for authorship and creation that is built about the construction of the proposal of DE at PUCRS VIRTUAL.

Event though teacher skill development in DE is considered by us as a vital strategy for the success of such modality, it does not bring definite solutions for the fact that its implications encompass not only technical but also ideological, social and various economical components that still call for explanations.

Differently from foregoing innovations, the nature of the changes brought about by infotelecommunicational means promoting teacher practice affects not only the teacher but also the student. The latter starts to be requested to interact with different subjects, and to share knowledge so as to construct new relations, by working and unworking out given information, reconstructing it into new spaces, according to new meanings and new forms of organization.

The educational proposal, as required as a challenge in DE, involves radical changes not only in the teaching but also in the ways of learning as well as in the way knowledge is thought about. There are changes in the dimensions of teacher practice such as the distribution of special times and spaces, now associated with the use of educational strategies relying upon technological tools, that alter and enhance the dimensions of effectiveness and quality in educational processes; however, we are aware that these mediations, if extended over to their final purposes, are not enough for the installing of background transformations in the sense of "accounting for" learning possibilities.

It is worthwhile to emphasize that, for a change in the culture of education; teacher as well as student actions do go through radical changes. It is not about a technical mechanism such as: "the teacher steps into a traditional door and leaves through a virtual portal."

We finish by quoting Deleuze, "for getting updated, the virtual shall not proceed by limitation but rather ***create*** own updating lines through positive acts."

REFERENCES

1. MEDEIROS, Marilú Fontoura de. *Projeto de credenciamento da PUCRS para Educação a Distância*, Porto Alegre, PUCRS, 1998.
2. COLLA , Anamaria Lopes; MEDEIROS, Marilú Fontoura de. Technological Interfaces as Promoting the Autonomy, and Descentralization, *20th ICDE World conference*, Düsseldorf, april, 2001. Session Posters.
3. DELEUZE, Gilles ; GUATTARI, Félix. Mil platôs. Vol. 4. Rio de Janeiro, Ed. 34, 1997.
4. DELORS, Jacques et al.. *Educação, um tesouro a descobrir*. Relatório para a UNESCO da Comissão Internacional sobre Educação para o século XXI. São Paulo, Cortez, 1999.
5. MEDEIROS, Marilú Fontoura de; NICOLLETTI FILHO; VARGAS, Rubem Mário Figueiró, PERNIGOTTI, Joyce Munarski. *Relatório circunstanciado ao MEC acerca do Curso de Engenharia Química, ênfase em operação petroquímica na modalidade a distância /PUCRS/OPP*. Porto Alegre, VIRTUAL PUCRS, 2001.
6. DELEUZE, Gilles ; GUATTARI, Félix. Mil platôs. Vol. 4. Rio de Janeiro, Ed. 34, 1997.
7. DELEUZE,Gilles. Bergsonismo. Rio de Janeiro, Ed. 34, 1999.
8. DELEUZE, Gilles; GUATTARI, Félix. O que é filosofia? Rio de Janeiro, Ed. 34, 1995.
9. DELEUZE, Gilles; GUATTARI, Félix. Op. Cit., 1997.
10. ALLIEZ, Eric (org.). Gilles Deleuze: uma vida filosófica. Rio de Janeiro, Ed. 34, 1996.
11. MEDEIROS, Marilú Fontoura de; MEDEIROS, Gilberto Mucilo de; COLLA, Anamaria Lopes. A produção de um ambiente de aprendizagem em educação a distância com o uso de mídias integradas: a VIRTUAL PUCRS. In: *VII CONGRESSO INTERNACIONAL DE EDUCAÇÃO A DISTÂNCIA*, 2001, Brasília. Associação Brasileira de Educação a Distância/ABED, Anais do Congresso, 2001.
12. FRANCIOSI, Beatriz Tavares, COLLA, Anamaria Lopes, MANGAN, Marco Aurélio, MEDEIROS, Marilú Fontoura de. Algumas Reflexões Sobre a Capacitação de Professores em Educação a Distância.. *IX Simpósio Brasileiro de Informática na Educação - SBIE* - Maceió/Alagoas , 2000.
13. BOFF, Elisa, GIRAFFA, Lúcia Maria Martins. Construindo um ambiente de ensino-aprendizagem cooperativo: uma experiência interdisciplinar. *SBIE 2000*, Maceió/Alagoas, p.112-119. 8-10 novembro, 2000. Proceedings.
14. MEDEIROS, Gilberto Mucilo de. ; MEDEIROS, Marilú Fontoura de. PUCRS' brazilian topology in DE: technological support in its learning environment (ID: P1866). *20th ICDE World conference*, Düsseldorf, april, 2001. Proceedings.
15. MEDEIROS, Gilberto Mucilo de; MEDEIROS, Marilú Fontoura de. Op. cit., 2001. Proceedings.
16. DELEUZE, Gilles; GUATTARI, Félix. *Op.cit.*, 1997.

17. HARDT, Michael. *Gilles Deleuze. Um aprendizado em filosofia.* São Paulo, Ed. 34, 1996.
18. MONTERO, Maritza. De la realidad, la verdad y otras. In. : *Conocimiento, realidad y ideologia.* AVEPSO. Caracas, 1994.
19. IBAÑEZ GARCIA, Tomas. La construccion del conocimiento desde la perspectiva socioconstruccionista. In.: MONTERO, Maritza et al. *Conocimiento, realidad y ideologia.* AVEPSO, Caracas, 1994.
20. DELEUZE, Gilles ; GUATTARI, Félix. Op.cit., 1995.
21. HABERMAS, Jürgen. *Para a reconstrução do materialismo histórico.* Rio de Janeiro: Brasiliense, 1990.
22. HABERMAS, Jürgen. *Direito e democracia.* Rio de Janeiro, Brasiliense, 1998.
23. NITZKE, Julio A.; CARNEIRO, Mara L.F.; GELLER, Marlise. *Criação de ambientes de aprendizagem colaborativa.* SBIE 99. Disponível em http://penta.ufrgs.br/pgie/sbie99/acac.html.Acessado em janeiro de 2003.
24. PANITZ, Ted. *A definition of collaborative vs cooperative learning.* Disponível em http://www.lgu.ac.uk/deliberatios/collab.learning/panitz2.html, 1999. Acessado em Janeiro de 2002.
25. ROGER T and JOHNSON, David W.. *An overview of cooperative learning.* Disponível em http://www.clcr.com/pages/overviewpaper.html. 1999. Acessado em janeiro de 2003.
26. TIJIBOY, Ana Vilma; MAÇADA, Débora Laurinó; SANTAROSA, Lucila Maria Costi e FAGUNDES, Léa da Cruz. Aprendizagem cooperativa em ambientes telemáticos. *Informática na Educação: teoria e prática.* V.2, n° 1, maio, 1999, p. 19-28.
27. MEDEIROS, Marilú Fontoura de ; Gilberto Mucilo de Medeiros. Uma Topologia de Educação a Distância no Brasil, Porto Alegre, VIRTUAL PUCRS, *IX Reunião da RECLA*, Porto, Portugal, setembro, 2001.
28. COLLA , Anamaria Lopes; MEDEIROS, Marilu Fontoura de. Technological Interfaces as Promoting the Autonomy, and Descentralization, *20th ICDE World conference*, Düsseldorf, april, 2001. Session Posters. Proceedings.
29. DELEUZE, Gilles. *Diferença e repetição.* Rio de Janeiro: Graal, 1988.
30. DELEUZE, Gilles. *Gilles Deleuze. Seminar session at Vincennes, 27 february, 1979*, p 1-13. Acessado em dezembro de 2002.
31. DELEUZE, Gilles and PARNET, Claire. *Diálogos.* Rio de Janeiro, Ed. 34, 1998.
32. DELEUZE, Gilles. *Diferença e repetição.* Rio de Janeiro: Graal, 1988.
33. ALLIEZ, Eric (org.). *op. Cit.*, 2000.
34. DELEUZE, Gilles ; GUATTARI, Félix. Op. Cit. , 1995.
35. MEDEIROS, Marilú Fontoura de; MEDEIROS, Gilberto Mucilo de; COLLA, Anamaria Lopes. Op. Cit., 2001.
36. MEDEIROS, Marilú Fontoura de; MEDEIROS, Gilberto Mucilo de; COLLA, Anamaria Lopes. Concretizando um Paradigma em Educação a Distância com o uso de Mídias Integradas: a PUCRS VIRTUAL VIII Congresso Internacional de Educação a Distância - Brasília/DF, 2001.
37. MEDEIROS, Marilú Fontoura de; MEDEIROS, Gilberto Mucilo de; PERNIGOTTI, Joyce Munarski; VARGAS, Rubem Mário Figueiró; FRANCIOSI, Beatriz Regina Tavares; COLLA, Anamaria Lopes; HERRLEIN, Maria Bernadette Petersen. Algo de novo sob o sol? Capturas de traçados possíveis em EAD. 2002. In.: SILVA, Marco (org.). EAD on line. Rio de Janeiro, Papirus, 2003 (no prelo).
38. MEDEIROS, VARGAS, MEDEIROS, HERRLEIN, FRANCIOSI, COLLA, WAGNER, ANDRADE, PERNIGOTTI. PUCRS VIRTUAL: Concretizando um Paradigma para

Educação a Distância na Realidade Brasileira. International Conference On New Technologies In Science Education - Aveiro/Portugal, 2001.
39. VYGOTSKY , Lev S., A Formação Social da mente, São Paulo: Martins Fontes, 1984.
40. HABERMAS, Jürgen. Op. Cit., 1998.
41. DELEUZE, Gilles ; GUATTARI, Félix. Op. Cit., 1995.
42. MORIN, Edgar. Ciência com consciência, Rio de Janeiro: Bertrand, 1996.
43. LÉVY , Pierre, Cibercultura, Rio de Janeiro: Editora 34, 1999.
44. DELEUZE, GillesOp. Cit. , 1988.
45. TOTARO, Donato. *Gilles Deleuze's Bergsonian film project.* 1999. Disponível em http://www.horschamp.qc.ca/9903/offscreen_essays/deleuze2.html Acessado em 14/03/2002.
46. ARIGONY, André. Project 00100 in Chemistry. Chemistry Faculty. Porto Alegre, PUCRS, 2002.
56. DELEUZE, Gilles and PARNET, Claire. *Diálogos.* Rio de Janeiro, Ed. 34, 1998.
47. HARDT, Michael. *Op. Cit.*, 1996.
48. RAJCHMANN, John. Existe uma inteligência do virtual? In.: ALLIEZ, Eric (org.). *Gilles Deleuze: uma vida filosófica.* Rio de Janeiro, Ed. 34, 2000.
49. HARDT, Michael. *Op. cit.*, 1996.
50. DELEUZE, Gilles ; GUATTARI, Félix. *Op. cit.*, 1995.
51. DELEUZE, Gilles ; GUATTARI, Félix. *Op. cit.* , 1995.
52. HARDT, Michael. *Op. cit.* , 1996.
53. HARDT, Michael. *Op. Cit.*, 1996.
54. HARDT, Michael. Op. Cit. 1996.
55. MEDEIROS, Marilú Fontoura de. Capacitação docente em EAD, Porto Alegre, PUCRS, PUCRS VIRTUAL, 2000.Disponível em http://www.ead.pucrs.br.

Chapter 6

USING E-MAIL AND WEB PAGES TO DEVELOP WRITING SKILLS OF ELEMENTARY STUDENTS: AN EXPERENCE WITH FIFTH GRADERS[2]

Octavio Henao Alvarez, Doris Adriana Ramírez S, Luz Estella Giraldo L.

Abstract: The purpose of this project was to design and test a teaching program to develop both individual and collaborative writing skills in primary school students, thus creating a more real, significant, and stimulating classroom environment for written communication, supported by electronic mail and other computerized tools. In this study participated forty fifth grade students from four co-ed schools in different sectors of the metropolitan area of Medellín, Colombia. The results show that electronic mail and Internet are effective devices to support a classroom atmosphere that stimulate collaborative writing activities between students of various schools. As a whole, the findings of this research show evidence that these technologies are powerful tools to support educational strategies that promote in children a better relationship with writing and a greater capacity to produce expository, poetic, narrative, and epistolary texts.

Key words: New technologies, collaborative writing, electronic mail, Internet, written communication.

[2]This paper is derived from a research approved and financed by COLCIENCIAS and Universidad de Antioquia.

M. Llamas-Nistal et al. (eds.), Computers and Education. Towards a Lifelong Learning Society, 63–74.

1. INTRODUCTION

For many students writing is a difficult, tedious activity, associated to the concept of task. School needs to reassess its teaching approaches, by creating learning environments in which students can have real, pleasant, and significant writing experiences. This will allow them to assume the written language as a true communication instrument.

Electronic mail offers teachers multiple possibilities to design teaching strategies that promote true communication, thus transcending the classroom's time-space barriers. Moreover, the Internet generates wide possibilities for information exchange, representing thereby the most revealing globalization symbol in the current world. These technological resources also allow materializing the principle of curricular integration, permitting those students, along with the development of writing skills, access information and build knowledge on different disciplines.

This research offers the region's and country's learning community a teaching program to stimulate and develop the written expression of primary school children, supported by the use of electronic mail, the Internet, and collaborative work strategies. Therefore, it represents a contribution to solve a problem evidenced by many studies on the limitations of the school to promote in students a good level of competence for written communication.

2. PROBLEM DESCRIPTION

In all school levels, it is evident that many students do not enjoy writing; their written productions amount to a minimum and their quality is very poor. On these grounds it is necessary to: (1) Create a school context that generates dynamic communication, and an agile, permanent information exchange; (2) address writing as a means of expression of thought, imagination, memories, reality perception, and feelings, (3) promote in school a culture in which writing is a communication means that transcends the institution, and makes possible the contact with different people and cultures from around the world.

Although many of the country's institutions have invested important resources in the acquisition of equipment and computer programs, they still lack a new pedagogical or curricular framework to use these technologies. In this research, a teaching program was designed and tested to stimulate and develop the capacity of written expression of primary school students by using electronic mail and the Internet. Therefore, this is a contribution to the creation of a school culture that incorporates both computerized and telematic resources in the teaching, learning, and knowledge-construction processes in the area of language.

3. JUSTIFICATION

In order to train the citizens that a globalized world increasingly demands, schools must break the barriers imposed by their physical spaces, while offering the students multiple possibilities to access and exchange information. Electronic mail is a communication device through which you can establish links with various people and institutions of any place around the world. As Cummins [1] indicates, computers offer students the possibility of making real the notion of a global village, and imply great potentiality for cultural interchange. Through written interaction with peers who live in various regions of the world, students explore the values and history of other cultures, discovering through this process unsuspected aspects of their own culture.

The results of this project constitute an innovating and strategic contribution for our school system. The Colombian Ministry of Education includes among its short-term plans the Internet connection of a great amount of primary schools and high schools from all over the country. Several experiences have demonstrated that if technical equipment does not come along with pedagogical proposals that show teachers the sense and value of the incorporation of these technologies to their teaching practice, we run the risk of underusing these resources, or of using them in an inadequate, trivial, or sterile way.

4. OBJECTIVES

4.1 GENERAL OBJECTIVES

- To contribute to the generation of policies and strategies about the incorporation of new technologies to the school system.
- To promote in schools a vision of writing as a tool for social and cultural interaction.
- To renew the models and practices of teaching writing in school, by using collaborative strategies mediated by telematic and computer resources.

4.2 SPECIFIC OBJECTIVES

- To design and test a teaching program that incorporates collaborative learning strategies supported by electronic mail and the Internet, to improve the writing competence of primary school students.
- To construct writing environments that stimulate and qualify the production of narrative, expository, poetic and epistolary texts.
- To improve, through a writing program, the skills of information search and retrieval of primary school students.

5. CONCEPTUAL FRAMEWORK

5.1 The Social and Cultural Nature of Writing

The conceptions of writing and of teaching writing cannot be reduced to an association of visual symbols and hearing references, nor to a simple motor ability. Writing is a complex and active cognitive process of representations and interpretations that includes an instrumental knowledge, a formal knowledge, and a socio-cultural background. Written language is not simply the graphical expression of oral language; it is a code system with its own characteristics. Writing is a cultural instrument that allows man to control and transform himself and his own environment [2].

The writing activity involves socio-cultural, linguistic and communicative dimensions. It is frequent that school practices ignore these essential aspects of writing, turning it thereby into a mechanical exercise of textual reproduction whose only addressee is the teacher. In order to have writing recover its true sense and value, it is necessary that its teaching incorporates varied interactive situations and real communication contexts.

In the learning of written language, the importance of social context stands out. Communicative interaction not only allows to share experiences and ideas, but also to construct knowledge collectively. The classroom should be a privileged space for this interaction, but the strategies and models that dominate the teaching of writing do not adequately take advantage of the possibilities of information exchange and communication among the members of the group.

5.2 Collaborative writing

The power of computers and telecommunications allows us to create an environment rich in possibilities for the promotion and practice of collaborative writing. The current technology allow a student of Sidney and a student of Madrid to write together a letter, collaborating in the writing process more closely than if they were seated one next to the other [3].

Collaborative writing is an activity oriented to the production of a collective text where each one of the participants must complete a specific task that contributes to the attainment of a common objective. In its development there take place cooperation actions between classmates that combine interests, experiences, and knowledge of different text bearers.

The quality of texts written collaboratively is determined by the level of conceptual development of the students and the type of information that they interchange. According to Teberosky, the written interchanges among children are nothing but instruments to socialize what each one knows, and to help to attain a joint construction [4].

Participation in collaborative writing projects may boost and develop in students skills such as the capacity to research, formulate, and solve problems; capacity to infer and generalize; critical-reflective thought; group-work ability, and the cooperation between students and teacher.

5.3 Writing supported in new technologies

Since the mid-80's research have been carried out about the effects that the computer mediation has in learning writing and the writing process. The results obtained in most of these studies positively praise the use of computers as writing tools. Poole presents some important conclusions on this regard: students show a more positive attitude towards writing, improve the quality and fluency of their texts, show a greater motivation about the topic of their writing, and show a greater interest for learning to write thanks to computer's audiovisual and physical support. They present a better attitude for checking drafts, and take more time to perform the process. They are more concerned about the quality of their text in terms of their presentation and design. They make much better documents about scientific topics. They make less grammar, punctuation, and capitalization mistakes [5]

Some interesting remarks and suggestions regarding the use of these technologies for supporting the writing process, reported in the literature are: (1) the age of the writer, his/her cognitive development, and his/her writing style are determining factors in the use given to the computer as a writing tool. (2) In order to ensure the development of the writing skills, it is important that the collaborative work be combined with the production of individual texts. (3) The use of computers in the teaching process must respect the different learning styles and rhythms of the students. And (4) a lot of people prefer to review a written work printed in paper than viewing it on a screen [5].

A word processor alone does not turn anybody into a better writer. It makes the design, checking, and correction processes of the text easier, which in handwriting tend to be exhausting tasks. In addition, this tool eliminates obstacles related to the psychomotor nature of writing. According to Daiute, writing with a computer is more similar to a dialogue. This tool highlights the writing communicative functions, not only because it interacts with whom writes on it, but also because it provides a way to communicate with each other. The computer is a communication way and at the same time a tool for writing. It is used at the same time as pencil, eraser, typewriter, printer, scissors, glue, duplicating, filing, notebook and post office [6].

5.4 The electronic mail in the school

Currently telematic and computer resources are amplifying the possibilities of synchronous and asynchronous communication at a worldwide level, offering new options for interactive learning, information search, and the contact with institutions, academic communities, and people from over the world.

Computer networks offer the school different alternatives to innovate and dynamize its teaching and learning processes such as: permanent communication among students; teachers and family parents searching common objectives; students' contact with peers from other schools in different countries in the world; teachers and students have access to a great variety of research sources, knowledge tools, and learning environments.

The electronic mail is probably the Internet's tool more widely used at the present time. It is a quick and efficient communication means through which information and ideas are interchanged almost in an instant way. This technology has been being used in schools, high schools and universities, allowing the students to communicate with teachers and students from other institutions for sharing information, discussing ideas, and carrying out joint projects, stimulating this way the students to produce more significant texts. Likewise, using the Internet opens the perceptions that students have about the world, and strengthens cognitive skills related to the retrieval, interpretation, and synthesis of information, knowledge of other cultures, and new ways of thinking.

6. A COLLABORATIVE WRITING PROGRAM BASED ON ELECTRONIC MAIL AND INTERNET

Schools must design writing environments offering students stimulating and innovating conditions for producing varied, significant texts. These environments may include reading activities, analysis of good texts of different literary genders, as well as the production, edition and socialization of individual and collaborative writings. For this research, a writing program was designed involving the students in reading activities, production and analysis of lyric, epistolary, narrative, and expository texts in individual and group ways

As an individual writing experience, children produced texts of different genders with the support of models and the guiding of the teachers. Multimedia and printed resources such as books, encyclopedias, texts of different genders, dictionaries, and different Internet web pages were used. The experience of collaborative writing took place in a virtual environment, supported by the electronic mail. Two modalities of collaborative text production were used in the program: (1) the production of a written text in group, (2) the writing of a short story in couples. Likewise, short stories were individually written and analyzed critically by a student of other school.

Three kinds of communicative interchange took place among the participating children: (1) Interchange activities one to one, in which the child sends and receives messages about concerns of his/her family, school or personal life. (2) Writing activities between two children of different schools oriented to the collaborative production of texts about a previously chosen topic. And (3) writing activities among groups of four students of different schools regarding interesting topics.

7. RESEARCH QUESTIONS.

1. How does a writing program supported in collaborative work, electronic mail, and other computer resources influence in the meaning , value, and functionality that the students attribute to writing?
2. In a comparative way, what impact does this writing program have in the quality of narrative, expository, lyric, and epistolary texts produced by the students?
3. What impact does this writing program have on the information search strategies used by the students?

4. How does electronic mail support a collaborative program to develop writing skills?

8. METHOD

8.1 Sample, Design and Variables

Sample Forty fifth grade students were the sample for this study. These students were chosen proportionally from four mixed schools of different sectors of the metropolitan area of Medellín. The selection was made by the teachers by taking into account their relatively good academic performance as well as an equal distribution by gender.

Design For this research a quasi-experimental intra-subjects design with pre-test and post-test was used, combining two types of analysis; quantitative and qualitative.

Variables *Independent Variable*: The writing program which incorporates experiences of individual and cooperative work supported by electronic mail and Internet. *Dependent Variables:*1) Meaning, value and functionality of writing; 2) Information search strategies; 3) Quality of written production.

8.2 Hypothesis

H_1: The participation of children in the writing program determines qualitative changes in the meaning, value and functionality attributed to the writing.

H_2: The participation of children in the writing program determines qualitative changes in their information search strategies.

H_3: There is a significant difference in the quality of poems, tales, letters and written works produced by children before and after their participation in the experimental writing program.

8.3 Instruments

Each student was assessed before and after the experience by using the following instruments:

Questionnaire about meaning, value and functionality of writing, which includes 32 items concerning aspects such as: What is writing, why do you write, importance of writing, interest on writing, topics of writing, personal relationship with writing, knowledge of some genres as narrative, expositive, lyric, and epistolary; evaluation and production experiences concerning group written work

Questionnaire about information search strategies composed by 11 items which explore aspects such as: steps to do research about a topic; notions about consultation sources, criteria adopted to select a source, and the procedures followed to perform an information search.

Scale to evaluate poetic production. Composed by10 items that explore aspects such as: structure, continuity, the emotivity that it induces, the level of fantasy , the metaphoric richness and the originality.

Scale to evaluate the narrative text. Composed by 13 items which explore aspects such as: expressive strength, organization, originality, lexical richness, grammar, methaporical dimension, formative value, interest it awakes, semantic complexity, etc.

Scale to evaluate the epistolary production: Composed by 10 items which explore aspects such as: formalities and conventions, strength and argumentative logic, lexical diversity, grammatical and orthographic correction etc.

Scale to evaluate the expository text: Composed by 18 items that explore aspects such as: structure and components, coherence, updating, conceptual rigidity, organization and presentation, orthography, references, lexical richness etc.

8.4 Procedures

The tests, "Questionnaire about the meaning, value and functionality of writing", and "Questionnaire about information search strategies", were applied as pre-test and post-test.

To evaluate the quality of the texts produced by the children during the pre-test and post-test, a jury was conformed by three B.A teachers of Spanish and Literature, who independently evaluated all the texts using as a criteria an scale designed for each type of text. The final score given to the texts produced by the children was the arithmetic average of the scores assigned by the three members of jury.

Each child had an electronic mail and his/her own web site, which contained his/her photography and their most relevant bibliographic data. This allowed the children to choose the addressee of their messages, their couples and the members of the groups

9. RESULTS

The analysis of the results shows that the quality of poems ($t=8.71$, $p<0.001$) the tales ($t=6.72$, $p<0.001$, the letters ($t=12.24$, $p<0.001$) and the written work ($t=7.96$, $p<0.001$) was significantly better in the post-test than in the pre-test.

The program had an impact particularly notorious on the relationship the children made with the poetic genre. At the start of the experience, the students manifested not only a complete lack of knowledge of poetry but indifference and rejection which were slowly transformed into a clear interest and love for poetry. This was possible because the program offered multiple options of contact with poetry: poems of excellent quality were read, they played to replicate "good poets", they also had access to poetic plays of very well known poets, they had interlocutors to speak about poetry and finally they enjoyed a good audience in the socialization stage of their poetic productions. Besides, they had the perspective of making public their poems in a web page.

Undoubtedly, this program built an environment capable of revealing the magic of poetry to the children, by seducing them towards the reading and writing of this lyric genre.

Once the program was concluded, a larger number of children manifested their interest in writing tales. According to the data of the pre-test, the main reason for writing was the "school requirement" which notably changed during the post-test, producing other arguments concerning their likes, interest for expressing and the possibility of learning.

A conceptual mobilization was also evident, from a traditional point of view of tales, closely related to the teaching of values into another conception of the same, as a means to know the world, to improve their intellectual capacity, and as an instrument to dominate this genre.

The notion that the children had about written work also changed, which at the moment of pre-test was unknown for some of them; it had been considered as a school task or a simple copy of texts. Once the program was concluded, most of the children got to structure a definition of this written genre as an organized text around a topic.

The idea that the written work is only a school task lost credibility, and the notion that this type of written production is a means of communication and intellectual development strengthened At the same time, some variations were observed specially concerning their motivation for performing written works. What became more important was the reasons they had about pleasure and learning over the ones referred to school requirements

In this experimental program, children were allowed to devote enough time to writing. They had the option of choosing a topic, its contents and the consultation resources; at the same time, they could organize, illustrate and edit their work in a cooperative way. The texts being generated were revised, widened or supplemented by their classmates; likewise, the teachers team acted as interlocutor and mediator, guiding the quality of the work and stimulating self-correction. These conditions could explain the advances in the conceptualization, appropriation and quality of text production made by children.

The interest of children in publishing their written works increased considerably at the end of the program. This could be a result of their experience on sharing their writing, and on the exhibition of their works on the web page, which all children had access to. The most formal, conventional aspects of writing which are privileged in many school practices, lose their value in the post-test. At the same time, the search activities were more valued as a quality warrant of a written work.

At the end of the program a high percentage of the children conceived the process of research as a sequence of actions which included searching about the topic, reading, extracting ideas, revising and writing. In the mean time, they recognized the importance of using various research sources among them, internet, dictionaries and encyclopedias in multimedia format. Besides, many children who before the experimental program only used printed materials or people as sources of consultation, turned out to use a combination of different sources after the experience.

10. CONCLUSIONS AND PEDAGOGIC IMPLICATIONS.

The reflection and analysis of the results suggest the following conclusions:

- It is possible to get the children enjoy their writing experiences and achieve important improvements in their written communication skills, if their schools create a learning environments which includes: (1) Real and significant activities about written communication (2) the reading; analysis and discussion of good representative texts of different literary genres; (3) the use of computer and telematic tools that support writing; (4) teacher's mediation; (5) academic peer work which improves the cooperative production of texts.
- The electronic mail showed to be an effective device to stimulate and support cooperative writing activities among students of different schools. With the support of this tool, a significant writing context was

generated which promoted continuous communication among the participants of this project. Writing for a particular reader implies an effort to precise and organize the ideas so they become understandable; this only requirement favors the development of writing skills. The findings of this project show evidence that electronic mail is a powerful support for designing didactic strategies that support the development of writing skills.

- The proper conditions of the program made it possible to have a mediation which combines the teacher's support and the versatility of computer tools to promote the development of writing skills. The computer screen makes the text visible for others, thus making it easier to explore it, to analyze it , and to develop it cooperatively. The support the teacher can give to his/her students at revising, editing and organizing a text, is more accurate, fluid and immediate, if they use a word processor, than when they hand-write. It is also important, that the teacher guides the process of writing, not as evaluator but an advisor, allowing therefore a freer, personal writing in children in accordance with both their points of view and their level of development.
- The experimental program positively impacted the meaning, value and functionality that children give writing, which is evident in the conceptual changes such as: (1) a more accurate valorization of writing as a tool of expression and communication; (2) they associate the quality of writing with a better handling of the topic and the appropriate communication of ideas,: (3) they relate the domain of writing with possibilities of professional success; (4) they give functionality to writing beyond the school context.

REFERENCES

1. J. Cummins, "De la ciudad aislada a la aldea global: el microordenador como catalizador del aprendizaje cooperativo y del intercambio cultural". *Comunicación, Lenguaje y Educación,* vol. 1, pp. 58-59, 1989.
2. L.L. Tolchinsky, "Aprendizaje del lenguaje escrito: Procesos evolutivos e implicaciones didácticas," Barcelona: Anthropos, 1993, pp. 344.
3. F. Smith, "De cómo la educación apostó al caballo equivocado," Buenos Aires: Aique Grupo Editor, 1998, pp. 95.
4. A. Teberosky, "Construcción de escrituras a través de la interacción grupal". En. E Ferreiro, y M. Gómez P. (comp.) *Nuevas perspectivas sobre los procesos de lectura y escritura.* México: Siglo XXI, 1982, pp. 155-178.
5. B. Poole, "Tecnología educativa" Madrid: Editorial Mc Graw Hill, 1999.
6. C. Daiute, "Writing and computers". Reading, MA: Addison-Wesley, USA, 1985, pp. xiv.

Chapter 7

DIDACTIC ERGONOMY FOR THE INTERFACE OF INTELLIGENT TUTORING SYSTEMS

Gloria M.J. Curilem Saldías [1], Fernando Mendes de Azevedo [2].
[1] *millaray@ufro.cl. Engineering Department of the La Frontera University, Francisco Salazar 01145, Temuco, Chile.* [2] *azevedo@ieb.ufsc.br. Biomedical Institute of the Federal University of Santa Catarina, Campus Trindade, CEP 80040-900, Florianópolis, Brazil.*

Abstract: Personalization problematic is a central aspect of educational changes. That is why it is a central aspect in the research area of pedagogical software. The development of pedagogical software depends, on one hand, of the pedagogical paradigms considered to manage the teaching-learning process and, on the other hand, of the available technologies to implement these paradigms in computers. The problem of personalization is today in full effervescence, because pedagogical paradigms leave in open many aspects involved in educational processes and there is not consensus in determining how to use technology to support students' learning. The present article presents a research about the construction of a didactic ergonomy for the interface, integrating pedagogical strategies and technologies to support the apprentice's interaction with the studied object. As a result of this research, a method to implement Adaptive Interfaces in Intelligent Tutoring Systems is proposed.

Key words: Adaptive Interfaces; Intelligent Tutoring Systems; Hypermedia and Pedagogical Software.

1. INTRODUCTION

A new culture based on information is changing the way people learn, work, interact and live. Education is seen today as a key for development [1]. In this new context a great research effort is being made to find technological tools to support the new demands of education. Pedagogical software is one of the most important results of these researches. But two

M. Llamas-Nistal et al. (eds.), Computers and Education. Towards a Lifelong Learning Society, 75–88.

questions are still unanswered: can technology really empower teaching – learning processes? And, if it does, how should it be inserted to support the educational needs [2]?

To answer these questions, the actual situation of education should be analysed, to know which its new requirements are. Actual educational structure is based on the old relationship between a master and his pupils. This relationship supported two aspects considered important for the educational process: the process was highly personalised and it was significant for the student. The increase of the number of pupils transformed the master in teacher and the pupils in students, losing the advantages of the initial relationship. Many variables of the teaching-learning process are lost, for example motivations, personal capacities, cognitive styles, emotional states, etc. The process also loses meaningful, because learners are confronted to pre-established and pre-organised knowledge: Institutions decide what to teach, when and how to do it.

To be considered as a valid alternative, pedagogical software should incorporate several learners' characteristics to propitiate personalised processes [3] and they should offer significant pedagogical activities [4]. The hypothesis is that different activities offered by these systems should increase the efficiency of learning, because the content is adapted to learners' needs and interests, and the presentations are adapted to their cognitive styles, all this based on solid pedagogical strategies.

Intelligent Tutoring Systems (ITS) try to implement these concepts [5]. These systems use Artificial Intelligence (AI) techniques to adapt the activities proposed to a learner to his/her learning types. In first place, AI was used to model the contents that should be presented to the learner [6],[7]. Second, AI was used to model the pedagogical decisions of a tutor [8]. Third ITS incorporated a Student´s Model to better interact with the student [9]. These two models (Tutor and Student) allowed improving the adaptation capacity. However, the limitations of human being models didn't allow the construction of efficient systems, slowing down ITS development.

New approaches place the interfaces as a vital element of the learning process: they become the communication mean to improve learning environments. Researchers are working on the application of AI techniques to develop Intelligent Interfaces. In pedagogical software, these researches should be oriented to obtain a didactic ergonomy [10]. ***Didactic Ergonomy*** means the creation of an interface configured according two axes: the learner and the pedagogical strategies. The first should guarantee the ergonomics concept, that is to say, to facilitate the interaction between the learner and the studied object. The second axis should guarantee the didactic concepts, offering an interface highly adapted to the pedagogical strategy. To do so, it can be necessary to provoke conflicts in the learner, as repetitions, etc. That is why the function of the didactic ergonomy is not to facilitate the use of the system, but to support the educational process.

2. DIDACTIC ERGONOMY

The work presented in this article is focussed on the construction of a didactic ergonomy for the Interface. The approach is based on two observations. First, computers can create rich and motivating pedagogical environments, using the available technologies for interface construction (multimedia, icons, activities like encyclopaedia, games, simulations, etc.). The second observation is that some cognitive theories define many learner's characteristics, classifying them according to cognitive preferences. The recognition of these elements allows configuring technological tools for personalised pedagogical activities. So, the objective of this work is to define a didactic ergonomy and propose a method to implement it.

To construct a didactic ergonomy, it is necessary to know how the environment influences learning, which elements define a learner, how can a computer identify these elements and, at last, which elements define the environment. To answer to these questions, an extensive bibliographical research on pedagogical paradigms and cognitive theories was developed. The results of this research are presented below.

2.1 Pedagogical Considerations

Research on learning has a long past, but only since the XIXth century, researchers investigate how learning happens, with rigorous scientific methods. Even if the results of these researches have been significant in this area, it is not possible to highlight a theory over the others: the different conceptions point out different and complementary teaching-learning aspects [11]. That is why different theories were combined to create a pedagogical base for the didactic ergonomy proposed here.

Some pedagogical theories establish which environment can enhance the learning process for several student types, which they define [12]. Once a student type is obtained, the theory orients on, which are the elements that should be present in the environment to support learning. So, once obtained a student definition, the interface can be configured to respond to the specific learner's requirements. In this work, all the variables that define a learner are called ***characteristics***, and the variables that define an interface are called ***attributes***.

Pedagogical strategies guide the general actions needed to support learning. Two pedagogical strategies, extracted from behavioural [13] and constructivist [14] theories, were considered to design the Pedagogical Activities. Environments compatible with these two conceptions can be built in a same system (e.g. Tutorial like activities allow implementing the behavioural phases, and "Microworlds", or exploration activities allow to implement constructivist environments). As the strategy guides on the general actions, it is necessary to obtain criteria to decide which specific actions must be implemented. For example, in the behavioural phase of "Apprehension", it is necessary to call the learner's attention for the most important elements of a lesson. However, behaviourism does not specify how to call his/her attention.

Pedagogical tactics refer to the specific actions that should be executed to support a pedagogical strategy. The implementation of pedagogical tactics was based, in this work, on theories that define capacities and individual styles in the learners. Learning Styles [15] and Multiple Intelligences[16] theories were considered and also elements of the Situated Learning theory [17]. These theories allow to obtain characteristics, possible of being detected by a computer, that guide the ITS decisions over specific aspects of the interface. In the example above, when a strategy suggests "call learner's attention", the learner's learning styles visual or verbal can determine if texts or images will be activated. It is important to point out here, that the research didn't questioned the validity of the considered theories, but the aim was to know how these theories orient the definition of the interfaces given a Student's Model.

To define the student and the interface, many characteristics and attributes were considered. Some of them are presented next. These sets of variables are not closed. Other variables can be incorporated, according to the interest, objectives or pedagogical conceptions adopted by the system designers. In this stage, the goal was to obtain a set of variables (characteristics and attributes) and their relationships (which characteristic activates which attribute and inversely). This information allowed projecting a system that, acquiring information on learner's characteristics, "decides" how to configure interface attributes.

2.2 Learner Characteristics

The Learner's characteristics are the elements that define a Student. They are contained in sets that refer to a same variable type. Some of these sets are presented next. Questionnaires were used to identify these characteristics. It's important to remind that these characteristics define the Student's

Model.

1) *Stages of Development:* these characteristics were extracted from the constructivist theory. The stages are inferred from the learner's age.
2) *Interests*: the learner's interests are represented by a set of specific questions that the learner can select. Each of them corresponds to specific information on the content: when the learner selects a question he/she is selecting a subset of topics.
3) *Learning styles:* they are personal characteristics, imposed by biological or environmental factors. They make that a same teaching method is effective for some students and ineffective for other [18]. The Learning Styles theory suggests environments and technologies that can empower learning for each style. 8 styles were considered all of them are used in the Student's Model.
4) *Multiple intelligences:* they are different facets in cognition [19]. The theory suggests that individual possesses different intelligence in different degrees and several technologies can be used to better reach each intelligence. The theory considers 8 intelligences, five of them are included in the Student's Model.
5) *Topic:* this variable describes the interface, but is also considered as a student's characteristic. It is used to identify the Contents that were already passed. The passed topics are inhibited, so they will not be offered to the learner again.

2.3 Interface Attributes

The Attributes are the elements that define the interface. To conform a pedagogical activity, the interface should be decomposed in elements that can be enabled or disabled independently, according to the student's characteristics. The attributes are contained in sets. In each set the number of attributes can vary from project to project. Some of them are presented as example next.

1) *Topic*: the domain that is being covered by the ITS is divided in units, called topics. Each topic is a set of information, related to a specific object, concept, etc. of the domain. The Topic attribute identifies the specific Content that will be presented to the learner. The number of topics depends on the specific domain.
2) *Navigation:* indicates the degree of freedom that will be given to the learner to move among the topics. Free Navigation (LIV) is considered when the system determines that the user should be able to reach all the topics he/she desires. Predetermined Navigation (PRE) is considered when the user can only reach specific topics, going forward or backward,

in a pre-determined sequence.

3) *Interaction Level*: is related to the number of links (hyperlinks) available in the screen, during an activity. Links allow the learner to interact with the information presented by the ITS. The interaction level is high (ALT) when the system offers a high number of links, or low (BAX) otherwise. Links associate information within a specific topic, which is why Interaction is different from Navigation.

4) *Media*: this attribute specifies the means used to represent the information and to construct communication channels with the learner. The following media were considered: text (TXT), speech (FAL), music (MUS), sound (SOUND), images (IMG), animations (ANI), video (VID) and animated characters (PER).

5) *Pedagogical activities:* they are specific contexts inside which learners interact with the contents, with different degrees of student and system intervention. Pedagogical activities respond to different pedagogical strategies, mainly to the behaviourism (tutorial presentations, question-answers) and to the constructivism (exploration environments, encyclopaedia and games) and to the "Situated Learning" theory (examples activity and problem resolution). Therefore when the system selects an activity it is selecting a pedagogical strategy.

2.4 Characteristics and Attribute Relationships

Once defined the variables of the problem it's necessary to establish the relationships between them. Knowledge on these relationships will allow designing a system that, identifying the learner's characteristics, can configure a compatible interface. Inversely, if the learner selects some attributes on the interface, knowledge of the relationships allows inferring which characteristics are related to these selections, so the Student's Model can be modified.

The relationships between the Characteristics and the Attributes were obtained from the cognitive theories. These define Learner's characteristics and associate them with elements of the environment. For example, the "verbal" style is related to text and speech media. The "global" style is related to free navigation, etc.

Some of these relationships are presented in Table I. In the lines are presented some characteristics and in columns some attributes, like Media (1), Navigation (2) and Interaction Level (3). The 1's represent a positive influence between the characteristic and the corresponding attribute (in the system implementation these values are fuzzy, so the strength of the relationship can be adjusted).

	(1)								(2)		(3)	
Characteristics	TXT	FAL	SOM	MUS	VID	ANL	IMG	PER	LIV	PRE	ALT	BAX
OpC		1		1		1	1	1		1	1	
VERBAL	1	1										
MUSICAL			1	1								
ACTIF											1	
GLOBAL									1		1	
SEQUENTIAL										1		

Table 7-1. Example of the relationship between some characteristics and attributes.

3. ADAPTATION MECHANISM

The general objective of the adaptation mechanism is to implement an ITS, based on didactic ergonomy. A methodology was proposed to model the problem incorporating the elements that define the pedagogical base of the system, the student's characteristics, the interface attributes and the relations between them [20].

An ITS is defined by four modules that correspond to the four types of knowledge that should be present in any pedagogical process. The methodology proposed in this work, establishes how to design each module, to guarantee flexibility and adaptation of the interface. It is important to observe that many pedagogical considerations, as the cause of the student's mistakes, traditionally treated in ITS, are not treated in this work, whose objective is focussed on the adaptive interface.

3.1 Specialist Module

The Specialist Module stores the contents that will be introduced to the learner. These contents cannot be stored without a form, which is why the study pointed out the need to implement, for each topic, a great variety of files, with different media, activities, scenarios and links. The form of storing the information should be compatible with learners' characteristics and with interface attributes. So it is necessary to construct the content considering all the variables of the process. The contents, the presentation forms, the links, etc., should be stored in separated files that should be loaded in the screen independently. One of the advantages of structuring the contents is that technology is used in the exact measured established by the pedagogical considerations. The different types of students that are being considered determine which activities should be implemented. The methodology proposes some steps, presented next, to design the Specialist Module.

1) *Subdivision of the contents:* The domain should be divided in topics that can articulate the different student's characteristics that influence the selection of the content of a Pedagogical Activities (theoretical contents should be separated from practical, to reach global, intuitive and sensitive styles, etc.).
2) *Activities design:* some contents are more adapted to one environment than an other. This adaptation must be used to project a minimum of environments that have high development costs.
3) *Media:* Each pedagogical activity should be implemented using all the media available
4) *Navigation and Interaction:* a maximum number of links should be projected for each pedagogical activity. So the system can carry them in the screen, according to the Interaction Level or the Navigation attributes.

A table can be built to facilitate the combination of all the factors that intervene in the construction of the Specialist Module. This table facilitates creation and manipulation of the attribute files. The method proposed for activities implementation assures that no variable of the teaching-learning process will be discarded involuntarily. The process is still long and complex, however the development of the interface is no more "blind" but guided, at each stage, by the pedagogical strategies and tactics considered in the project. All this demands a great processing speed from the system, as well as storage capacity for so much amount of information and variety of formats.

3.2 Student Module

The Student Module has the important task to maintain the Student's Model updated. The Student's Model consists of the group of characteristics previously defined. The Student Module should guarantee that the characteristics identify the learner as exactly as possible. The learner's identification has two different objectives and is accomplished in two different moments of the process.

First, the objective of the identification is to determine the Initial Student's Model. This model is obtained by means of an interview that uses questionnaires, in an activity called Diagnosis Activity. This is only offered to the student in its first interaction with the system, before starting pedagogical activities. An Expert System was implemented to analyse the questionnaire's answers to get the student's characteristics values. This Initial Model is the starting point of the system operation: with this model, the system configures the first pedagogical activity and waits for the learner's actions.

Second, the learner's identification has for objective to update the Student's Model. This process is accomplished during the learner's interaction with the pedagogical activities. In the whole process, the learner's interactions are analysed by the system. When the learner acts on the interface, during his/her ongoing across the activities, the actions are analysed to detect Student's Model changes.

A special consideration established that small children will not be submitted to the complete Diagnosis Activity. Characteristics as Learning Styles and Multiple Intelligences won't be searched so the system can offer more activities to them.

3.3 Tutor Module

The Tutor Module stores the knowledge on the variable relations, necessary to take pedagogical decisions. This Module accomplishes two functions: it configures the interface and updates the Student's Model. The Tutor Module analyses the Student's Model and determines which interface attributes should be activated. The Tutor Module also analyses the learner's actions on the interface and updates the Student's Model, according to the student selections in the interface. This process is represented in Figure 1.

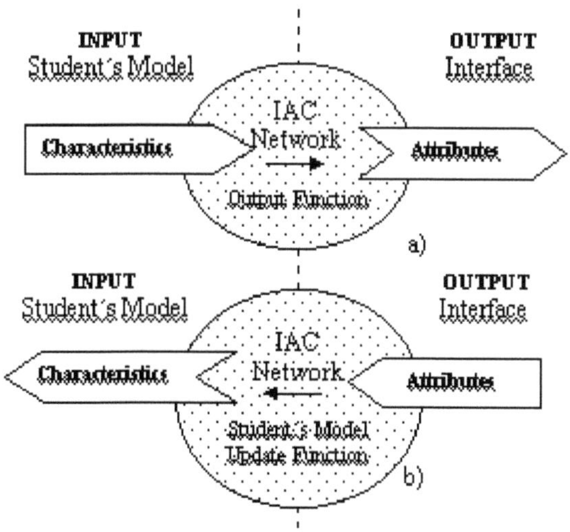

Figure 7-1. Tutor Module functions: a) Interface configuration. b) Student's Identification

To implement the Tutor Module, it must be observed that this module has three important properties: parallel processing, bi-directionality and uncertainty. An "Interactive Activation & Competition" (IAC) Artificial Neural Network (ANN), Azevedo Model [21] was used to design the Tutor Module. This ANN type is composed by processing units organised in groups that represent similar concepts. The interactions inside a group are competitive, that is, neurons of a same group have inhibitory connections and between groups, they are excitatory or null. IAC networks have no learning phase: the programmer establishes the value of the weights of each connection. In this project, the variables of the problem formed groups of neurones, so, there are groups that correspond to characteristics and groups that correspond to attributes. The weights matrix stores the knowledge about the relationships between characteristics and attributes. The weights are configured with fuzzy values. These values depend on the designer pedagogical conceptions.

The groups' architecture and the competitiveness inside each group do a very close representation of the problem (characteristics groups, for example, Learning Styles or Interests and Attributes groups, for example, Media). Having "winning" neurones within the groups, allows the activation of few attributes, what increases system's individualisation. Another important aspect is that the operation of the net, similar to a BAM, assures an acceptable result, even with incomplete information at the inputs.

3.4 Interface Module

The user's actions on the interface are the system's inputs and the interface configurations are the system's output. So interface is the central component of the system [22], [23]. Traditionally interfaces' adaptability is based on "navigation" or "presentation." In the first, the system controls the possibilities of displacement among the whole domain. The second adaptability is focussed on the presentation forms of the contents. In this project, the learner is analysed in a more detailed way, by means of his/her characteristics. This enables to control more elements of the interface and not only navigation and presentation. The intervention degree of the system can go from the total control, as in a traditional tutoring system, to total freedom of the learner, like in reactive systems.

To configure the screen, the Tutor Module processes the user's characteristics, obtained from the Student's Model. This allows to activate the attributes that should be offered for that student, determining the content (topics), the form (media) and the hyperlinks (navigation and interactivity) of the interface. According to the characteristics, the system also selects a pedagogical activity, that is why, the pedagogical strategy, used to implement that activity, is also reflected in the interface. This way, for each Student's Model, the system can determine which attributes should be activated. As all the components of the screen are stored in independent files, in the Specialist Module, the activation of the attributes determines which files should be loaded in the screen. So, pedagogical activities that are offered to the learner, are being created at run time, during the learner's interactions with the system, generating a process highly dynamic and adaptive.

Changes of the model happen when the learner is submitted to an evaluation or when he/she selects attributes that were not supplied by the system. When evaluated, if he/she succeed the past topic is disabled and a change in the model happens. If he/she fails the evaluation, there will be a change in the form of presenting the same topic, because the system determines that it's necessary to offer to the learner other activities: the initial model is considered inadequate, so the Student's Model is modified. The student can modify the attributes supplied by the system manually. A button is available in all the activities, to configure the interface manually, passing over the system decisions. If other topics or other media are selected, the planning proposed by the system is being modified. The Student's Model changes and the corresponding changes in the environments happen.

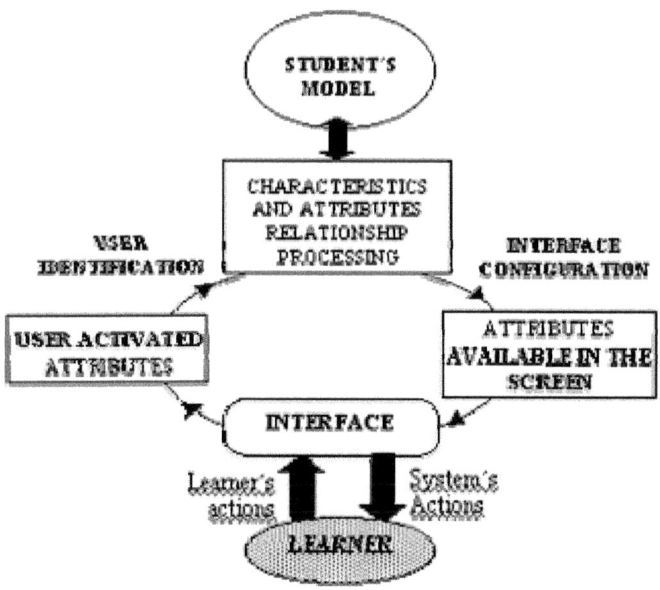

Figure 7-2. Interface Adaptive Process according to the Student's actions and Model.

This way, the user can follow the suggestions of the system, acting in the environment that was offered by the system. If he/she decides to change the offered environment, the user can provoke a change in his/her Model, provoking changes in future activities. Another environment will be generated for the user, in agreement with his/her choices. Figure 2 represents the adaptation cycle proposed by the present methodology. This process guarantees a dynamic and user adapted interface. As seen in this figure, the processing unit (Tutor Module) configures the interface considering the information supplied by the Student and the Interface Modules. Loading the corresponding files from the Specialist Module does this.

4. FINAL CONSIDERATIONS

Can technology really empower teaching – learning processes? How should it be inserted to support the educational needs? The pedagogical domain establishes strategies and tactics that influence the learning environment, suggesting actions and elements that should be present to support teaching-learning processes. The technological domain offers tools to implement these actions and elements. Most of all, technology can support the construction of personalised environments, which respond to many learners' specificities. Based on that, the present project validated the hypothesis that learning process can be empowered by technology. A methodology was proposed to configure the learning environments, setting the interface attributes, according to some learner's characteristics. This methodology proposes how to insert technology to effectively empower learning.

The difficulties found in the student modelling process have slowed down the development of ITS. The approach of this project is to contribute with a modelling that uses simple learner cognitive characteristics. This is a starting point to incorporate new characteristics until obtaining a Student's Model more and more reliable and complete. Interface Attributes can also be improved considering more elements (colours, font size, and also other technologies like Telecommunication, Virtual Reality, etc.) The variables presented in this article represent, therefore, an initial proposal that can be modified as other theories are incorporated to it.

To implement an adaptive and dynamic ITS it is necessary to update the learner's model. For this reason, the Diagnosis Activity was complemented by a continuous learner's evaluation. The IAC neural network presented a good performance. The Tutor Module stores pedagogical information, so it can be seen like a 'Teacher Model". It has more or less intervention degree in the process, according to the strategy, that is to say, according the Student's Model. So the behaviour of this Module goes from a Tutor (behaviourism) to a Moderator (constructivism).

A set of experiments were realised to validate the Adaptive Mechanism. These experiments determined that the Tutor Module took right decisions in more than 85% of the cases. Research is being developed in the IAC network, to increase this result, but it is considered a good performance.

Didactic Ergonomy validation is one of the next steps of this project. To do so, a system must be implemented to evaluate the degree of effectiveness of the pedagogical conceptions considered in it. In this way, the proposed system can be used to evaluate, in practice, the considered theories and their influence in the learning process of a specific area.

ACKNOWLEDGEMENT

We thank the valuable help of the CAPES (Coordination of Improvement of Superior Level Personnel. Brazil) for the financial support without which the development of this project would not be possible. We also thank the UFRO (University of La Frontera. Chile), for having supported the accomplishment of the first author's of this article Doctorate, that took to the accomplishment of the present research.

REFERENCES

1. R. Larson. (1999). *As novas realidades e os desafios da educação tecnológica superior.* Site : http://www.engenheiro2001.org.br/teleconferencia_3.htm#tele2
2. W. Winn. (1997). *Constructivism in practice : The case for Meaning-Making in the Virtual World.* Human Interface. Technology Laboratory. Washington Technology Center. University of Washington. http://www.hitl.washington.edu/publications/r-97-47/three.html
3. C. Kolski, M. Tendjaoui, P. Millot. (1992). *A process method for the design of "intelligent" man-machine interfaces. Case study: "The decisional module of imagery".* International Journal of Human Factors in Manufacturing, 2(2), p 155-175.
4. J. R. Carbonell, (1970). *AI in CAI: An artificial intelligence approach to computer-aided instruction.* IEEE Transactions on Man-Machine Systems, Vol. MMS-11, N 4, p. 190-202.
5. E. Wenger (1987). *Artificial intelligence and Tutoring Systems. Computational and Cognitive Approaches to the Communication of Knowledge.* Morgan Kaufmann, San Francisco.
6. J.S. Brown, R.R. Burton, and A.G. Bell, - (1975) *SOPHIE: a step towards a reactive learning environment.* International Journal of Man-Machine Studies, 7, 675-696.
7. R.R. Burton, and J.S. Brown, - (1976) *A tutoring and student modeling paradigm for gaming environments.* In Colman, R. and Lorton, P. Jr. (Eds) Computer science and education, ACM SIGCSE Bulletin, 8, 1, 236-246.
8. J.S. Brown, and R.R. Burton, - (1978) *Diagnostic models for procedural bugs in basis mathematical skills.* Cognitive Science, 2, 155-191.

9. W.J. Clancey, (1992). *New Perspectives on Cognition and Instructional Technology.* NATO ASI Series v91. Series F, Computer and System Sciences.
10. J.F. Rouet. (2001) *Cognition et Technologies d'Apprentissage.* http://perso.wanadoo.fr/arkham/thucydide/rouet.html
11. N.S. Pfromm (1987). *Psicologia da aprendizagem e do ensino.* São Paulo: EPU/EDUSP
12. S.G.M. Curilem, F. de Azevedo. (2001). *Estratégias Pedagógicas e Gerenciamento da Interface de um Sistema Tutor Inteligente.* XII Simpósio Brasileiro Informática na Educação, 21-23 Novembro 2001, Vitória, ES, Anais: pp.565-568.
13. [13].B.F. Skinner. (1968). *The technology of Teaching.* New York: Appleton-Century-Crofts
14. J. Piaget. (1967). *A psicologia da Inteligência.* Editora Fundo de Cultura S.A Lisboa .
15. R. Felder. (1996) *Matters of Style.* ASEE Prism, 6(4), 18-23. A. Harrison, private communication, May 1995.
16. H. Gardner (1993) *Multiple Intelligences: The Theory in Practice.* NY: Basic Books.
17. H. McLellan, 1995. *Situated Learning Perspectives.* Englewood Cliffs, NJ: Educational Technology Publications.
18. R. Felder, B. Soloman. (1997) *Learning styles and strategies.*
19. http://www2.ncsu.edu/unity/lockers/users/f/felder/public/ILSdir/styles.htm
20. L. Campbell, B. Campbell, D. Dickinson (2000). *Ensino e Aprendizagem por meio das Inteligências múltiplas.* Porto Alegre: Artes Médica Sul.
21. S.G.M. Curilem, F.M. de Azevedo. (2001). *Implementação Dinâmica de Atividades num Sistema Tutor Inteligente.* XII Simpósio Brasileiro Informática na Educação, 21-23 Novembro, Vitória, ES, Anais pp.453-460.
22. F.de Azevedo, L.Brasil, R. de Oliveira. (2000) *Redes Neurais com aplicações em Controle e em Sistemas Especialistas.* Ed. Visual Books. Florianópolis.
23. P. Brusilovsky, (1997) *Efficient Techniques for Adaptive Hypermedia.* Intelligent hypertext: Advanced techniques for the World Wide Web. Lecture Notes in Computer Science. Vol. 1326, pp. 12-30.
24. S,A. Güven. (1999). *Applications of Machine Learning Algorithms in Adaptive Web-based Information Systems.* Tese para obtenção do grau de PhD em Ciências da Computação, Middlesex University. UK.

Chapter 8

TE@R PORTAL
A Web Tool to Support Collaboration

Rafael G. Machado and M. C. A. Gomes
21st Century Nónio Competence Centre at Viseu Higher School of Education - Portugal : Coordinator of the 21st Century Nónio Competence Centre at Viseu Higher School of Education - Portugal

Abstract: TE@R is a collaborative space being developed in the scope of the project of the 21st Century Nónio Competence Centre at Viseu Higher School of Education. In this context, it is especially directed at a real community of students and teachers who have collaborate on this project. The greatest expectations are placed on them to enliven this space, whose growth, implantation and diffusion depend on them. We present the strategies followed for the conception and implementation of TE@R as well as the first results of its use and the evaluation carried out by a group of teachers.

Key words: communities of practice, collaborative work, learning communities, Internet

1. INTRODUCTION

The approaches to the problem of managing and organizing learning has emphasized the value of social interaction and the processes of social development, inspired by the social theories of learning, such as those presented by Vigotsky [1] and followers. Such learning theories demand situated and contextually rich social environments. In this light, models of management of learning are proposed, which emphasize the importance of the organization and of the community in the learning process of every individual.

The concept of learner organizations introduced by Senge [2], which the author proposes be applied to the specific context of the School [3], is linked to some convictions: organizations, and consequently the School, are a result

M. Llamas-Nistal et al. (eds.), Computers and Education. Towards a Lifelong Learning Society, 89–100.

of how their members think and interact; learning involves communication and interchange; learning is driven by motivation or vision. In this framework, learning communities have risen, as the structure that supports the collaborative work between its members in pursuit of common objectives or goals, reinforcing the sense of identity of the community itself.

Wenger [4] introduces the concept communities of practice as the focus of the learning process. Assuming that the involvement in social practice is the basic process by which we learn, the author proposes a social learning theory and identifies the necessary components for the characterization of social participation as a learning process: meaning, related to experiencing; practice, related to doing; community, related to belonging; identity, related to being.

According to Wenger [5], all communities of practice are structured around three elements: the domain, which frames the sense of identity; the community, which frames social interaction; practice, which frames the specific knowledge that a community develops within its domain.

The epistemological sources of Senge and Wenger are not discordant, and the concept of a learning and collaborative community maintains its centrality in their approach to the problem of management of learning. These are the general terms that frame the conception of the TE@R space.

2. MOTIVATIONS OF THE DEVELOPMENT OF TE@R

Viseu Higher School of Education is a real place of encounter between students/future teachers and teachers who collaborate with us, developing various projects or attending courses, from short training courses to master's courses. The Nónio Competence Centre at Viseu Higher School of Education has been developing its project of following the implementation of Information and Communication Technologies in primary and secondary schools since 1997 [6]. This project allowed the supervision of concrete projects in 14 schools, and simultaneously involved about 1100 teachers from many schools from the Viseu region in several practical courses.

Not forsaking the contribution of all involved, strategically we wager on this real community to find the elements that give TE@R meaning and identity.

This space intends to explore the facilities of information technologies in the sense of providing a place where the members of this community can assume their identity, define their domain and describe their activities.

Considering we are dealing with teachers on duty at their schools, at distant workplaces, but with similar problems and challenges, this type of space becomes important in animating a community whose members can effectively participate in its construction.

3. DESCRIPTION OF THE TE@R PORTAL

The TE@R Portal (URL: http://www.esev.ipv.pt/tear) is structured in 5 main functional areas:

Services; Resources; Information; Incubator; Evaluation of Educational Software

Figure 8-1. Opening page of TE@R Portal

The different areas developed on a platform written in Microsoft ASP (Active Server Pages) [7] and resorting to a set of databases in Microsoft Access. The linking mechanism between the ASP and the data kept in Microsoft Access is obtained at the expense of the access component of the database included in the ASP, designed by ADO (ActiveX Data Objects) that offers a set of objects, organized in a hierarchical manner, permitting in this way, the link form an ASP to practically any type of database, through Microsoft's ODBC. SQL Commands [8][9] were used for consulting, inserting, deleting and changing data.

An OMT (Object Modelling Technique) approach [10] was used, given that it allows the manipulation of elements that are better identified with the real world, obtaining this way a higher level of abstraction [8]. The result of its use was the design of the Objects' Model, with the definition of classes, with its respective attributes and types, generalization hierarchies, associations and restrictions of integrity, serving as a support to the construction of various databases. From the objects' model, the equivalent relational model [11] was designed, achieving a set of standardized tables, with the respective primary keys.

The implemented areas were subject to usability tests. For example, before making the forum available, it was tested by a group of 20 teachers during a training course. The results of this test contributed towards the improvement of the interface and error detection.

3.1 Services

In this area 2 tools are available to ease the exchange of questions and information between the various TE@R Portal users, supporting also the creation of small virtual communities.

3.1.1 Electronic Mail

This tool allows any Portal user to create and configure an internal electronic mail account, in a closed Web Mail system.

The system allows the exchange of correspondence between the different users (allowing the inclusion of attachment files) and disposes numerous facilities such as the possibility of defining an address book and a digital signature [12].

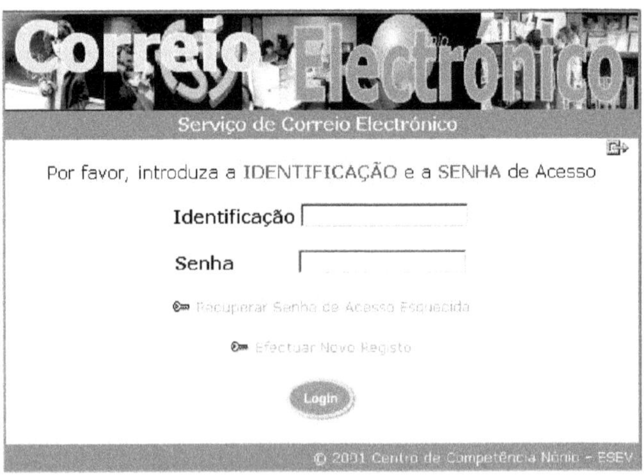

Figure 8-2. Opening page of the Electronic Mail service

3.1.2 Discussion Forum

The discussion forum claims itself as being the space that promotes the sharing of knowledge by all TE@R Portal users, or small sub-groups of users.

Besides other facilities, the service allows the request of the creation of new forums, which is later validated by the system administrator.

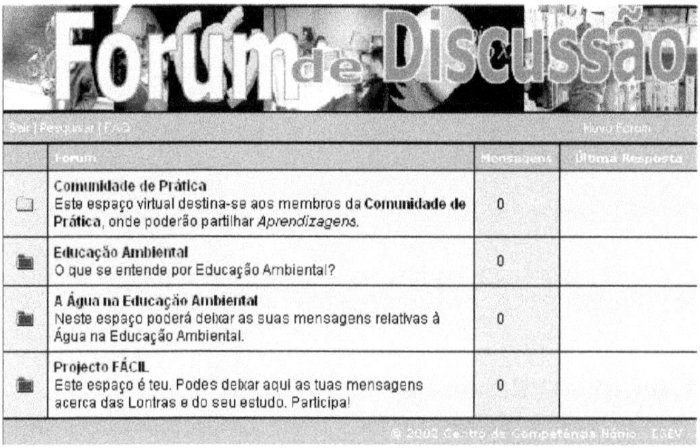

Figure 8-3. Opening page of the Discussion Forum

3.2 Resources

In this area, 2 services with a common interface were made available, offering the users material that can be proposed and used by the different interveners, teachers or students, in a class situation or in a study and research situation. An attempt is made to offer a selection of documents that express the community's database of knowledge.

3.2.1 The Link Archive

The Link Archive, as the name suggests, contains duly classified links according to themes, within their respective areas.

Besides the availability of links, the system also allows the user to suggest links that, because of their appropriateness, are considered of relevant interest to the community.

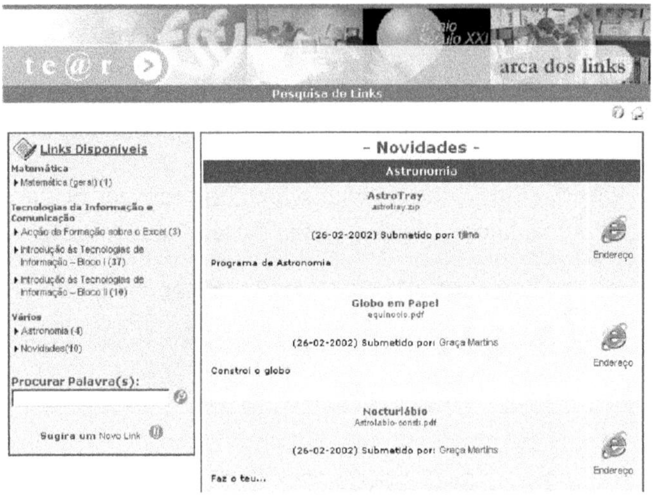

Figure 8-4. Opening page of the Link Archive

3.2.2 Educational Resources

In this space, the interveners have at their disposal several educational resources, namely: notes, tests, exams, worksheets, projects, books, magazines, newsletters, etc. This type of information can be searched for in a personalized way, facilitating its quick access.

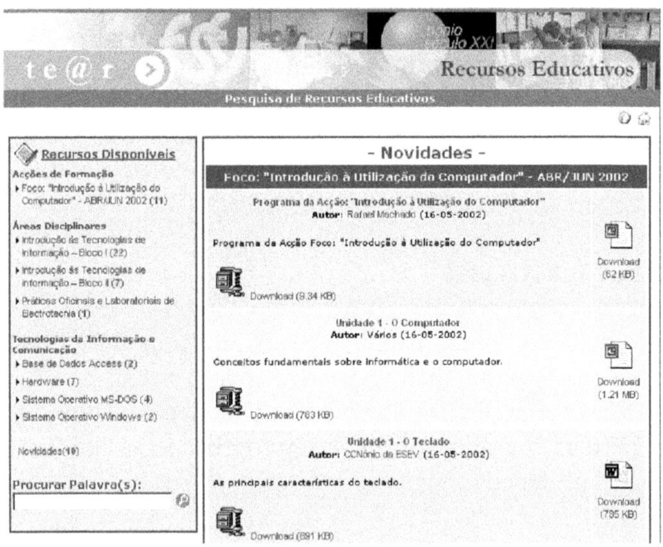

Figure 8-5. Opening page of Educational Resources

3.3 Information

This area is reserved for information considered of interest to the different TE@R Portal users. This space is composed of the day's news, novelties, activities and events that are to take place.

3.3.1 News

The News service consists of the daily collection of news that is of interest to the community, and its subsequent insertion in the database.

3.3.2 Events

The events and activities hosted by the different entities can be found at the TE@R Portal Events service. Besides a personalized search with themes, the service also has, for those interested, an online form to suggest events.

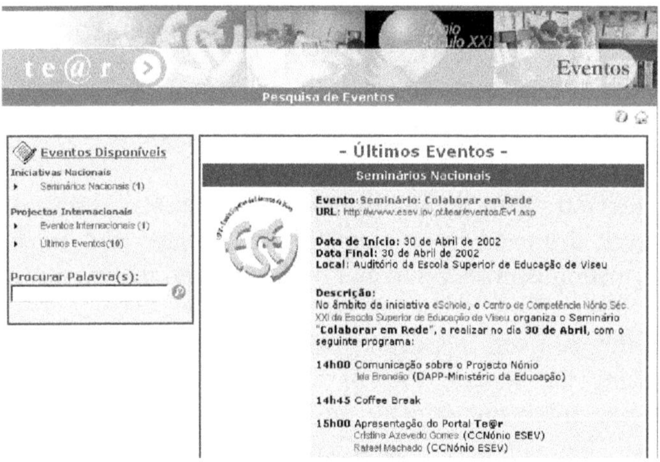

Figure 8-6. Opening page of Events

3.4 Incubator

Alike any incubator this space intends to offer conditions for growth of projects. The Project Incubator area was created in order to provide a physical space for the sheltering of pedagogical projects.

Besides pedagogical support, technical support is also guaranteed, whenever it is requested, as well as the possibility of using the available collaborative tools (Electronic Mail and Discussion Forum).

The incubator promotes the recognition of projects and schools and makes them visible.

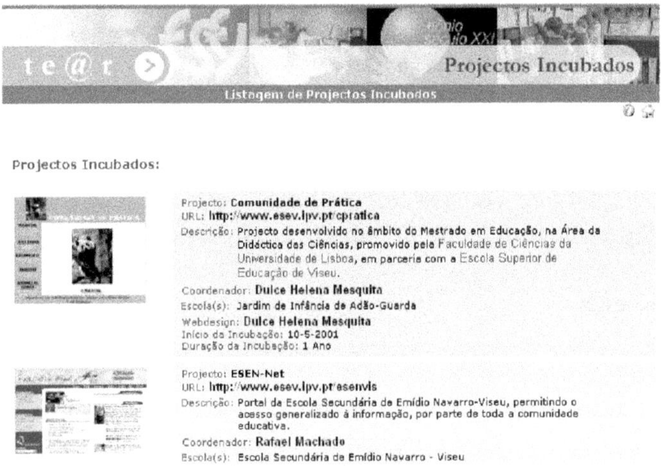

Figure 8-7. Opening page of the Incubated Projects Area

3.5 Evaluation of Educational Software

The area referring to the evaluation of educational software rises as a result of work achieved by students/future teachers and teachers in the different formation courses promoted by VHSE and the Nónio Competence Centre.

During the courses, applicants are invited to evaluate educational software, using the support tool of evaluation 'Hyper List' [13]. These evaluations are filled out directly on the database, which contains items referring to the software identification, its technical, didactic and pedagogical characteristics.

In the presentation of the evaluation there were matters that rose related to either the facility at the search software level, or to the way the obtained results were presented.

The search results allow the choice of the software desired to obtain an evaluation in order to decide on the appropriateness or not of its use in the activities to be developed.

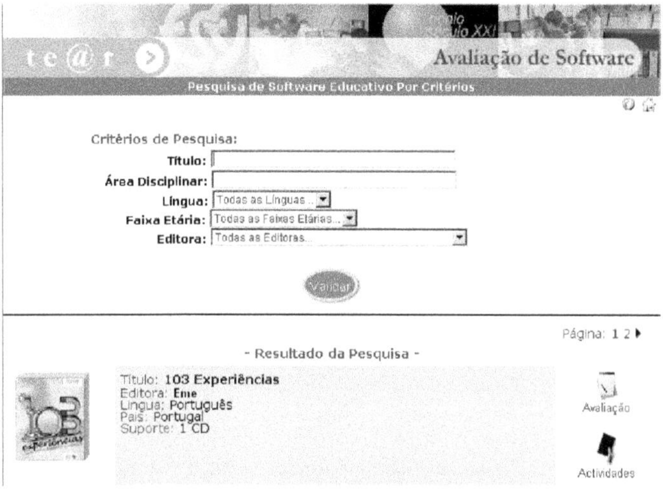

Figure 8-8. Result of the Search Criteria application

After that, the user can choose one of the many available evaluations.

For each evaluation the respective evaluators are identified and the different application analysis items are presented.

Besides the evaluations regarding the software, other documents are provided, when existent, that allows the performance of a set of activities, using the particular software.

4. FIRST PHASE OF EVALUATION

In a first phase, TE@R Portal was presented to teachers and directors of primary and secondary schools, in a seminar held at the Higher School of Education of Viseu Polytechnic Institute.

The seminar's main objective was the diffusion of the Portal in the educational community, as well as to hear the participants' opinion about two relevant issues. The importance of the developed areas and the interest in using the different services provided.

A short inquiry distributed at the end of the seminar allowed the gathering of data that is presented in graphic form.

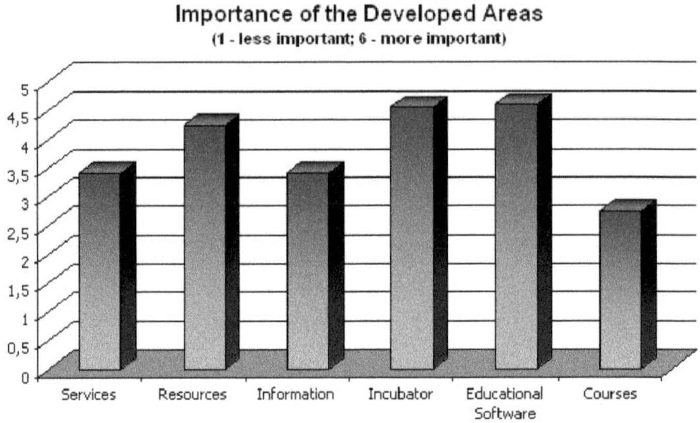

Figure 8-9. Classification of the importance of the developed areas, N=20

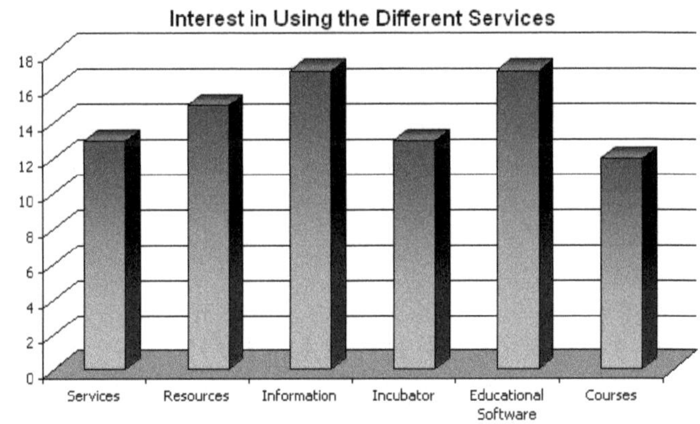

Figure 8-10. Intention of using the provided services, N=20

By analyzing the graphs, it can be easily concluded that all the developed areas reveal a strong interest by the participants, particularly the areas related to the Incubated Projects and the Evaluation of Educational Software services, which are probably the most innovative and unusual services provided by this portal.

Regarding the use of the provided services, the participants indicated that they would consider using the available information service since vital information never reaches, or delays at reaching schools. On the other hand, they also showed a strong motivation in the use of the Evaluation of Educational Software service, given that most of the participants were unaware of the existence of interesting applications for their scholastic activities during the year.

It must be noted that the fact that the incubator was referred to as one of the most important services, it is not reflected on the expectancy of use, denouncing the difficulties the teachers still have regarding the animation of projects using the Internet.

Besides the gathered data, some comments and suggestions were also obtained:

- It was pleasant, enlightening, useful and relevant.
- Very useful. It will be interesting diffusing and promoting its use.
- Its diffusion should be done at the schools' Executive Boards.
- An excellent job that should be divulged and stimulated.
- A very good service for the whole community.
- The image and interface are fantastic, and exploring it is simple.
- We hope that the acceptance level is worthy of the site.
- It is a pity that schools with no computers cannot intervene in the TE@R Portal.

During the first month of activity, TE@R Portal accepted the incubation and provided the due technical and pedagogical support to five projects:

- *Esen-Net*: the Portal of Emídio Navarro Secondary School in Viseu
- *Projecto Fácil (Easy Project)*: Project of the Science Education Area of Viseu Higher School of Education.
- *Comunidade de Prática (Community of Practice)*: Project in the context of the Master's degree in Science Education.
- *Água na Educação Ambiental (Water in Environmental Education)*: Project supported by the European initiative "Erasmus Project".
- *A Primeira Página da Minha Escola (The First Web Page of my School)*: Workshop of the Information and Communication Technologies' area held during the Cultural Week of Viseu Higher School of Education.

The Discussion Forum had a good acceptance, and was quite crowded, serving mainly as a support of sharing and gathering of information and opinions between interveners of the different incubated projects.

5. CONCLUSION

The conception and implementation of TE@R Portal aspires to enliven a vast community of students/future teachers and teachers in the context of the training project of Viseu Higher School of Education and of its Nónio Competence Centre.

The first evaluations carried out, and the usage verified in this first month of activity, permitted, in a first phase, the validity of the usefulness of this space for the community it is preferably directed to.

The increase of participation in this space is expected, naturally, at the beginning of the next school year. The fact that TE@R was only made available in May made it impracticable that more schools join the project, especially the incubator service, since it was too late to launch new projects in schools. It will be at that time that we will proceed to the second phase of the evaluation of TE@R, trying to test its usage and relevance with effective members of the community.

The models of learning management based on the concept of learning communities place very interesting challenges, in initial training as well as continuous training of teachers, adjusting the roles of the people involved, opening space for the statement of the individual's learning. It is in this sense that the TE@R Portal can play an important role in the animation of a learning community, in the context of teacher training.

REFERENCES

1. Vigotsky, L. S: (1974). *Thought and Language* Massachusetts: MIT Press
2. Senge, P. (1990). *The Fifth Discipline. The art and practice of learning organization*. New York: Currency Doubleday.
3. Senge. P. et al (2000), *Schools That Learn*, Nicholas Brealey Publishing, London.
4. Wenger, E. (1998) *Communities of Practice: Learning, Meaning and Identity*. Cambridge University Press, New York.
5. Wenger, E. et al (2002) *Cultivating Communities of Practice*, Harvard Business School Press, Boston.
6. Rego, B., Gomes, C. A., Andrade, M. C. (2000). *O Centro de Competência Nónio – Século XXI da Escola Superior de Educação de Viseu. Millenium*, 4 (17), pp. 159 – 173.
7. Fedorov. A. et al.. (1999) *Professional Active Server Pages 3*.0, Wrox Press.
8. Date C. (1995) *An Introduction to Database Systems*, Addison-Wesley Publishing Company.
9. M. Loomis, M. (1995) *Object Databases: The Essentials*, Addison-Wesley Publishing Company.
10. Rumbaugh, J. et al. (1991) *Object-Oriented Modelling and Design*, Prentice Hall.
11. Aloke, N. (1991) *Introducing SQL-Server*, Addison Wesley.
12. Machado, R. (1999) *Sistema de Informação Baseado numa Intranet para a Gestão Pedagógica de uma Escola do Ensino Secundário*, Porto, Portugal: Faculdade de Engenharia da Universidade do Porto, Tese de Mestrado.
13. Gomes, M. C. , & Silva, M. J. (1996). Avaliação de aplicações educativas no ensino das ciências da natureza: formar para utilizar. *Actas do Simpósio Investigação e Desenvolvimento de Software Educativo*. Monte da Caparica: Universidade Nova de Lisboa.

Chapter 9

THE PROVIR SYSTEM

Adaptation of a distance learning system for a course with high practical load

Juan J. Villacorta-Calvo, Alberto Izquierdo-Fuente
E.T.S.I.Telecomunicación, Universidad de Valladolid

Abstract: This contribution presents a distance learning model based on the traditional educational model that joins synchronous and asynchronous communication components. We also analyze the integration of the proposed model to teach a subject whose educational methodology is based on the resolution of practical exercises in a laboratory. This adaptation process is divided in two phases and in this paper we explain the tele-education tools used in both phases and how to take advantage of the specific characteristics of each tool to improve the learning. Finally, the results obtained during first implantation stage are exposed and we show the changes that will take place in order to reach the second phase.

Key words: validation, distance learning, real-time multimedia, tele-teaching tools

1. INTRODUCTION

In the last years, computer systems and communication networks have experienced an advance that can be described as revolutionary, since it has a massive penetration in all sectors, indicating a transition from the industrial society to the society of the knowledge. The education is not free of this influence and, as answer to the changes in the social needs, new models of education have arisen. These models introduce the use of the new technologies in the educational process [1, 2] and are called tele-education systems.

Although the major use of the tele-education systems is the distance learning, they represent an important support for the presence and semi-

M. Llamas-Nistal et al. (eds.), Computers and Education. Towards a Lifelong Learning Society, 101–113.

presence education. The objective of these new education models is not to replace the traditional modalities of education, but complement them and improve all the educational process [11]. The integration of traditional and tele-education systems can optimize the result.

1.1 Concepts and definitions

We can give several definitions to the term tele-education. Surely, most of them can be given as correct although they do not include all the contexts in which this term can be applied [3]. The first definition could be obtained from the etymological origin of the word: education in the distance, or better, distance education. That is, tele-education could be understood as an education in which there is a separation between professors and students, and in which another medium is provided to fill up the physical gap.

However, this definition has important deficiencies. It implies that ideal education is the traditional one in presence classrooms, whereas tele-education is a lower quality version that tries to emulate the traditional model [4]. Although this has been certain in some cases, the present technological advances and the recent investigations in the pedagogical area allow that new tele-education techniques would be an alternative of such good quality as traditional education.

The second deficiency of the previous definition is that it considers only a space separation between the professor and his students [4]. One more generic definition adds the time as separating element. Finally, the initial definition contemplates only professor-student communication, forgetting any other type of interaction produced in a classroom and limiting the learning model to the traditional lesson, in which the professor is the only source of information.

One more general definition is that tele-education is the education that provides the same educational opportunities to any person in any place and at any time [3]. We will consider tele-education like the remote education that makes use of computers networks and other telematic tools to provide those educational opportunities.

1.2 Tele-education tools

We will consider a tele-education tool as any telematic tool that allows computer networks to be used as mediators in the communications between professors and students, student and students and, even, between the students and the teaching material [9]. This is a general definition that includes both the specific tele-education systems, and those traditional education systems that use computers to help themselves in the educational work.

Therefore, this type of tools does not have to be specific for their use in education. Any tool, including the most general, can be considered a tele-education tool if it is used in the educational scope. From this point of view, no tool can be considered good or bad, everything depends on how professors or students make use of the tool [5].

In this way, there are numerous examples of the application in the teaching of the general tools [7, 8] such as the electronic mail [10] or the web [6]. Nevertheless, most of these general tools lack enough flexibility to adapt to the education model that is required by the professor, or they are too complex to be used in a comfortable and rapid way. In these cases, it is necessary to resort to a tele-education tool specifically designed for each situation.

2. PROVIR TELE-EDUCATION MODEL

The tele-education model presented in this section has been oriented to be used to teach courses and subjects within the degree of Engineer on Telecommunication and similar. The characteristic we try to exploit with this system is its high experimental degree: on the one hand, in the theoretical lessons is frequent the use of the blackboard to write formulas and equations from mathematical demonstrations and to draw graphs and figures that help in the explanations. On the other hand, the theoretical classes are complemented with the realization of practical exercises where the acquired knowledge is applied. These practical exercises are frequently made in laboratories, with simulation programs executed in personal computers.

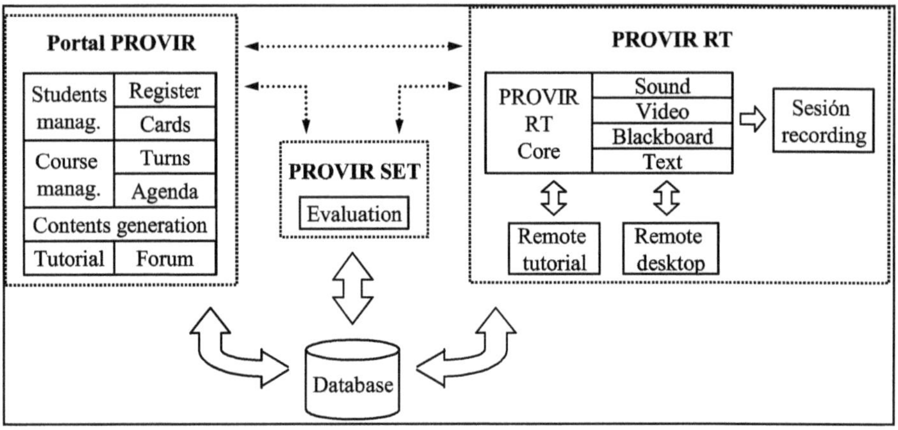

Figure 9-1. PROVIR tele-education model

PROVIR system is based on the adaptation of the traditional model of education so that: i) the professor can keep his particular way of teaching providing him the same teaching experience than in the traditional classroom, ii) the students can eliminate the present space-temporary restrictions and iii) the learning is maximized.

In order to obtain the proposed objectives three elements have been integrated in the system. In the first place, a direct communication channel between professors and students is required. A teleconferencing tool, called PROVIR RT, is used to implement this element. It allows the communication through the transmission of video and sound in real time. Around this central element of communication we have added a complete toolset useful in the educational process.

The second element of the system is Portal PROVIR, which complements the real time tools by providing a permanent place in which to find all the information related to the subject. This information is stored in a database accessible via a web interface.

The last component consists of a complete system of evaluation that includes all the tasks implied in the evaluation, called PROVIR SET or SET.

2.1 PROVIR RT

PROVIR RT is the central element of this tele-education system whose main elements are:

- Real time transmission of sound and video: oral language is the more natural communication medium, so that PROVIR transmits the voice from the professor to all the students and from them to the professor. The professor's video is also transmitted to all the students, although its contribution is minor but it is used to create a presence sensation.

- Virtual blackboard: where the professor can show images and documents previously created and indexed. It is also possible to write and to draw directly in the blackboard, either in a new empty page or on an existing image. The use of a tactile digital tablet allows the professor to write directly on the screen just as he would make it on a real blackboard, facilitating the adaptation to the system.
- Text channel: this additional communication channel allows that the students send text messages to the professor and vice versa. This communication channel is less natural but it allows the intervention of the students without interrupting the professor teaching.

These features are common to other commercial teleconferencing tools, but PROVIR is an asymmetric system that follows the structure of a traditional classroom: on one hand there is the professor, who has a total control over all the elements of the virtual classroom, whereas on the other hand, the students can only access the elements allowed by the professor. Another difference is that PROVIR allows the integration of other tools or modules that improve the system with greater benefits. At the present time PROVIR incorporates the following tools:

- Contents generation: it is used to select the images and documents that will be shown in the virtual blackboard of PROVIR RT.
- Remote desktop: this tool allows the professor to see the computer screen of any student and even work remotely on it. The professor can also send his own computer screen to all the students.
- Session recording: this module stores all the events that take place during the class: the voice of the professor, the virtual blackboard changes, the text channel... These recorded sessions can be viewed at any time by the students to review the lesson.
- Remote tutorial: this service allows knowing if the professor is connected to the system and if he is available for a consultation, initiating a private conference to solve the student doubts.

With the introduction of all these tools we can use PROVIR RT in other situations apart from the theoretic lesson. Thanks to the modular design of the system we can add new elements or modify the existing ones based on the necessities or on the technological evolution.

2.2 Portal PROVIR

During the teaching of a course, much information is generated that must be stored and, in most cases, made public to the students. Within this information we can include the list of the students, the groups' distribution, the scheduling, the practices calendar, the bibliography and any other document that the professor considers necessary. A complete tele-education system must provide a way to store and manage all this information. The most efficient way to store the information is the database.

Because this information does not have the real time characteristic of PROVIR RT, we have designed a separated component to manage and access the information stored in the database. Portal PROVIR provides a simple web interface, based on forms, to simplify the maintenance of the information, at the same time that it provides automatically a central information point to consult all information related with the course.

Portal PROVIR is divided in different sections, some of them are public, while others are only available for professors. The main modules are:

- Electronic card: that stores all information related to each student is stored (personal data, evaluation results…). Automatically the system generates a list of all students that can be consulted by the professor.
- Course documents: in this area, the professor will be able to add all documents, in electronic format, related to the course.
- Scheduling: to plan the practical classes to be done every day.
- Discussion forums: they provide asynchronous communication channels used to establish public discussions between the educational communities.

2.3 PROVIR SET

The main objective of PROVIR SET is to facilitate all the tasks implied in the process of educational evaluation. It includes a series of tools that allows automating the evaluation as far as possible. The tools including in SET can be divided in two categories based on who can access them: management tools that include creation and correction of exams, and examination tools, including exams fulfilment and results consultation.

The management tools are only accessible for the professor and allow him to define the questions included in the exams and the set of options that provide more flexibility to the examination model. The exams can include test questions, in which the student can choose between a set of fixed answers, or open questions in which the student can write his own answer. The system makes an automatic correction of the test questions, but the questions with free answer must manually be corrected by the professor, although the system includes a tool to correct these questions ant to add commentaries to the answers given by the students.

The students, on the other hand, can access PROVIR SET to fulfil the questions during the period of accomplishment established by the professor. Once the correction process has finished, the student can consult the obtained qualifications and, if the professor allows it, review his examination accessing the correct answers and the commentaries from the professor.

As last element, SET can make a statistical analysis of the exams results. We can get graphics with the number of students who have answered each question and obtain histograms of the qualifications. This statistical analysis and the flexibility of the questions allow using the system to make scoreless surveys or polls to obtain the users opinion.

3. INTEGRATION OF PROVIR IN THE COURSE DIGITAL TREATMENT OF SIGNALS

The course Digital Treatment of Signals or TDS is an obligatory course to obtain the degree of Telecommunications Engineer by the University of Valladolid (Spain). The course consists of 90 hours, 30 of them are theoretic classes and the other 60 hours are exercises and training in laboratories.

3.1 Course description

This course tries to reinforce the knowledge and use of the tools for signal processing in the discrete time scope. Together with the analytical resolution of the exercises two techniques appear:

- Modelation and simulation of signals and systems using Simulink.
- Real-time implementation with the signal processor TMS320C31.

We pretend that the student, based on the theoretical knowledge, acquires the capacity to model and simulate the behavior of the main systems and, eventually, he will be able to implement them in real time.

The educational methodology used tries to exploit the practical character of the course, being promoted the learning of the contents through the resolution of practical exercises in which the theory previously explained must be applied. The teaching is divided in weekly modules composed by 2 hours of theory in the classroom, in which the theoretical concepts are explained, and by 4 hours of practical exercises that take place in laboratories where the professor propose 2 or 3 exercises, that the students will solve during the practical hours. The objective is that the theoretical concepts are not reduced to a set of mathematic formulas without physical sense, but that the students can experiment with their practical application on real signals.

The resolution of the exercises will be made in groups of students to reduce the work load and to allow the resolution of greater number of exercises, promoting the work in group.

The evaluation of the course is made of mixed form, averaging the results of the exercises done during the practical exercises along the entire course with the obtained qualification in a final evaluation. In this way, we pretend to value both the work done during the course, reflected in the exercises results, and the level of knowledge reached, obtained from the exam taken at the end of the course.

The evaluation of the practical exercises is made exclusively in the laboratory, verifying in-situ, during the practical classes, that the designed programs and simulations work. The final exam follows the same structure than the exercises made during the course.

3.2 Strategy of implantation

The course Digital Treatment of Signals has been used to validate the application of PROVIR in the teaching of a real case and its adaptation to the concrete educational methodology of this course.

In order to guarantee the reliability of the system we have established that all the tools developed must past a period of validation before their use in the official teaching. For each one of the integral tools of model PROVIR three phases or states are defined:

- Debugging: the tool is tested intensively to detect and to correct the possible errors.
- Validation: the tools are used in controlled circumstances, like nonofficial and seminaries.
- Operation: after validating the tool during a minimum period of 50 hours, it can be used with no limitation.

The integration of the educational methodology of TDS with PROVIR takes place progressively in two phases: the first step, that is transitory, presents a moderate integration with PROVIR. During this phase, we use only those tools that have been passed to operational state. Also, this transitory phase is used to obtain the students opinion about the use of the tele-education tools.

The final purpose is to teach the course using PROVIR system. It will be reached in the second phase, during the year 2002-03, once all the tools have passed the number of hours established as validation and are in operational state. This phase will present a full integration with PROVIR.

3.3 Educational contributions of PROVIR

The objective when using PROVIR system with this course is to use the available telematic tools to improve the quality of teaching and to increase to the communication professor-student without having to change the used methodology.

In the following sections the integration of TDS with PROVIR is detailed, specifying in each area of operation the integration grade reached during 2001-02 and its final evolution that will be obtained in the next year.

3.3.1 Teaching preparation

The preparation of the course Digital Treatment of Signals is divided in two tasks: creation of the web site with all the information related with the course and registering and grouping the students for the practical exercises and their distribution in the four existing turns.

In the first step we have to determine the web site contents, the information that is going to be included in the web site. These contents can be divided in two great categories: permanent information and dynamic information. The permanent information consists of all the information related with the course that does not change during the year. The documents included in this category are: course description, objectives, bibliography, methodology of evaluation and general scheduling.

The dynamic information is composed by all the contents of the course that do not remain constant throughout the course, either reflecting the advance of the course program or adding new information as it is generated: news, lists of students and groups, qualifications, practice scheduling and…

The main objective for the year 2001-02, during the transitory phase of integration with PROVIR, is to verify the validity of the web site contents and its acceptance from the students. We have registered the number of visits to each one of the pages during the course; there were a total of 28000 visits to the course pages, that is, an average from 240 visits per student. The more visited pages were the news page and the scheduling that maintained a constant average of views throughout all the year. This fact can be explained because these pages contain information that changes almost every day.

The other task in the course preparation is the registration and grouping of the students. In 2001-02 this task was achieved electronically with the tools integrated in Portal POVIR, facilitating the students' management. In figure 9-2 we can observe the high number of student registration during the first days. A week after the beginning of the course all students were registered and had chosen his group, so that the practical classes could begin.

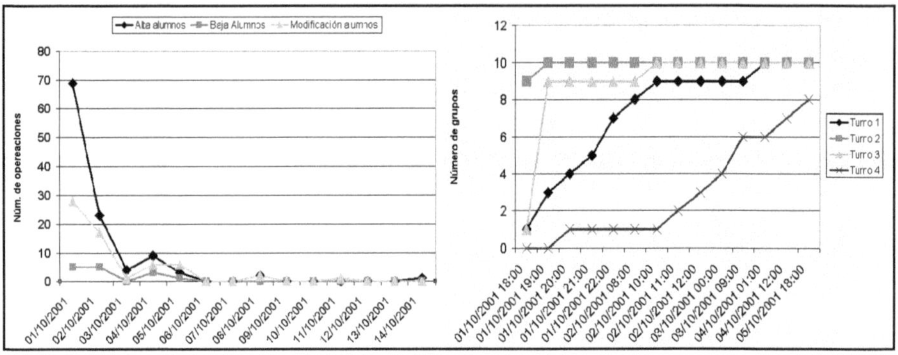

Figure 9-2. a) Operations of student registration, b) Number of groups created

3.3.2 Theoretic lesson

The integration of PROVIR with TDS makes possible the remote explanation of theoretic lessons using the teleconferencing tool PROVIR RT. Nevertheless, in the transitory phase we have not used this tool, partly because the tool was not in operational phase, but also because we did not have the necessary resources to allow its use for all the students. In the year 2002-03, PROVIR RT will be already in operation state and it is hoped to have the necessary resources, so that PROVIR RT will be used to teach the theoretic lessons.

The use of this synchronous tele-education tool to teach the theoretic lessons has special importance to explain the operation of the computer programs that are going to be used later in the laboratory. The professor can use the remote desktop tool integrated in PROVIR RT to show all the students how to perform the basic operations of each simulation program.

Another advantage of the use of PROVIR RT is that the recording session tool can be used to store each theoretic lesson to make an electronic library that can be reviewed by the students when they want.

3.3.3 Control of the laboratory

PROVIR RT not only can be used for the theoretic classes of the course, but also it will be used during the practical hours to facilitate the control of the work done by the students. The professor must observe what the students are doing and solve the doubts that arise while they solve the exercises.

During year 2001-02, this control is made in person, the professor moving around the laboratory, from student workplace to student workplace, while he verifies the progress of each group and solves their doubts. This method limits the number of groups that can work simultaneously in a same laboratory. In the year 2002-03, as part of final integration, PROVIR RT will be used to make the control of the laboratory. In this case, the professor will stay on his own workplace and will check the students work using the remote desktop of PROVIR RT.

The use of PROVIR RT for the control of the laboratories improves the time usage because the professor does not have to move from a workplace to another one, allowing to improve the control of students work and to increase the number of groups in each turn.

3.3.4 Auto-evaluation

PROVIR SET has been used to make auto-evaluation tests which can be used by the students to verify their knowledge. The professors have generated a compendium of questions about all the chapters of the course and each test consist of a reduced set of questions chosen randomly from this compendium, so that they are different for each test. The number of questions created initially in the first year oscillates between 50 and 80 per chapter. During the next years the number of questions will be increased progressively. As the number of questions increases, we will classify the questions by their degree of difficulty so that there will be several tests of increasing difficulty per chapter.

The auto-evaluation uses the automatic correction of SET to show the test score just after its completion. All the tests are optional and their scores do not influence the final qualification, but the answers are stored in the database with statistical purpose. The analysis of these data allows us to identify the study methodology of the students: most of them only study immediately before their knowledge is going to be evaluated. However, there is a small percentage of students who study continuously throughout the year.

3.3.5 Continuous evaluation

The continuous evaluation exams consist of the resolution of one or more exercises using several methodologies: analytically, through simulation and with real-time implementation.

The evaluation of the analytical resolution of each exercise uses PROVIR SET to obtain the most important results of the resolution and the following analysis to obtain them.

The practical resolutions require that the professor check if the simulations and programs created by the students work, so that they cannot be evaluated using PROVIR SET. During 2001-02 this practical resolution is qualified while the professor makes the round of consultations. In the next years, the professor will be able to use the remote desktop tool to verify if the simulations and programs created by each group of students work without moving from his own computer.

3.3.6 Educational poll

At the end of each year, the students of Digital Treatment of Signals fill a poll in order to express their opinion about the course and about the professors. Traditionally, this survey has been made in paper, and so that it is necessary to introduce the answers database to analyze the results statistically. From year 2001-02 this laborious process has been eliminated thanks to the use of PROVIR SET to perform the educational poll.

The objective of the surveys is to know the opinion of the students about the course and then the professors can use it to plan futures changes in the educational methodology. The survey made in year 2001-02 has special interest because is the first year in which the tools enclosed in PROVIR are used. We have added a set of questions related to the used tools that will serve like subjective evaluation of PROVIR. The poll results show a high degree of acceptance of both the used methodology and PROVIR system.

4. CONCLUSION

The use of PROVIR system in the course Digital Treatment of Signals, that requires the presence of the students during the practical exercises, demonstrates the adaptability of tele-education systems in general, and PROVIR in particular, to any educational methodology and that they are not limited to remote teaching in the strictest sense of the word.

The use of the tools integrated in PROVIR for teaching purposes allows the teacher to reduce the workload, facilitates the access to the information, facilitates the control of the students progress, and, in summary, it improves the quality of teaching

On the other hand, the strategy of implantation in two phases used in TDS provides a progressive transition to the new tele-education model allowing the previous evaluation of its impact on the course.

REFERENCES

1. R. M. Palloff y K. Pratt, Lessons from the Cyberspace Classroom: The Realities of Online Teaching. Ed. Jossey-Bass. 2001
2. P.Penfiel y R. Larson, "Education Via Advanced Technologies". IEEE Transactions on Education, Vol. 39 (3). 1996
3. M. Mariani, "Distance learning in postsecundary education: Learning whenever, wherever", Occupational Outlook Quarterly, vol. 45 Issue 2, Summer 2001
4. E. F. Spodick, "The Evolution of distance Learning". Honk Kong University of Science &Technology Library. August 1995. Available: http://sqzm14.ust.hk/distance/evolution-distance-learning.htm
5. L. Sherry, "Issues in distance Learning". International Journal of Educational Telecommunications I (4), pp. 337-365. 1996
6. D.H. Jonnassen, "Applications and limitations of hypertext technology for distance learning". Distance Learning Workshop, Armstrong Laboratory. 1992
7. D.R. Garrison, "An analysis and evaluation of audio teleconferencing to facilitate education at a distance". American Journal of Distance Education, 4(3), pp. 16-23. 1990
8. P. Zhang, "A case study on technology use in distance learning". Journal of Research on Computing in Education vol. 30 (4), pp. 389-411. 1998
9. A.W. Bates, "Third generation distance education: The challenge of new technology". Research in Distance Education, 3 (2), pp. 10-16. 1991
10. A. Duin y R. Archee, "Collaboration via e-mail and Internet Relay Chat: understanding time and technology". Technical Communication, 43(4), pp 402-412. 1996
11. J. P. Merisotis y R. A. Phipps, "What's the Difference? A Review of Contemporary Research on the Effectiveness of Distance Learning in Higher Education". The Institute for Higher Education Policy. Change, 31(3), pp. 13-17 April 1999,. Available: http://www.ihep.com/difference.pdf

Chapter 10

SHARING LIVE EDUCATIONAL RESOURCES IN UNIVERSAL WITH ISABEL

Juan Quemada, Joaquín Salvachúa, Blanca Rodríguez, Gabriel Huecas
Universidad Politécnica de Madrid

Abstract— This document describes the design, architecture and implementation of the Isabel live delivery platform integrated in the Universal Brokerage Platform. Isabel enables live delivery of Educational Learning Activities, such as courses, lectures, talks or interactive collaborations over the Internet. We will discuss both the design decisions and the actual implementation, which makes use of the new Semantic Web technologies at the UBP side and of the Internet .multimedia architecture at the Isabel side.

1. INTRODUCCION

The use of new information and communication technologies to improve the overall effectiveness of the educational system is an area of intensive research. The use of new technologies enables new forms of collaboration among educational institutions, which can have a significant impact in those institutions. Therefore many initiatives aim at the creation of educational materials based on open standards which allow exchange and reuse over the network [14, 15, 16], as well as at the design of services which support the exchange and collaboration among educators [2, 3, 7, 8, 9, 10, 13, 19, 20, 21], which are known as educational mediators.

This work has been partilly funded by the European IST UNIVERSAL Project.

M. Llamas-Nistal et al. (eds.), Computers and Education. Towards a Lifelong Learning Society, 115–126.

The Universal project has created the EducaNext service [3, 4, 8] for supporting the exchange of learning resources among members of academic institutions and knowledge communities. Academic institutions, as well as knowledge communities hosted by EducaNext, allow their members --- educators or knowledge producers--- to collaborate and exchange knowledge resources. The service can be accessed at http://www.educanext.org.

EducaNext has been created using the brokerage platform produced in the Universal IST project, known as the UBP (Universal Brokerage Platform) [4]. The portal which provides access to the service has been created at the Vienna University of Economy.

Educational mediators exchange usually educational objects, which are also referred to as packaged content, which is aimed at supporting learners in their learning process or at supporting educators in the learning activities under their control. The Universal approach goes one step further and supports not only the exchange of learning materials, but also the exchange of learning activities over the network. More concretely Educanext supports the brokerage of

- Educational materials, such as electronic textbooks, recorded lectures and presentations, case studies, quizzes, lecture notes, problem statements, project assignments, etc.
- Educational activities, such as lectures, tutoring sessions, synchronous group collaboration, on-line courses, etc.

The rationale [22, 23] behind the support to the exchange of learning activities is that the majority of the educational system is based on presential education, because of the higher effectiveness of the school paradigm as compared to self study approaches. The broadband networks and applications existing today allow an effective sharing of educational activities in synchronous collaborations over the network with advanced collaboration applications, which make use of videoconferencing, remote presentation, as well as other shared media.

EducaNext shall enable an electronic market place of learning resources as depicted in Figure 1, where a broker holds metadata representing the offers and bookings of learning resources, whereas the learning resources exchanged will be offered by content providers which will offer them over separate delivery channels which make use of separate servers.

2. SERVICE ARCHITECTURE

The UBP is an open platform which has the goal of allowing the integration of users, as well as learning object offers or even existing learning resource repositories. The design has been therefore based in open standards, mainly from based, such as, XML/RDF metadata representations

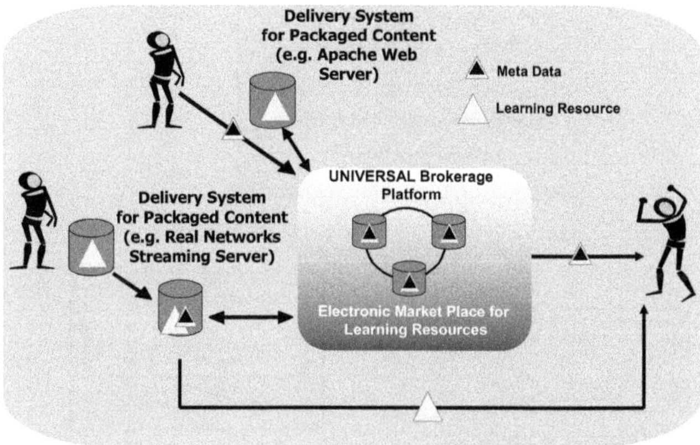

Figure 10-1. User view of EducaNext

of the learning resource offers, SOAP interfaces for communication or URN for object references. The IEEE LOM standard [14] has been used for metadata representation although extensions have been necessary to support the representation of educational activities [22, 23]. Offers describe and link resources available over the Internet, which have been made by members of EducaNext and which may be booked by other members of EducaNext.

In order to decouple the brokering functions from the content delivery functions, the UBP includes a generic delivery interface for the integration of existing content delivery servers or platforms. This interface is known as the DME (Delivery Management Engine). This architecture creates a two layer system where the upper layer deals only with brokerage of learning object metadata, whereas the lower layer deals with learning resource delivery, as shown in the next Figure 2.

The learning object metadata are represented in XML/RDF, because in order to make the UBP an early example of the W3C Semantic Web initiative. Each learning object which is made available over the UBP is therefore represented by a 3 element tuple including the resource URN.

The open and distributed architecture of the UBP has several benefits. Delivery servers or platforms may have a distributed architecture, which facilitates the integration of existing repositories or content servers. The existence of an open interface allows the integration of the brokering function of the UBP to existing eLearning delivery platforms or to future ones. The DME interface has been designed to allow the interworking with packaged content servers, as well as with live delivery platforms which allow collaborative educational activities among Universities.

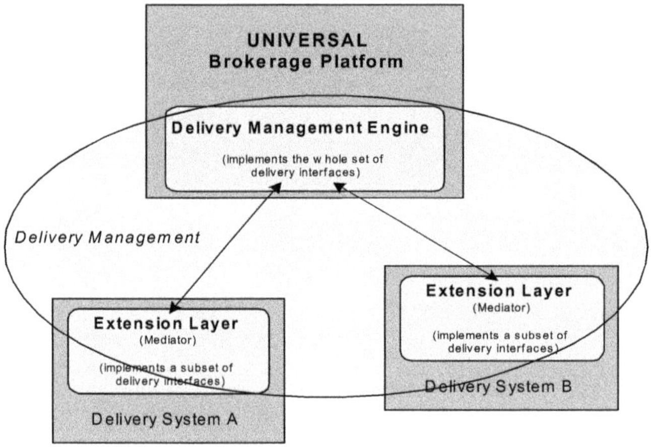

Figure 10-2. Service Architecture

The interface defined between the UBP and the Delivery System is described in more detail in Figure 3. It supports operations like booking, availability, billing and payment.

The DME interface has the following functionality:

- Check the availability of the system and if all requirements for the delivery are meet.
- Grant, Deny and Check security access for a user.
- Check the availability of a Learning Resource and check if the requirements for the delivery are meet.
- Report each delivery and access to the Learning Resources from the delivery system to the DME in order to allow billing.

The following table shows a couple of delivery platforms which have been integrated in the UBP in the UNIVERSAL project.

Learning Management Systems:	Hyperwave e-Learning Suite
Standard Web Server repository:	Apache server
Streaming Audio- and Video:	Real Networks Servers
Video Conferencing and Collaborative Work:	The CSCW Isabel application

The CSCW Isabel application [24, 25, 26] has been chosen for live delivery of UBP events, because of the support provided for interactive activities in a multipoint scenario and because it enables the realisation of various types of collaborative activities supported over the network, such classes, seminars, meetings, etc.

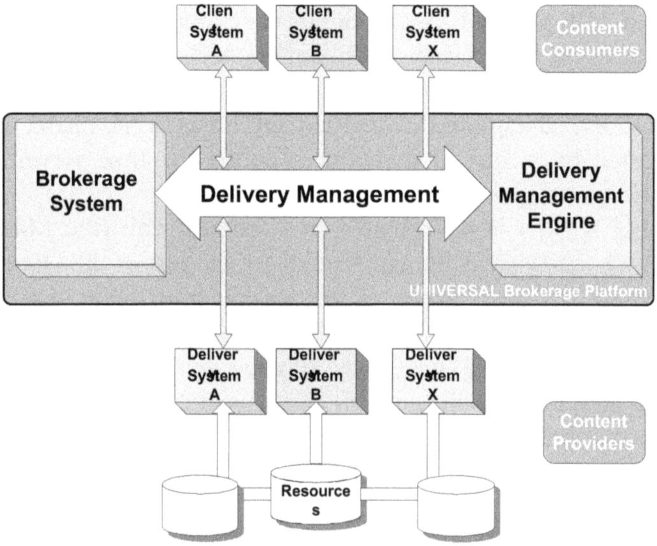

Figure 10- 3. DME Architecture

3. INTRODUCTION TO ISABEL

The Isabel CSCW application [24, 25, 26] is a group collaboration tool for the Internet, which uses standard TCP-UDP/IP protocols. Isabel platforms complement the UNIVERSAL Brokerage Platform by supporting the realisation of the various types of collaborative activities over the Internet. Isabel supports the following types of services:

- Tele-training, which provides a strict control by the lecturer or educator of the interactions taking place. For example, the lecturer can bring any site into scene at any time, the students or trainees must request intervention to the lecturer intervention, etc.
- Tele-meeting, which supports a fairly free way of interacting, allowing each participant to react in a fairly free way.
- Tele-conference, which is script driven and is based on a centralized control which guaranties a timely delivery of the program.
- Other services defined using the Isabel service description language.

Isabel Platforms are constructed over IP networks using either IP unicast, IP multicast or mixtures of both. A flow server is the Isabel equivalent to a videoconferencing MCUs and must be used for creating multi-points over unicast connectivity. Terminals can be used as flow servers as they always include one. Dedicated flow servers can be also used.

UDP and TCP packet flows in an Isabel session are as follows: First, the management agent of the Isabel terminal connects to the Master site with a TCP connection. Then, media components are exchanged between the Isabel terminals as UDP Datagram flows. The UDP flows of the media components are aggregated by a special component called the flow-server. The UDP flows can be exchanged over unicast or multicast.

An Isabel session is coordinated by a control unit (the Master) of the session, which acts also as the entry point for the rest of the Isabel terminals to the session. The participants to the session must connect via an Isabel terminal, which has to request to the Master the acceptance into the session. Once the Isabel terminal has been allowed by the Master to enter the conference, he will enter the session and participate in the activities taking place in the session.

4. DELIVERY OF EDUCATIONAL ACTIVITIES

The organization and management of distributed educational activities is an effort-consuming task, which requires the collaboration of different actors (lectures, tutors, network experts, etc.) and institutions.

Live activities require a live videoconferencing platform to be set up between the institution offering the live resource and the institutions booking the resource and the exact topology of the platform will not be known until all the bookings of the resource have been made.

The interface between the Broker and the live delivery platform includes two components: a platform server which manages the setup of the delivery platforms, and a language for the description of live videoconferencing platforms. The language is called EDL (sEssion Definition Language) and allows incremental definition of sessions, as well as authentified access.

Initially the interface between the Delivery Management Engine and the Deliver System was implemented using a proprietary protocol over HTTP. Now this interface has been defined using the W3C Web Services framework and uses SOAP and is offered in WSDL.

5. EDL DATA MODELLING

An EDL file (confErence Description Language) is composed of a generic session description and a set of participating site descriptions. The generic session description must include all the session parameter as well as the generic elements of the session, such as the master and the Isabel MCU's (Flow Servers) used for the session. Each site must define the type of participation, (interactive or not), the bandwidth, the Flow Server used, etc. EDL is platform-independent, allowing the definition of application and networking platforms. EDL has been successfully used on the live trials on 2001.

EDL used in the first definition a proprietary syntax, but has been redefined in a second version in XML/RDF to make it an open resource usable by third parties in the context of the Semantic Web. In this section the EDL data model is presented, with both XML and RDF serializations.

5.1 XML and RDF Serializations

The eXtensible Markup Language (XML) [12, 17] is a development of the World Wide Web Consortium (W3C) derived from the more complex Standard Generalised Markup Language (SGML), and aimed mainly at structuring data over the web. Like HTML, XML makes use of tags (words bracketed by '<' and '>') and attributes (of the form name="value"). A well-formed XML document creates a tree of tags, each of which can include several attribute-value pairs.

In XML there is no fixed tag vocabulary or set of allowable combinations. This may be done in two ways: by using a document type definition (DTD) or an XML Schema. Both of them define the structure of a XML document. The EDL XML Schema is partially shown in Figure 4.

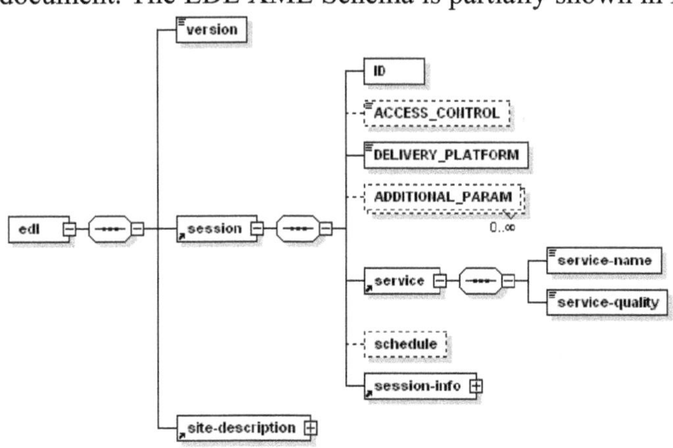

Figure 10-4. EDL XMLSchema

The EDL XML document is an instance of the EDL XML Schema, which means that it must conform the XML Schema to be valid. For example, an EDL XML document defining an Isabel telemeeting conference, etc would be serialized like this:

```
    <edl xmlns:xsi="http://www.w3.org/2001/XMLSchema-instance"
xsi:noNamespaceSchemaLocation="esquemaEDL.xsd">
        <version>1.5</version>
        <session>
            <ID>Universal</ID>
            <DELIVERY_PLATFORM>
                Isabel
            </DELIVERY_PLATFORM>
            <service>
                <service-name>telemeeting</service-name>
                <service-quality>2M</service-quality>
            </service>
    ...
        </session>
</edl>
```

The Resource Description Framework (RDF) [1, 11] is another World Wide Web Consortium initiative, building upon earlier developments such as the Dublin Core and the Platform for Internet Content Selectivity (PICS).

RDF is a foundation for processing metadata; it provides interoperability between applications that exchange machine-understandable information on the Web. The basic concept in RDF is that an identifiable, addressable 'resource' may be described by means of a selection of 'properties', each of which has an associated 'value'. These properties may, as well, form, in their selves, a further 'resource'.

The specification shows three representations of the RDF data model: as 3-tuples (triples), as a graph, and in XML. These representations have equivalent meaning [11].

Graphical RDF directed graph descriptions add clarity, allowing the distinction between resources, properties and values to become clear. At their most basic, such diagrams are as shown in Figure 5.

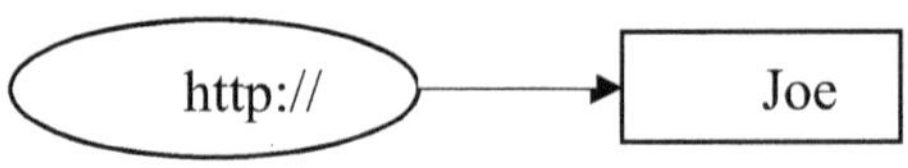

Figure 10-5. RDF Graph

Here, a 'resource', webpage.html, has a 'property', author, with the 'value' Joe Smith. In this diagrammatic form, resources are represented as ovals, properties are represented by arrows and the value of the property is represented as a rectangle, if it is a literal; but this property may, in turn, be a resource itself, and in this case, it would be represented as an oval.

This information can also be represented in the form of 3-tuples (triplets): {predicate, subject, and object}, where predicate is a property, subject is a resource, and object is either a literal or a resource. In the previous example the triple would be expressed as {author, webpage.html, Joe Smith}.

XML provides the default syntax used to encode RDF descriptions. The previous example would be coded in XML as follows:

```
<?xml version="1.0"?>
<rdf:RDF
   xmlns:rdf="http://www.w3.org/1999/02/22-rdf-syntax-ns#">
 <rdf:Description rdf:about="http://webpage.html">
    <author> Joe Smith </author>
 </rdf:Description>
</rdf:RDF>
```

RDF properties may be thought of as attributes of resources and, in this sense, used to represent traditional attribute-value pairs. RDF properties also represent relationships between resources.

As XML Schema allows defining a vocabulary, RDF Schema allows to define a vocabulary for properties and specify to which objects can be applied [11]. But, unlike an XML DTD or Schema, which gives specific constraints on the structure of an XML document, an RDF Schema provides information about the interpretation of the statements given in an RDF data model. While an XML Schema can be used to validate the syntax of an RDF/XML expression, a syntactic schema alone is not sufficient for RDF purposes. RDF Schemas may also specify constraints that should be followed by these data models. In the next Figure, an example of an EDL RDF document is represented, using a graph:

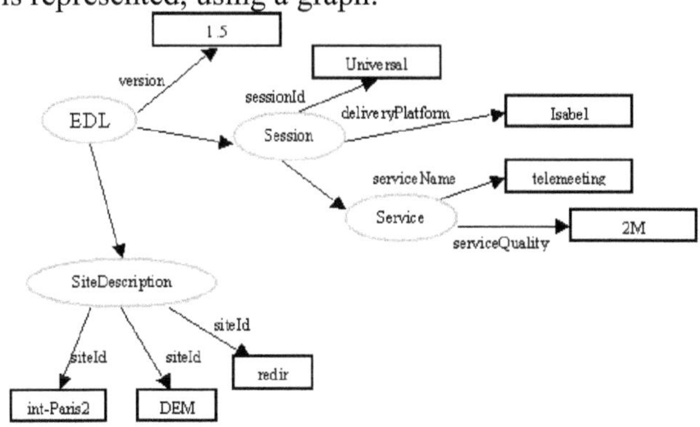

Figure 10-6. Example of an EDL RDF Document

Some of the corresponding triples for the graph above would be:

{version, /EDL, 1.5}
{session, /EDL, /EDL/Session}
{sessionId, /EDL/Session, Universal}
{deliveryPlatform, Session, Isabel}
{service, /EDL/Session, /EDL/Session/Service}

6. CONCLUSIONS

This paper describes the extension of an educational content mediator to allow the brokerage of educational activities, which is based on a new taxonomy for learning resources that differentiates "educational activities" from "educational material". This taxonomy has led to an enrichment of the standard LOM metadata model and serves as a vehicle for defining generalized educational offers which should be acquired or consumed by third parties with the help of educational mediators. The model can represent a variety of educational offers available since the dawn of the Internet, ranging from traditional courses in the classroom to courses over videoconferencing or over learning management systems.

The term "educational activities" is used to refer to events of which the primary goal is to educate and train persons, whereas "educational material" is used to refer to units of content that support educational activities. A clear differentiation between these two categories of learning resources seems necessary for deriving proper exchange models for educational mediators. Besides, we support the argument that educational activities as a special type of learning resource are not sufficiently covered by the IEEE LOM.

The integration of "educational activities" in an educational mediator is straightforward, although the organisation of distributed educational activities requires complex coordination procedures among academic reponsibles. The realisation of live activities creates also new IPR issues [18]. The live broadcasting of the sessions and the recording and redistribution of the activities need to be addressed in each offer/booking process.

The availability of European broadband networks is a necessary condition for the realization of live experiments. The deployment of GEANT and the improvements taken place during the lifetime of the project have greatly simplified the organisation of live events at the end of the project, when the broadband European Internet (GEANT + NRENs) where generally available at the participating institutions. This was not the case at the start of the UNIVERSAL project, when the MBS ATM service had to be used.

Isabel has fulfilled the needs of the collaborative educational activities done in the trials. EDL has also fulfilled the requirements for which it was designed, namely the incremental generation of live platform according to the offer/booking process of each learning resource brokerage.

7. ACKNOWLEDGEMENTS

This work was supported by the UNIVERSAL project and is partly sponsored by the European Commission (IST-1999-11747). The authors would like to express their gratitude to the consortium members who actively participated in the UBP design, in the integration of Isabel, in the trials with Isabel and in particular to Arno Wagner, Bernd Simon, Gustav Neuman, Stefan Brantner, Katherine Maillet, Vana Kamitsou and Effie Law.

REFERENCES

1. W. Nejdl, W. Siberski, B. Simon, J. Tane: Towards a Modification Exchange Language for Distributed RDF Repositories, Proceedings of the 1st International Semantic Web Conference, Sardinia, Italia, June, 2002.
2. H. Ahmed, L.K. Stergioulas and C.S. Xydeas An adaptive, on-line, data acquisition/presentation engine for the pedagogical assessment of learning resources, in: Proceeding of the EU conf on e-Learning in a life learning perspective, Lund University, Sweden, 24-26 Oct 2001.
3. S. Brantner, T. Enzi , S. Guth, G. Neumann, B. Simon: UNIVERSAL - Design and Implementation of a Highly Flexible E-Market Place of Learning Resources, in: Proceedings of the IEEE International Conference on Advanced Learning Technologies. Madison (WI), USA, August, 2001.
4. G. Vrabic, B. Simon: Learning Resource Catalogue Design of the UNIVERSAL Brokerage Platform, in: Proceedings of ED-MEDIA 2001. June, 2001.
5. B. Simon: Erfolgsfaktoren Elektronischer Märkte im Hochschulsektor - Eine Studie im Rahmen des UNIVERSAL-Projekts, in: Virtueller Campus - Szenarien - Strategien - Studium, Hildesheim (Deutschland), September, 2001.
6. M. Hämäläinen, A. B. Whinston, and S. Vishik, "Electronic Markets for Learning: Education Brokerage on the Internet," Communications of the ACM, vol. 39, pp. 51-58, 1996.
7. P. Meier and B. Simon, "Reengineering Undergraduate Teaching by Introducing Internet-based Learning Information Systems," in Proceedings of the 8th European Conference on Information Systems, vol. 1439-1444, Vienna: Springer, 2000.
8. S. Guth, G. Neumann, and B. Simon, "UNIVERSAL - Design Spaces for Learning Media," in Proceedings of the 34th Hawaii International Conference on System Sciences, Maui (USA), Maui, USA: IEEE, 2001.

9. K. Stanoevska-Slabeva and B. F. Schmid, "Requirements Analysis for Community Supporting Platforms Based on the Media Reference Model," International Journal of Electronic Markets, vol. 10, pp. 250-257, 2000.
10. F. Arcelli and M. De Santo, "An Agent based Internet Infrastructure for Learning Commerce," in Proceedings of the 33rd Hawaii International Conference on System Sciences - 2000, O.A., Ed. Maui, 2000.
11. D. Brickley and R. V. Guha, Resource Description Framework (RDF) Model and Syntax Specification: W3C Recommendation: REC-rdf-syntax-19990222, 1999.
12. T. Bray, J. Paoli, and C. M. Sperger-McQueen, Extensible Markup Language (XML): W3C Recommendation: REC-xml-19980210, February 1998.
13. S.-G. Han, J.-B. Park, J.-E. Jung, and G.-S. Jo, "Intelligent Gathering of Contents on Distance Education using Mobile Agents," in Proceedings of the International Conference on Electronic Commerce 2000, Seoul, Korea: 2000, pp. 267-273.
14. "IEEE Learning Technology Standards Committee (LTSC) Learning Object Metadata - Draft Document v3.8" http://ltsc.ieee.org/doc/wg12/LOM3.8.html, 1999.
15. T. Anderson, D. McArthur, S. Griffin, and T. Wason, IMS Meta-data Best Practice and Implementation Guide: Educause, 1999.
16. F. Dawson and T. Howes, vCard MIME Directory Profile. The Internet Society: http://andrew2.andrew.cmu.edu/rfc/rfc2426.html, 1998.
17. Wang, Extensible rigths Markup Language (XrML): http://www.xrml.org, 2000.
18. R. Iannella, "Open Digital Right Languages (ODRL)," W3C Workshop on Digital Rights Management, 2001.
19. E. Duval, E. Forte, K. Cardinaels, B. Verhoeven, R. Van Durm, K. Hendrix, M. W. Forte, N. Ebel, M. Macowicz, K. Warkentyne and F. Haenni (2001). The Ariadne Knowledge Pool System. *Communications of the ACM*, 44 (5), 73-78.
20. W. Nejdl, B. Wolf, C. Qu, S. Decker, M. Sintek, N. Ambjörn, M. Nilsson, M. Palmer and T. Risch (2002). EDUTELLA: A P2P Networking Infrastructure Based on RDF. In: Proceedings of the 11th International World Wide Web Conference, Hawaii, USA,
21. L. E. Anido, M. J. Fernández, M. Caeiro, J. M. Santos, J. S. Rodríguez and M. Llamas (2002). Educational metadata and brokerage for learning resources. Computers & Education, 38 (2002), 351-374.
22. J. Quemada, B. Simon, A Use-Case Based Model for Learning Resources in Educational Mediators. IEEE Educational Technology & Society Journal, ISSN 1436-4522, 2003.
23. B. Simon and J. Quemada. A Critical Reflection of Metadata Standards Based on Usage Scenarios. In Medien in der WissenSChaft. Proceedings of GMW Tagung 2002, Basel September 2002, pp:241-250. ISBN 3-8309-1191-2.
24. Isabel CSCW Application http://isabel.dit.upm.es
25. Juan Quemada, Tomas de Miguel Arturo Azcorra, Santiago Pavón, Joaquin Salvachua, Manuel Petit, David Larrabeiti, Tomas Robles, Gabriel Huecas, Daniel Rodriguez, Fernando Echevarrieta, Eva Castro, Teleservice creation with Isabel in heterogeneous network environments, Interoperability of Networks for Interoperable Services, ISSN 1385 9501, Ottawa, July 1998.
26. J. Quemada, T. P. de Miguel, E. Castro, S. Pavón, G. Huecas, T. Robles, J. Salvachúa, E. Apolinario, J. Sedano, Mª J. Perea. Isabel distribution of the Madrid Global IPv6 Summit 2002 over an IPv6 transition network. Proc. of the 2003 Symposium on Applications and the Internet Workshops, IEEE. Orlando Florida. ISBN 0-7695-1873-7, pags: 200-203, January 2003.

Chapter 11

ACCESSIBILITY: DISCUSSING HUMAN-COMPUTER INTERACTION ON THE WEB

Débora Conforto
Lucila Maria Costi Santarosa

Abstract: This paper intends to reflect upon the structural concepts of a new ethnic-cultural basis for society, and legitimize the potential of new communication and information technologies as efficient agents of democratization of spaces, which can allow knowledge experiences. We discuss the problem of Web accessibility and we present a digital library with the objective of creating strategies that increase the participation of all individuals with full rights, creating equality of opportunities and respect for differences in the emerging cyberspace.

Key words: Accessibility, Human-computer Interaction, Digital Inclusion, and Digital Library

1. INTRODUCTION

Advances in graphic representation, animation and dynamic information are often excluding factors for an increasingly and significant great number of user with special needs (whether physical, motor or cognitive), and even for those having incompatibility problems with many platforms for the support of certain software or hardware.

This excluding process has been conditioning the discussion about Web Accessibility and Computer-Assisted Technologies and establishing conditions for the structuring of projects connected to current world movements supporting digital inclusion.

M. Llamas-Nistal et al. (eds.), Computers and Education. Towards a Lifelong Learning Society, 127–137.

Challenged by the new possibilities created by the incorporation of new digital tools and believing that the changes implemented by computer resources cannot be clung to history and, mainly, aware that each new technology created by humanity brings in itself a high inclusive or excluding power, we intend to discuss the necessity of a conceptual revolution to empower new information and communication technologies as co-structuring elements for the overcome of digital exclusion and present the project of a Web Accessibility and Computer-Assisted Technologies Digital Library designed by the researchers at RedEspecial -Brazil., a non-governmental organization (NGO) in collaboration with NIEE UFRGS and with financial support from FAPERGS[3].

2. INTERNET ACCESSIBILITY

Internet accessibility is the flexibility of access to information and interaction of users who have some special kind of need. In this perspective, accessibility is understood as a synonym of approach, a way of providing each user with an interface that respects his / her needs and preferences. Current investigation carried out by international researchers who seek to articulate a project of social inclusion has revealed the importance of developing a global process of discussion about accessibility. Official documents, such as the European Union documents, have already revealed the need to implement public actions to face the problem of digital exclusion.

It was believing in the construction of a society based on the possible utopia of inclusion for all its social actors, that international groups - GUIDES, SIDAR, W3C-WAI, among others - and companies such as Microsoft and IBM are researching on Web accessibility. Many times, discussions about accessibility remained limited to the physical and sensorial limitations of users with special needs, but these aspects can bring benefits to a greater number of users, making knowledge available on the Web reach a much greater audience, without damaging its graphic or functional characteristics.

To deal with the diversity of specificities, researchers such as Neto[3], Zúnica [8], Group GUIDES [2] and W3C-WAI [6], point to actions in key areas, establishing and guaranteeing accessibility to new information and communication technologies. These actions are related to: accessibility characteristics incorporated in the hardware or in the operating system that

[3] A prototype of *Biblioteca Digital de Acessibilidade à Web e Tecnologias Assistivas Informáticas* is available at www.redespecial.org.br.

promote its accessibility to users with or without special needs; utilities that modify the system to make it more useful to a greater number of users and more practical to install in all platforms, such as output systems in Braille or keyboard or mouse modifications; special applications for people with disabilities, such as word processors designed to integrate voice and text with the objective of helping users with limited writing and reading abilities; the characteristics of usability that can be incorporated to the main special needs, making them easier, such as the standardizing of colours or keyboard accelerators.

The main objective of Web accessibility principles is making all Web content available to all users in the worldwide network of computers – the Internet. According to W3C-WAI – Web Accessibility Initiative del Word Wide Web Consortium – the most frequent causes of lack of accessibility for users in many web pages are often associated to the absence of a structure, which disorients the user making navigation a difficult process, and the abusive use of graphic information - images, image maps, tables to format content, Java scripts, multimedia elements - without providing adequate alternatives of text or another kind of comment. This kind of web page modelling generates problems of accessibility mainly for users who use screen readers that send the content of an image to a voice synthesizer (such as pwWebSpeak) or for those who use browsers that only display the text of web pages (such as Lynx or Net Tamer).

Accessibility principles or directives were organized having this perspective in mind. They were made to be followed by all Web content authors – site owners and creators – and by those who create computer tools to model Web content. Accessibility principles, according to W3C-WAI [6], involve two axes: assuring a harmonious transformation and making all available content browsable and understandable.

The harmonious transformation of a Web page can be guaranteed by observing some key points in the creation of a Web page: separating the presentation structure, differentiating the content (the information to be conveyed), the structure (the way the information is organized in logical terms) and the presentation (the way the information is reproduced, for example, printed, displayed in a bidimentional graphic presentation, exclusively in a graphic form, as a synthesized talk, in Braille, etc.); creating pages that achieve its purpose, even when the user cannot see and/or hear, supplying information that fills the same purpose or function that the audio or video, in a way to adapt, in the best possible way, to alternative sensorial channels and to the available support technologies; creating pages that do not depend exclusively on a single kind of equipment, because they should be accessible to users who do not have a mouse, who receive voice or text, etc.

Creators of Web content need to make their productions understandable, using a clear language and providing means to access and understand the information presented. Providing site orientation and navigation tools are factors that increase Web accessibility because they guarantee perceptibility and browsability within the site. Without these elements, the users may not, for example, understand tables, lists or extensive menus.

The general principles about the concept of Web accessibility were posted in the site of the group GUIDES [2] and W3C-WAI [6], created in an International Forum of Specialists between December 14 and 18, 1999. These principles or directives should be applied only to information considered relevant to the comprehension of the navigation and content. Its application should allow the interaction with the system without requiring vision, pointing devices, precise movements or simultaneous actions and the comprehension of information and navigation through auditory or visual means. Accessibility verification points were established for each proposed principle or directive as a way to explain how each one is applied to typical developing environments for Web content.

3. ACCESSIBILITY PRINCIPLES

The creators of content for the worldwide network of computers – the Internet, when conceiving a page or a site, should have in mind the multitude of situations and the diversity of users on the Web. In order to make each project of a page an accessibility stimulator, researchers elaborated a set of principles or directives with the objective of sharing the benefits of the Web to all its users. The document elaborated by the W3C – Web Content Accessibility Guidelines 1.0 [6], presents fourteen principles or directives that deal with Web accessibility questions, detailing the verification points with the respective priorities, presenting solutions for accessible projects:

1°. To supply alternatives to sound or visual content - providing the kind of content that, when presented to the user, conveys, in essence, the same functions and purposes of the sound or visual content.

2°. Not to appeal only to color - assuring the perceptibility of text and graphic elements when viewed without colors.

3°. To use correctly notes and style sheets – through documents annotation with adequate structural elements. To control the presentation through style sheets, instead of doing it with presentation elements and attributes.

4º. To indicate clearly which is the language used – using notes that facilitate the pronunciation and the interpretation of abbreviations or text in foreign language.

5º. To create tables that are subject to a harmonious transformation – assuring that the tables have the necessary notes to be harmoniously transformed by accessible browsers.

6º. To assure that pages full of new technologies are transformed harmoniously – making pages accessible even when the more recent technologies are not supported or have been deactivated.

7º To allow user control over temporary alterations of the content – assuring the possibility of momentarily interruption of the movement, intermittence, display or automatic update of objects or pages.

8º. To allow the direct accessibility of integrated user interfaces – assuring an independent access of devices, operationality through the keyboard, voice emission (verbalization), etc.

9º. To approach the concept of independence when facing devices – using functions that allow page activation through input devices and commands. Generally pages that provide interaction through the keyboard are also accessible through interfaces of voice command or command lines.

10º. To use transition solutions – so that older support technologies and browsers work correctly.

11º. To use the technologies and principles of the W3C – to enable integrated accessibility functions, to guarantee that accessibility points are present in the content creation phase, because these specifications were developed according to an open and consensual process in the computer area.

12º. To supply context and orientation – to help users understand pages or complex elements.

13º. To supply clear browsing mechanisms – through coherent and systematized browsing mechanisms to increase user possibilities in finding information on the page or site. The existence of coherent and clear browsing mechanisms is important for users with cognitive or visual impairment, benefiting, also, all users.

14º. To assure clarity and simplicity of the documents – to guarantee an easier understanding by the user. The use of paging, this is, a coherent and systematic page distribution, with recognizable graphics and an easily understandable language is beneficial to all users, providing efficient communication.

4. WEB ACCESSIBILITY EVALUATION AND VALIDATION

Accessibility evaluation and validation should be made using automatic tools or using direct manual revision. Automatic approaches are generally quicker, but are not capable of identifying all accessibility aspects. Human evaluation can help guarantee language clarity and ease in browsing.

For the automatic accessibility validation of a page or site we can use the tools or services of analysis accessibility and compatibility, such as Bobby (http: //www.cast.org/bobby/); W3C validator (http://validador.w3.org/) and TAW (www.tawdis.net).

Zúnica [8] points out the advantages and disadvantages regarding automatic and human revisions/evaluations of WEB pages, considering combination of both as the ideal approach. The research team of W3C-WAI [6], point out, as an approach to test a page or site after the implementation of the accessibility principles, the following verification points:

• To use an automatic accessibility tool, and browser validation tools.

• To validate the syntax (e.g. HTML, XML, etc.) and style sheets.

• To use an only-text browser or an emulator.

• To use several graphic browsers with: sounds and graphics; without graphics; without mouse; without carrying frames, interpretable programs, style sheets or applets, and to use several browsers, old and recent.

• To use a browser with automatic speech emission, with screen readers, with enlargement software, monochromatic monitors, etc.

• To use spelling and grammar checkers. A user who uses a voice synthesizer to read a page may not be capable of choosing the best synthesizer approach for a word that has a spelling error. The elimination of grammar problems increases understanding.

• To review the document, verifying clarity and simplicity. Readability statistics, as those generated by some word processor programs, can be a valuable clarity and simplicity indicator. It is fundamental to submit the document to an experienced reviewer to check the written content and evaluate the clarity of the text and also identify potentially delicate cultural questions that can be a consequence of the kind of language or icon display.

• To validate pages with real users. These users, experienced or not, are a precious source of information about the page or site regarding its accessibility and ease of use.

5. WEB ACCESSIBILITY AND COMPUTER-ASSISTED TECHNOLOGY DIGITAL LIBRARY

The respect for human diversity requires an adaptation effort by the digital media and requires technical and theoretical competences that assure to web designers and engineers the necessary knowledge for the construction of a universal design for the promotion of accessibility to the ever-changing computer tools.

The project of a Web Accessibility and Computer-Assisted Technology Digital Library, coordinated by Redespecial BR, is another ongoing movement in searching for digital inclusion. Considering the accessibility problem, it proposes the modeling of an environment that enables the manipulation, edition, storage and retrieving of information in a digital collection dedicated to the themes: Web Accessibility and Computer-Assisted Technology.

The transition from printed to digital media has been leading to the problem of creating spaces that enable the manipulation and retrieving of information, imposing an endless number of challenges in order to adapt textual, symbolic, numerical, visual and sound data to the digital form. The concept of a Digital Library emerges as a possibility of redimensioning methodologies and creating strategies for the collect, handling and access to information in dynamic environments that, when respecting human diversity, empowers the social process of inclusion.

The interface between man and computer tools has becoming a critical element for a set of users with special needs, whether cognitive, physical or motor. The great motivation behind this project by Redespecial BR is the wish to contribute in the construction of a technical and theoretical base supporting international and national policies that, regarding the modeling of interfaces, may create strategies that allow full access to the new information and communication technologies to all social actors in the complex contemporary society towards the overcome of the current problem of digital-exclusion.

In the transition from a model, according to BARKER[1], of a traditional library that was created with the writing, enabling the implementation of the first mechanisms of collection automation, to the model of a modern or automatized library that provides a greater efficiency when cataloguing and organization information provided by the advancement of computer tools, we see, today, in the onset of the 21st century, the appearance of electronic libraries with an on-line collection.

The Internet, for Shaw [4], is the most important network for libraries, working as a conduit in the location and retrieval of information, creating new roles for librarians, now, information providers who interact with users mediated by computer tools. These new technological possibilities have created new concepts of time and space, which have increased the appearance of non-physical libraries, which begin to affect the environment and content of traditional libraries. Traditional libraries start to create a new environment – no more buildings, walls and furniture – and new ways to present their collection – from printed to digital – expressed in the different kinds of electronic media and empowered by a network of communication.

The Web Accessibility and Computer-Assisted Technology Digital Library intends to act as catalyst space and as an information provider, contributing with the construction of a knowledge base about the development of people with special needs supported by the new information and communication technologies. We try to create a channel where it is possible to socialize research and studies about accessibility for people with special needs in the computer network, taking advantage of all its potential to provide a set of information that supplies the theoretical support for the implementation of actions that enable the evolution and the interoperationalization of the Internet, reviewing its graphic standards and increasing the interaction of users with special needs.

Collaborating with the ongoing projects of building digital libraries - as the ones proposed by Rede Saci, by CNPq Information Portal – Prossiga, among others - we try to help in the discussion about the global process of digital inclusion, proposing the construction of a strategic time-space that enables the location and retrieval of information with a theoretical base that has as its main theme Web accessibility and Computer-Assisted Technologies. These are central topics in the process of building a true inclusive virtual community.

The team responsible for the project of a Web Accessibility and Computer-Assisted Technology Digital Library created actions for the implementation of its prototype, resuming, at first, all research linked to RedEspecial-BR, which served as a theoretical support in the framework of the structure and modeling of interfaces of the digital database. In the data structuring, we did not forget, initially, the most elementary forms of organization of a digital collection – the creation of a registry in a web page, with links that forward to accessibility and computer-assisted themes, therefore we believe that the greatest quality of the project is the richness of its collection much more than its graphic interface.

The opening interface of the digital library presents to the user two areas related to the central themes of the project – Accessibility and Computer-Assisted Technologies - and a specific area related to searching, through key words, author or topics.

To facilitate user navigation, the digital collection about Web Accessibility and Computer-Assisted Technology was previously organized according to the kind of technical help, guaranteeing a greater functionality for the user in the search for computer tools that can contribute to giving people with special needs a greater independence, quality of life and social inclusion, through the maintenance or evolution of its functional capacities.

To display the data about Web accessibility, we opted for an organization by themes with the objective of facilitating the search for information by the users. Our motivation when proposing such structure was offering the user a set of information that is previously organized for a qualified and updated theoretician base, as well as providing computer tools for the evaluation of products for the Web considering all accessibility principles.

To add more interactivity to the project of a digital library, it was created an interface for the inclusion of new information to the database, which enables the user, through forms, to collaborate in a remote way, qualifying the digital collection.

With the evolution of research, the growing volume of data points to the need of a more dynamic insertion and search of information, which is the phase we are working on at the moment. In this sense, we are evaluating the best language for the creation and generation of more dynamic sites for the Web, in order to create a more efficient search in the digital collection.

6. FINAL CONSIDERATIONS

Information and communication technologies promise to create a radical change in the life of society because they let us hear a plural voice, a key condition for the construction of a society with full participation and equality in opportunities for all its social actors.

Society needs to discuss the aspects that cause disadvantages in the performance of the roles of its social actors. Therefore, it is necessary to approach the relationship technology-social inclusion to discuss the strategies that act like limitators of social-political-cultural actions when they reject minorities and human diversity.

The creation of inclusive politics for the recognition of the difference becomes possible with a conceptual revolution that conceives the participation of all social actors with equality rights and respect for its specificities. The themes Web Accessibility and Computer-Assisted Technologies is part of this permanent movement in the search of construction strategies in order to break up social practices of exclusion and build a universal culture of accessibility.

The consequences of the technological innovations on the routine of society are undeniable. Those behavioral mutations have its consequences in the conditions of search, availability, storage and retrieval of information.

The Internet creates new concepts for the space-time of traditional libraries and assumes its central role in the support of research and in the implementation of libraries with digital collections, in the environment of our contemporary society.

When we believe that the full interaction of all citizens – one of the basic principles of our contemporary society - will only be guaranteed with the flexibilization of the access to information and with the effective participation of all users with special needs, we also believe that the project of a Web Accessibility and Computer-Assisted Technologies Digital Library is the possibility of building a technical and theoretical base in supporting national and international policies committed with the social model of disability. The actions of RedEspecial Brazil are generated by the motivation of building a reference in the construction of strategies that redirect the actions of programmers and web designer for the exercise of a universal design, enabling the full access to new information and communication technologies and, thus, increasing the important and necessary process of digital inclusion.

The greatest motivation of this group of researchers is participating in an effective way for the implementation of a network of solidarity for the construction of a truly inclusive society. In this perspective we are only one of the twenty-one threads of the Ibero American Special Nets that begin to weave the web of the International Special Net, a web that is being created by this stream of information constructed in an interactive way by researchers in twenty-one countries.

REFERENCES

1. BARKER, Phillip. Eletronic libraries: visions of the future. *The Eletronic Library*. V,12, n.4, Agu, 1994.
2. GUIA – Grupo Português pelas Iniciativas de Acessibilidade. [Online] Disponível na Internet via WWW. URL: http://www.acessibilidade.net. Capturado em 31 de maio de 2000.
3. NETO, Miguel de Castro. *Ergonomia de interfaces WWW para cidadãos com necessidades especiais*. [online] Disponível na Internet via WWW. ULR: http://agricultura.isa.utl.pt/equipa/neto.asp. Arquivo capturado em 31 de maio de 2000.
4. SHAW, Debora. Libraries of the future: glimpses of a networked, distributed, collaborative, hyper, virtual world. *Libri*, v.44, n.3, p.206-223. Sept. 1994
5. SIDAR – El Seminario de Iniciativas sobre Discapacidad y Accesibilidad en la Web. [online] Disponível na Internet via WWW. URL: http://www.rppapm.es/sidar/. Arquivo capturado em 31 de maio de 2000.
6. W3C-WAI – Iniciativa de Accesibilidad a la Web - WAI. [online] Disponível na Internet via WWW. URL: http://www.w3.org/TR/1999/WAI-WEBCONTENT. Arquivo capturado em 31 de maio de 2000.

7. ZANG, Nelson et al. *Biblioteca Virtual: conceitos, metodologia e implantação*. Revista de Pós-graduação. Erechim, RS, Brasil, 2000
8. ZÚNICA, R. R.. Metodologia práctica de revisión de la acessibilidad de sítios WEB. Internet para todos "diseño de sitios WEB acessibles". Ciclo de invierno de la Universidad Cmplutense de Madrid – março 2001.

Chapter 12

THE CONSTRUCTION OF BLIND CHILDREN'S COGNITION BY INTERACTING WITH SOUND

Jaime Sánchez
Department of Computer Science, University of Chile

Abstract: Blind children tend to cognitively represent spatial environments with some difficulty and inexactness. We think this can be partially corrected through spatialized sound software. The aim of this research was to analyze the impact on cognition of sound-based virtual environments. We also analyzed the issues involved in representing navigable structures with only spatial sound. The results confirmed our hypothesis concerning the development of cognition through the use of spatialized sound delivered through computers. Blind children can achieve the construction of mental structures rendered with only spatialized sound revealing that spatial imagery is not purely visual by nature, but can be constructed and transferred through spatialized sound.

Keywords: virtual acoustic environment, spatial representation, blind children, audio-based navigation, usability, spatialized sound

1. INTRODUCTION

Integrating Virtual Reality (VR) to assistive aids for users with special needs appears to be an attractive combination that has been received media attention interest recently. VR or more accurately Virtual Environments (VE) provides novel methods for visualizing and interacting with complex data sets (Mereu & Kazman, 1996, Morley et al., 1998; Sánchez 2000, 2001; Sánchez et al., 2002). Recently, VR and VE are used to ameliorate cognitive and navigation problems of blind users. Thus the literature provides diverse applications for blind users.

M. Llamas-Nistal et al. (eds.), Computers and Education. Towards a Lifelong Learning Society, 139–152.

Web speech browsers are designed for users that access to Internet in a non-visual or combined auditory and visual manner. This is case for systems such as BrookesTalk, WebSpeak, MarcoPolo, AHA (audio HTML access), and DAHNI, Demonstrator of the Access Hypermedia Non Visual Interface-(Morley et al., 1998). All these approaches explore the fundamental issues of auditory navigation through hypermedia information.

Universal access to computer systems provides generic access to the legacy of resources for standard computer systems. For example, Emacspeak (Raman, 1996) was designed to provide impaired users with productive access to the wealth of network computing resources available on Unix platforms. Other systems such as Mercator provide generic access to the X-Windows platform without visual cues, and the European GUIB (Graphical User Interface for the Blind) to enable access to Windows operating system.

To present information of graphical nature through sound is a promising area. It is the sensory substitution of information for visual nature by audio information for visually impaired users. Schemes for auditory rendering of maps and embedded diagrams are being developed. Some authors have developed means for scanning arbitrary visual images and presenting them through sound. Also, there has been increasing interest in augmenting haptic displays with sound for the purpose of presenting graphical information. Interactive 3D environments such as The Spatial Auditory Environment in a Ring Topology (Savidis, 1996) aims to give a multimedia toolkit for non-visual interaction to provide a 3D auditory navigation environment. This system enables blind users to review a hierarchical organization of auditory interaction objects by using direct manipulation techniques through 3D-pointing hand gestures and speech recognition input.

The use of VR as interactive technology to explore users representing and interpreting symbolic objects and simulated environments in their minds has received recently some attention in the literature. Blind children can not fully represent spatial environments, but our past research indicates that it is possible to render spatial structures without visual cues. This idea leads us to assist children to construct cognitive skills by interacting with acoustic stimuli delivered through spatialized sound.

A few studies have approached this issue by using interactive applications that integrate virtual reality and cognitive tasks to enhance spatial orientation skills (Chance et al., 1998; Loomis et al., 1998). In this study, by using acoustic interactive virtual environments fully described elsewhere (Sánchez, 2000, 2001), we attempt to assess cognitive and usability issues involved in rendering spatial structures in the mind of blind children through acoustic navigable virtual environments.

Vision plays a crucial role in our world knowledge. Most image representations are created from visual perception. This excludes people who lack the sense of vision. Kennedy (1993) studied the field of drawing and spatial image representation for the blind. After letting blind individuals draw spatial scenes, he concluded that they do not represent images with perspective, maintaining a flat bidimensional projection in their draws. Other studies have implemented systems to imitate children's drawings based on spatial models (Burton, 1995). Even though these and other related studies are very useful no systematic approach has been developed to design perceptual images maps of three-dimensional objects and scenes without visual cues.

As a response to this need, our first approach extended these concepts by testing the hypothesis that a sound navigable environment can create some mental images. These systems can also serve as aural representations of the space and surrounding entities such as the ones explored in previous studies (Lumbreras, Sánchez & Barcia, 1996; Mereu & Kazman, 1996; Savidis et al., 1996). Kobayashi & Schmandt, (1997) explores the idea of sound-space association to enable simultaneous speaker listening, but spatial navigation is not included. To deal with this issue we created a framework to describe and implement virtual acoustic navigable environments.

In this preliminary pilot study we explored how audio-based entertainment and spatial sound navigable experiences can create cognitive spatial structures in the minds of blind children. We also proposed a model to describe an acoustic navigable environment. In addition, we asked whether spatialized acoustic modality combined with haptic manipulation of the environment may allow blind children to construct mentally associated structures such as haptic/acoustic correlation, spatial navigation without visual cues, and object permanence in time through the virtual environment metaphor.

As a result of this work we then implemented a full research study to analyze more deeply cognitive and usability issues involved in the use of aural virtual environments by blind children. We centered on the characteristics of representing navigable structures through spatialized sound.

The interaction with the virtual environment was usability tested through a contextualized field-testing research with blind children using audio-based computer interactive environments. The cognitive spatial representations of blind children when interacting with sound-based virtual environments were analyzed (Sánchez 2000, 2001; Sánchez et al., 2002). We challenged, motivated and engaged blind children to explore, interact, and design with sound-based virtual entities to construct cognitive spatial mental representations invisibly.

2. METHODOLOGY

2.1. Participants

The research was implemented in a Chilean school for blind learners in Santiago during six months three times a week. We extracted an intentional sample of forty-two first and second grade children coming from social and deprived suburbs. The size of the sample was established by considering some restrictions such as: school time slots and space available, structural and topological conditions of the school, PC availability, and the number of special education teachers we had available. Some of these children live in their homes and others live in the school in an internship system that allows them to go home during the weekends. The ages of the children spanned from seven to twelve years old. There were children with total blindness and some with residual vision. In addition, some of them have some degree of cognitive and learning disabilities. The fact that we were not only dealing with different levels of blindness but also with different levels of cognitive and learning disabilities pushed our research design and implementation to a case study. Diagnostic tests were applied to develop a profile of each child that included ages, type of blindness, affective background (maturity, tolerance to frustrations, irritability, emotional capacity, and self-esteem), and cognitive (Wechsler verbal scale) and psychomotor level.

2.2. Apparatus and material

The virtual environment used to render the spatial environment was built on the concept of a large set of monoaural clips of sound preprocessed with FIR -Finite Impulse Response- filters based on HRTFs –Head Related Transfer Functions- to render the spatialized sound.The software runs in a PC Windows 95 and higher versions with a standard stereo soundboard. We also built a Kit of Cognitive Tasks for space representation (see Fig.1).

a. Software interaction with external

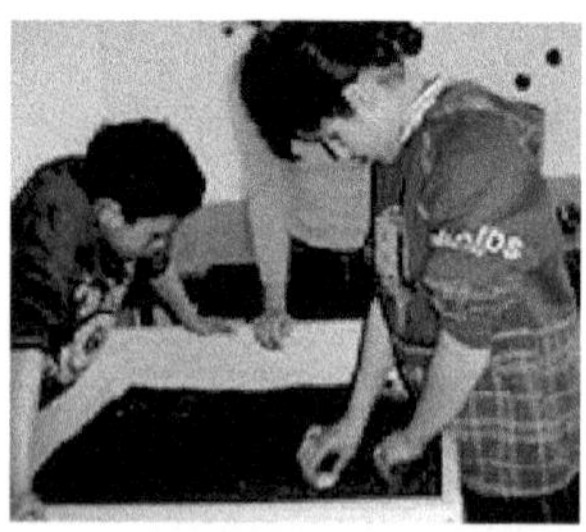

b. Model representation with the sand table

speakers

c. Model representation with Styrofoam and metal pin

d. Model representation with LEGO bricks

Figure 12-1. Sequence of activities from the interaction with the virtual environment to the building of the perceived space through the Kit of Cognitive Tasks

2.3. Procedure

Each child followed the same procedure by interacting with the virtual environment during thirty minutes each session, and then represented the navigated world through corporal movements in the school yard. After this, they made concrete representations of the navigated space by using the sand table, clay, Styrofoam, and Lego bricks. Each session was modeled by the Kit of Cognitive tasks (see Fig. 1).

The kit includes different levels of exposure to the interaction with the virtual acoustic environment, experiences with children performing corporal movements in the schoolyard, and model building by using sand tables, clay, Styrofoam, Lego bricks, plastic images, wood cubes, metal pins, small balls, and sand paper. The kit involved six specific tasks that were carefully planned by using a form that includes cognitive objectives, prerequisites, time, materials, activities, pedagogical sessions, and methodological procedures. It also includes learning activities to represent the perceived environment after navigating through the sound-based virtual environment, the organization of the space, and problem solving related to the interaction with the software.

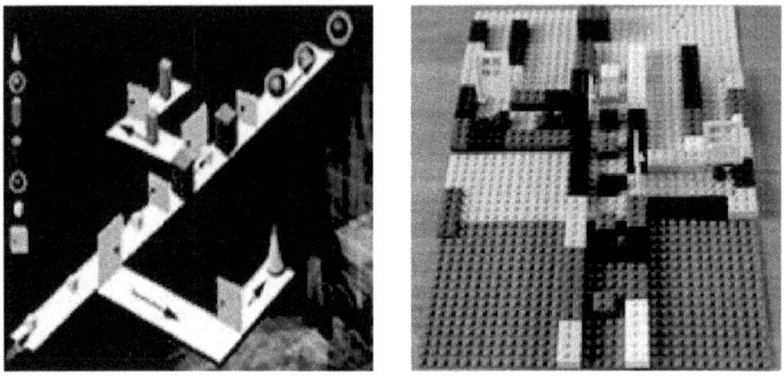

Figure 12- 2. Left, spatial map embedded in the virtual environment to be represented by the blind children. Right, final map built by a blind girl using Lego bricks.

The usability of the virtual environment was an explicit issue in the research. Thus we used both qualitative and quantitative research methods including interviews, survey methods, logging actual use, still pictures and video tape recording session analysis.

3. RESULTS

3.1. Cognitive achievement

As a result of the study we looked for regularities and grouped the performances of blind children during three months. We identified four developmental clusters depicted by blind children when interacting with virtual environments. The mental mapping of the spatial structure navigated virtually was crucial in our proposal manifested by different levels of fidelity in model design in comparison with the ideal structure embedded in the software (see Fig 2). Self-confidence, self-esteem, social interaction, learner's autonomy, and task control were also considered. Thus we ended up with four clear cognitive stages: Entry, Exploration, Adaptation, and Appropriation.

The *entry* is the initial interaction with the audio-based virtual environment. The child learns different spatial concepts that are prerequisite to make an adequate organization of the environment. The child develops self-esteem and autonomy when interacting with the environment. The child starts representing the space mentally through the story embedded in the virtual environment. The concrete representations made by the blind child are very incomplete and unclear. The main characteristic of this level is that the child interacts actively with the software and is highly motivated when doing this. The child's level of control of the software is low.

The *exploration* was represented by a general representation of the structure embedded in the sound environment (Fig 2 left) through corporal movement of the child in the schoolyard (see Fig 3, right). The main attention is centered on the exploration of the software. The child reaches the representation of the main corridor but no details and secondary corridors are represented with concrete materials (see Fig 3, left). The child develops spatial notions through virtually moving through a virtual space oriented by acoustic information. The child can represent the mental images of the virtual story space with concrete materials exclusively based on acoustic information, showing coherence between concrete representations and the story virtual space navigated through acoustic tools. The interaction with the software gives confidence and autonomy to the blind child. The child's level of control of the software is medium.

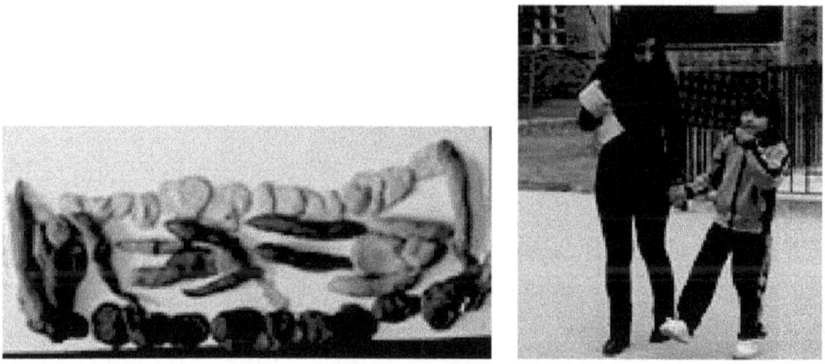

Figure 12-3. Left, concrete representation that reaches the idea of a main corridor. Right, corporal movement in the school yard made by a blind

The *adaptation* was attained by the representation of all corridors. The child understands that the structure embedded in the acoustic environment is composed of one main corridor and two secondary corridors. The child solves the conflict created by the entrance to the secondary corridors by understanding that this involves a change in the orientation of his/her movements. Even though the corridors are mapped the representation is incomplete (see Fig 4, left). The child's level of control of the software is high. The child makes complex representations of the virtual environment navigated virtually.

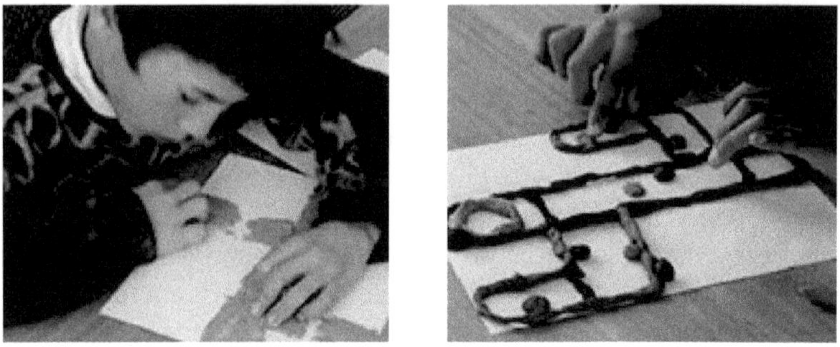

Figure 12-4. Model representations with clay when the child is in the adaptation stage (left) and the appropriation stage (right).

The *appropriation* was manifested through a complete understanding and mapping of the structure embedded in the sound environment. The main characteristic is the child's mastery of the environment. The child understands the story of the software and uses it effortlessly as an interesting tool. The child maps a main corridor with the possibility to move throughout divergent corridors passing by doors that make changes in the orientation of the movement. This reveals a full comprehension of the story virtual space (see Fig 4, right). The child's level of control of the software is complete. As a result, the child constructs a complete mental image of the spatialized environment and represents it concretely with high fidelity. The model is built with high quality and complexity in terms of the spatial structure of the navigated story, the elements used, and the entities involved.

A model of the child´s progress through time after exposed to audio-based virtual environments is depicted in Figure 5.

3.2. Levels of cognitive achievement

Not all children attained the appropriation stage. This was explained by the fact that there were other uncontrolled (but known) variables playing a significant role in the expression of our dependent variable, level of mental spatial representation. Actually, the sample was diverse. All of them were legally blind. Some children have total blindness and some have residual vision. Some could use their residual vision to interact with the visual interface and localize visually the keystrokes of the keyboard. Others have just color, light/shadow vision with almost no effect in the interaction. Some children have mental disorders and spasm hemiplegics.

After analyzing performances, behaviors, cognitive skills used to reach space-based tasks (see Table 1), models built, and cognitive stages attained by blind children we identified three levels of cognitive achievements: high, medium, and incomplete. *High cognitive achievement* was reached by students with residual vision and totally blind. They represent the virtual space with high fidelity, comprehend completely the spatial structure of the software, and move easily through the software making flexible changes in the orientation of their movements. They make correct design mock-ups with corridors and door distribution in the space, organizing elements and entities, and showing correctly the entry and end points of the story. There is a high coherence between concrete representations and virtual spaces navigated through sound. The narratives given by children when explaining their work included important details such as different modes to end the story depending on the corridor they enter.

Table 1. Cognitive skills to reach space-based tasks. To move through the environment is the lowest objective and path selection is the highest.

Objective	Required skill
To move through the environment	Software mastering, understanding of the interaction, sound semantic and positional recognition
To move from point A to point B	Landmark sequence organization and recognition, rotation understanding, path integration
To represent the embedded structure	Mental mapping of the topology, distance perception
To choose the best path from point A to point B	Full mental representation of the spatial structure and movement planning

Students with residual vision attained the level of *medium cognitive achievement*. They comprehend the existence of lateral and main corridors but cannot orient when passing through lateral doors. They are unable to make a complete second change in the orientation when moving through the virtual space. They do it with only one lateral corridor. The cognitive mapping of the story complexity is incomplete.

Students with cognitive and learning disabilities reached the level of *incomplete cognitive achievement*. Because of their limited cognitive development the performance stopped when we added complexity: more corridors, more elements, more entities, and more orientation movements. The children cannot relate corridors; they perceived them as entirely separated from the main corridor.

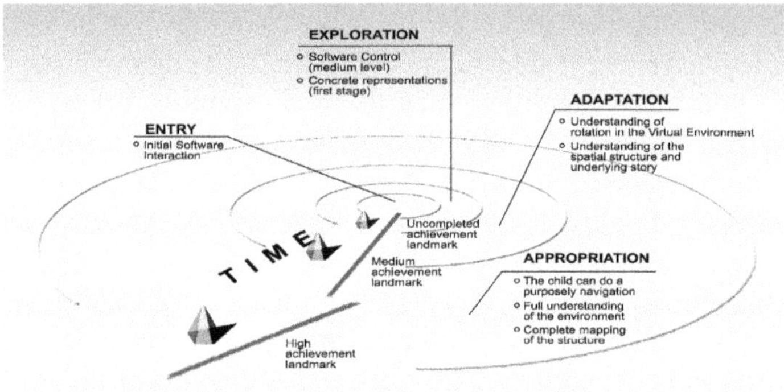

Figure 12-5. A Model Of The Child's Progress Through Time After Exposed To Audio-Based Virtual Environments

3.3. Comparative results between sighted and blind children

A group of sighted children of the same ages and cognitive characteristics of our blind children sample coming from a primary school were exposed to the interaction with the sound environment. Our goal was to observe how they behave and represent an audio-based virtual environment and compare their representations with the ones made by blind children.

As a result, the sighted children represented the navigated environment partially; the main corridor and some entities in the surrounding space (see left side of Figure 6).

In contrast, the blind children represented completely the main and additional corridors, mapping the main and additional corridors with high fidelity as designed in the original model embedded in the software (right side of Figure 6).

Figure 12-6. Comparative representations with Lego bricks between sighted (left) and blind (right) children after interacting with the audio-based virtual environment.

3.4 Logging actual use analysis

We recorded the child's interaction using a logging file to study the progress through subsequent sessions. The file log captures each event –user event or system event. With an ad-hoc analysis tool we studied variables such as the decreasing of time localization through sessions, error rate and pattern of interaction. As we have described, the virtual environment includes a main corridor with two divergent second corridors. To simplify the graphs we show below only some interactions that happened in the main corridor. The child can perform and receive events from three different surrounding sound units, voxels, labeled as left, middle, and right. In the following figures, each icon represents an event. The small box located in the upper left side of each icon is different grayed to indicate the class of the event.

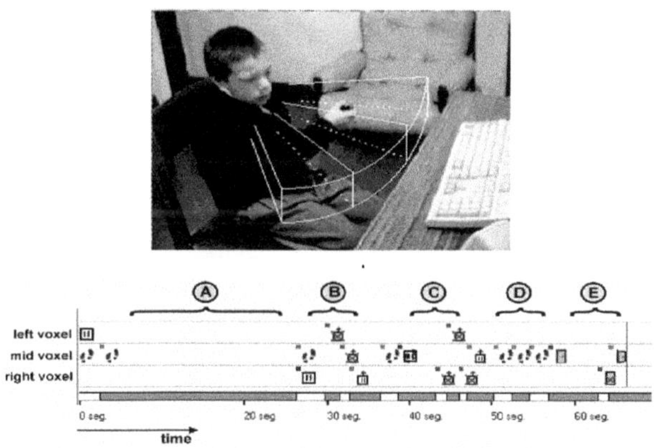

Figure 12-7. Above, the child's surrounds voxels depicted on the picture. Below, the trace of the initial interaction with the virtual environment.

Figure 7 shows the trace of an interaction. A indicates that there are almost twenty seconds without user activity, may be the child is confused. B illustrates a box of elements is encountered and the child tries to pick up the element box in the wrong voxel. In C the same pattern of B is displayed, the child cannot localize accurately the representative sound. D reveals that with a few steps the child arrives to the first door. In E, the child tries to open the door after 5 seconds; the first try was made in the wrong voxel.

After some training the child is able to pick up the objects almost immediately without errors. To reach to the end of the corridor the child took only 25 seconds instead of more than 60 seconds in the first try as displayed in Figure.7.

The trace of the pattern of interaction to reach the end of the main corridor is shown in Figure 8. At the end, the child encounters the final goal, the center of the flying source. In A the child localizes the box of elements and picks it up without errors. In B the child fails to detect the position of the door. In C after some tries the child can open the door, an entity appears and the child fails pointing a wrong voxel, then the child fixes the error and alters the entity after three shots. In D the child opens the last door of the main corridor. In E the mutant appears and moves from voxel to voxel after some seconds, then the child destroys it. In F the child arrives to the end of the main corridor and alters the center of the flying source.

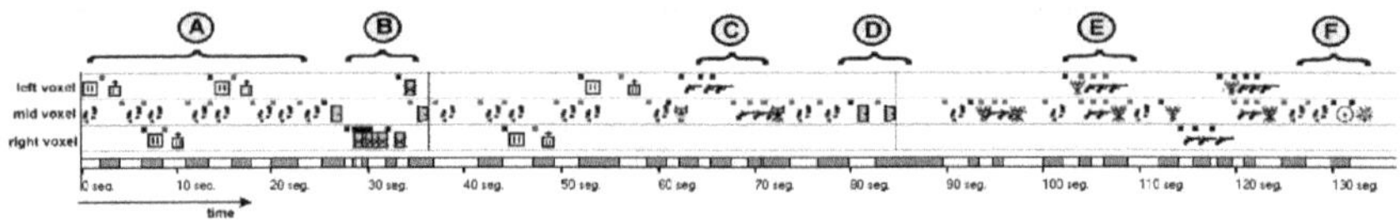

Figure 12-8. *The trace of the pattern of interaction to reach the end of the main corridor*

4. DISCUSSION

The results of this study revealed that it is possible to achieve the construction of mental structures rendered with spatialized sound in conjunction with a set of cognitive tasks. The sound environment by itself does not make any difference in the development of spatial structures in blind children. Cognitive tasks with pedagogical implementations are critical to get critical gains in spatial representation..

Spatial imagery can be transferred through spatialized sound delivered by virtual sound environments mediated with appropriate methodology. However, not all children reached the same cognitive stage in their spatial representation. The highest level we defined, the appropriation level, can be attained by most children but they showed different rhythm, pace, and emphasis. When they have another deficit besides blindness the development of spatial structures is more complicated and requires dedicated coaching with extensive time and slow pace. We believe that all blind children can reach the stage of appropriation if the design maps the needs, background, and requirements of each child.

Each child possesses unique skills and pace referred to mental and spatial development. This has a major impact on the quality of the topological features of the models designed in comparison to the spatial structure model embedded in the software.

When we compared sighted and blind children, the picture showed us that sighted children (and probably adults) do not rely on sound to construct their spatial structures as blind children could do. Learning through sound is very poor in sighted children. Sound environments can be used to enrich the cognitive experience of sighted children heavily based on images. An entire new story can be built in terms of using sound not just for emotions as we see mostly today, but rather to help to construct richer mental experiences.

Finally, we have reaffirmed the results obtained in a past pilot testing. This research study was deeper, longer, more systematic, cognitive focused, and full of diverse experiences with concrete materials. A clear picture of the role that virtual sound environments can play in the construction of mental spatial structures can be designed. We are exploring how exact are the representations made by blind children. Most children attain gross maps but detailed adjustment of model building to computer embedded model varies widely from child to child. With this idea in mind we have moved to a direction of making more powerful and flexible sound maps designed by teachers and parents by using sound-based virtual environment editors. This will lead us to study the impact of this software on the mental mapping of real spaces such as the subway and the school.

ACKNOWLEDGEMENTS

This report was funded by the Chilean National Fund of Science and Technology, Fondecyt, Project 1030158.

REFERENCES

1. Burton, E. (1995). Thoughtful Drawings: A Computational Model of the Cognitive Nature of Children's Drawing, in: *Proc. EUROGRAPHICS '95*; Maastricht, NL August 28 - September 1, C159-C170.
2. Chance, S., Gaunet F., Beall A. & Loomis J. (1998). Locomotion Mode Affects the Updating of Objects Encountered During Travel: The contribution of Vestibular and Proprioceptive Inputs to Path Integration, *Presence*, Vol. 7, No. 2, April 1998, pp. 168-178, MIT Press.
3. Kennedy, J. (1993). *Drawing & the Blind. (pictures by touch).* New Haven, London: Yale University Press.
4. Kobayashi, M. & Schmandt, C. (1997). Dynamic soundscape: Mapping time to space for audio browsing, in *Proceedings of ACM CHI 97*, pp. 224-228.
5. Loomis, J., Golledge, R. Klatzky. (1998). Navigation System for the Blind: Auditory Display Modes and Guidance, *Presence*, Vol. 7, No. 2, April 1998, pp. 193-203, MIT Press.

6. Lumbreras, M., Sánchez, J. & Barcia M. (1996). A 3D sound hypermedial system for the blind, in *Proceedings of the First European Conference on Disability, Virtual Reality and* Associated Technologies, pp.187-191, Maidenhead, UK.
7. Mereu, S. & Kazman, R. (1996). Audio enhanced 3D interfaces for visually impaired users, in *Proceedings of ACM CHI 96*, pp. 72-78.
8. Morley S., Petrie H., O'Neill M & McNally P. (1998). Auditory Navigation in Hyperspace: Design and Evaluation of a Non-Visual Hypermedia System for Blind Users. In *Proceedings of ASSETS '98, the Third Annual ACM Conference on Assistive Technologies*, April 15-17, 1998, Marina del Rey, California, USA.
9. Raman , T. (1996). Emacspeak – Direct Speech Access, in *Proceedings of ASSETS '96, the Second Annual ACM Conference on Assistive Technologies*, Vancouver, British Columbia, Canada.
10. Sánchez, J. (2000). 3D Usability and cognitive impact of the interaction with 3D virtual interactive acoustic environment by blind children. *Medicine Meets Virtual Reality: 7*, Newport Beach, California, USA.
11. Sánchez, J. (2001). Interactive virtual acoustic environments for blind children. *Proceedings of ACM CHI '2001, pp. 23-25.* Seattle, Washington, April 2-5.
12. Sánchez, J., Jorquera L., Muñoz E., Valenzuela E., (2002) Blin children cognition with sound-based virtual environments. *VI Ibero American Congress on Informatics and Education*, RIBIE 2002, Vigo, Spain, November.
13. Savidis, A. Stephanidis C., Korte A., Crispien K, Fellbaum K. (1996). Generic direct-manipulation of 3D-auditory environment for hierarchical navigation in non-visual interaction. In *Proceedings of ASSETS 96, the Second ACM Conference on Assistive Technologies*, April 11-12 1996, Vancouver, British Columbia, Canada.

Chapter 13

COGNITIVE FLEXIBILITY HYPERTEXTS IN THE DEVELOPMENT OF DIDACTIC MATERIALS

Reflexions Within The Context Of An Ongoing Study

Luís Francisco Pedro, António Moreira
Didactics Courseware Laboratory - Department of Didactics and Educational Technology, University of Aveiro - Portugal

Abstract: This article aims to present an ongoing study which has as its main objective to understand how teachers with different characteristics build didactic materials, in complex knowledge domains, by resorting to a cognitive flexibility hypertext. It will present some preliminary results pertaining to the representations of the subjects concerning the prototype as to three main dimensions: ease of use, usefulness and degree of demand of the prototype for the proposed task. The study is currently at the stage of collecting the final data, and treatment and systematisation of qualitative data, enabling us to put forward some perceived trends relating to some of the research issues.

Key words: Hypertext Systems, Teaching

1. CONSTRUCTIVIST THEORIES OF TEACHING AND LEARNING - COGNITIVE FLEXIBILITY THEORY

The constructivist perspective of teaching and learning defends that knowledge is an internal structure of the individual and is constructed through interactions with the environment and through negotiations of meaning with others. In this sense, some authors argue that learning occurs when new information is integrated into a structure of pre-existing knowledge in a self-regulating process of conflict between personal knowledge of the world and the new perspectives which individuals come across in their experience [1]. Such a position substantiates the belief that

M. Llamas-Nistal et al. (eds.), Computers and Education. Towards a Lifelong Learning Society, 153–165.

what is known is internally generated by the individual, rather than received from an external source [2]. The construction of meaning does not depend on correspondence with the world but will depend on understanding of the world on the part of the learner. Mental structures will therefore perform an instrumental and essential role in the interpretation of events, objects and views of the outside world and those interpretations contain a knowledge base that is personal and individualized [2].

Teaching from a constructivist point of view is therefore going beyond the simple representation of associations (knowledge representation), since cognitive processing requires stimulation so as to allow for the construction of meanings from those associations (knowledge construction).

Cognitive Flexibility Theory (CFT), according to its authors, is a theory of learning, knowledge representation and teaching [3]. One of its assumptions is that there is an intermediate stage of acquisition of complex knowledge between the learning of introductory aspects of a given knowledge domain and the attainment of expertise in that same domain. Both the aims and nature of these two moments of knowledge acquisition are different. The characterizing traits of holistic-integrative structuring of knowledge domains consubstantiate in the absence of general rules or principles that cover the majority of cases or real situations, illustrative of reality; the absence of structuring categories that determine appropriate actions in a given case or situation; the existence of different contexts of application that alter the patterns of significance for the same traits and the novelty of situations that results from the explosion of high order interactions between the various traits and relevant variables [4]. The presence of these characteristics, or of some of them, indicates the presence of a holistic-integrative knowledge domain.

Cognitive flexibility implies the selective use of knowledge to adaptively mould to comprehension and decision-making needs in a particular situation. Therefore, the potential adaptive construction of knowledge depends, above all, on a complete representation of the complexity that originates it. This holistic-integrative nature means that many concepts (interacting contextually) are pertinent in a specific case, but its patterns of combination are inconsistent across case applications of the same nominal type.

A great difference between CFT and other constructivist theories is the change of emphasis from the development of a structure of knowledge based on intact pre-existing knowledge towards the flexible adaptation of pre-existing knowledge so as to satisfy the needs of a novel situation.

Teaching in holistic-integrative knowledge domains is different from teaching in well-structured domains where knowledge can be taught in compartmented units, for future integration. In holistic-integrative domains, teaching should focus on general principles and on the inter-relationships of knowledge by means of a wide variety of cases or examples. This requires, on the part of who does the teaching, multiple representations of knowledge so that pre-existing knowledge be "assembled", flexibly, case by case. Through this process, adaptable knowledge is developed and flexible structures of knowledge acquired. Resorting to pre-existing knowledge with cognitive flexibility, the learner will be capable of transforming that knowledge and using it in a specific novel instance.

CFT suggests some teaching techniques that aim at facilitating the acquisition of knowledge at complex learning levels, simultaneously avoiding the learning problems that result from the inadequate use of simplifying approaches. Such suggestions include valuing the intricate and interwoven nature of knowledge rather than promoting compartmentalized and isolated knowledge; the use of multiple representations (themes, case examples, multiple lines of argumentation, interpretations of diversified origin); promotion of dynamic links between relevant knowledge from a diversity of cases and conceptual sources (instead of over reliance on intact retrieval of previously memorized information); the explicit connection of concepts to practice (situating conceptual knowledge in contexts that are similar to the ones required for the application of knowledge).

2. COGNITIVE FLEXIBILITY HYPERTEXTS

The term hypertext refers to computer based information systems that are characterized by changeability and restructuring capacity across different dimensions, purposes and times. Therefore, hypertexts differ from the so-called conventional (printed) media, given that they possess the ability to offer non-linear and multi-dimensional explorations of their contents [5]. The term hypermedia associates the characteristics referred to above to other types of media, besides text. We use the term hypertext, relying on its conceptual span [6] and also on the belief that this term transmits the idea of text as any object of study that permits a rich interpretation.

Several studies have been carried out on the potential and functionality of hypertexts [7][8][9][10]. The potential of hypertext is summarised in four main points: its associative and non-linear nature, the fact that it minimises the cognitive load of users, its distributed and coordinated architecture and its structure that can facilitate the capturing and communication of knowledge [10]. Nevertheless, these characteristics do not guarantee, *per se*, efficacy in the realm of teaching and learning. This can be confirmed by the markedly technological focus of the uses of these tools [6], neglecting the contributions of the cognitive sciences, educational psychology and the pedagogical and didactic assumptions of hypertext construction in the definition of use of these systems.

We believe that, in the definition of objectives, the choice of these tools should be made with a view to improving the teaching-learning process itself, and that the decision to use them should not be the result of inconsequential attitudes of *techno-idolatry* [11].

Interest in the use of hypertext systems with educational goals has been considerable [7][12][13][14]. Although a great deal of research and many of the developments of hypertext are related with aspects of flexibility in the capacity to organize and manage information in these systems [7], research related with the use of hypertexts in education has been much less explored and with at times controversial results. Some authors [2] state that some researchers in this area believe that hypertext information structures must reflect the structures of human memory as proposed by Bartlett with his *schema* theory. *Schema* theory is a non-linear model for the representation of knowledge. If the hypertext structure is similar to the way the brain codes information, this will allow bigger changes in the structures of knowledge of the learners. It is believed that as we explicitly map the semantic network of an expert into the hypertext, the learners will be able to think in the same way as the specialist.

These authors accept that the mere illustration of structures of content on the interface is not enough to help the learners acquire these structures. They maintain that it is the nature of the processing task and the learning objectives in the interaction with a hypertext that determines the effects of its use on the knowledge of the learners [2]. There have been few experimental studies on the required parameters for an effective *design* of educational hypertexts presupposing facilitation of the teaching-learning process in complex holistic-integratively structured knowledge domains.

Following this line of thought, a possible approach to the development of hypertext educational systems for teaching-learning situations at advanced levels, resides in the explicit definition of the *design* parameters in the research produced in the area of cognition in the teaching-learning process. On the basis of these principles, some hypertext systems have already been developed - in such areas as biomedicine, military strategy, cinematic/literary interpretation, the concept of perspective in visual education, the acquisition of concepts of grammatical nature, among others - that have as their goal the implementation of CFT assumptions [14].

The key characteristics of these hypertext educational systems based on CFT - Cognitive Flexibility Hypertexts [14] - include: the conceptual analysis of the domain through themes or multiple wide scope perspectives; the use of a vast range of examples based on cases that are subdivided in integral/complete educational units, called "mini-cases", generally materialized in short segments of text and/or images; the analysis and contextual association of a thematic vector for each educational unit that, given the holistic-integrative, complex and contextual nature of the structure of its content, will very rarely have an application for all the facets of a particular unit; the supply of specialized commentaries linking the thematic abstract dimensions of analysis (that is, the structural components of knowledge) to the specific manifestation of the unit (that is, the superficial components of knowledge); the supply of a thematic crossing or an exploration based on the themes of the mini-cases – the initial linear sequencing of units associated to a given case is re-edited, linking them to different unit sections in terms of their didactic relevance. This characteristic makes numerous new re-editions of the hypertext knowledge base possible.

3. HYPERTEXTS IN THE TEACHING-LEARNING PROCESS

There is no question that multidimensionality and complexity of knowledge finds in hypertext learning environments an amazing metaphor, and thus highlights the need to try to understand how, using these new means, the actors in the educational process (namely teachers and learners) respond to the increasing potential that the technological tools put to their disposal [15]. The need to develop program contents that make these technologies become true instruments of education is often referred, which implies, on the part of teachers, a willingness to question their pedagogical practice. In other words, it will not be enough for teachers to simply transmit knowledge to students: they will also have to teach them to search and relate diverse information, disclosing critical thinking.

This claim is made because learning cannot be seen in a reductive way – as the mere acquisition of knowledge – but must be regarded as the constant reconstruction of what one already knows. The learners do not simply add information to their knowledge stores: they review their mental structures, so as to accommodate new information or to formulate new structures based on the old ones when the existing structures are no longer enough [4].

According to constructivist assumptions and practices, teachers cannot simply map their interpretations of the world directly for the learners, since that they do not share with them the same extension and depth of knowledge and experience. So the way the teacher represents and structures knowledge is of crucial importance in educational contexts. Moreover, the use of *courseware* tools by the learners, namely the use of cognitive support tools, has the potential not only to change what the teachers teach in terms of contents, but also to change education in procedural terms.

Based on the characteristics of the holistic-integrative structuring of the majority of the domains of knowledge, namely regarding knowledge application activities, some barriers appear when our objective is oriented towards the mastery of conceptual complexity and the ability to use learned knowledge in situations that differ contextually from initial learning [4].

Some of these problems are addressed by the properties of the cognitive flexibility hypertext DIDAKTOS[4] as we will see in the next section.

4. THE COGNITIVE FLEXIBILITY HYPERTEXT DIDAKTOS

The prototype DIDAKTOS is an *open shell* that, in accordance with the principles of CFT, can be used in the didactic structuring of contents of any knowledge domain of a holistic-integrative nature.

Inspired in the pedagogical and didactic principles of random access instruction that imply the decomposition of illustrative elements of a given domain of knowledge into smaller fragments, it allows for the didactic organization of teaching materials, making possible the insertion of text, images, video and sound as well as their indexing to conceptual perspectives of analysis, commented in reference to their context of occurrence.

The incorporation of these didactic principles in the design of DIDAKTOS aims to promote in the learners the ability to acquire and transfer complex knowledge to novel situations. Its functionalities allow the teacher to make the selection of a given set of contents, to truncate them into smaller units so as to minimize the cognitive overload of the learner and, from the deconstruction of the illustrative examples, explain the example presented. These examples are automatically indexed and, although superficially identical, they bear distinct conceptualisations that are the result of their contextual unity. In the deconstruction of various cases into various mini-cases, a set of contents is established that can be reorganized automatically in special sequences. These materialize as "trails" or guided tours of the conceptual landscape of the content knowledge base, multiplying exponentially the conceptual approaches that the learner will be able to observe according to a proposal from the teacher. On the other hand, the learner will be also able to test hypotheses by looking for relationships between specific themes, up to a maximum of three possible correlations per search. It is thus possible to re-edit the content base automatically through a

[4] Acronym for Didactic Instructional Design for the Acquisition of Knowledge and Transfer to Other Situations.

search indexed to links of themes of conceptual complexity not suggested (or ignored) by the teacher in the special sequences.

5. THE ONGOING STUDY

There are several studies that prove the effectiveness of the use of Cognitive Flexibility Hypertexts on the part of the learners, suggesting that these systems constitute an effective educational aid, from the assumption of the facilitation of learning at advanced levels in domains of knowledge of a holistic-integrative nature [4][6].

In the ongoing study, we aim to understand how teachers (with different characteristics at the level of experience, epistemological preferences and attitudes towards computers and technology) select and organize information, in this type of systems, in an activity of construction of didactic materials. We aim also to assess its perceived effectiveness, for teaching. One other objective of the study is the evaluation of the cognitive flexibility hypertext DIDAKTOS itself. The didactic materials constructed by the subjects (evaluated in the pedagogical-didactic dimension and structuring of content according to CFT) will be the object of analysis, together with the results obtained in “Epistemological Teaching Preferences” questionnaires (ETP) and "Attitudes Towards Computers and Technology" (ATCT) and the factor “education experience”.

Some trends have already been detected that point to significant differences in performance in the construction of didactic materials, on the part of the different experimental groups (particularly if we look into the variable “experience”). However, at this moment, we cannot yet advance with concrete data, given the premature state of systematisation.

At this stage we can advance some data pertaining to one research goal: to assess the effectiveness of the tool used for the activity carried out by the subjects, in its theoretical, technical and functional dimensions.

5.1 Preliminary results concerning the effectiveness of the prototype DIDAKTOS, extracted from the analysis of the usage diaries

One of the activities conducted within the study aimed at surveying the progression, per session, of the perception of effectiveness of the prototype, on the part of the experimental conditions. This activity finds justification in the concerns disclosed by some authors [4][5] who alert to the fact that it is necessary to conduct research that evaluates the impact of the abilities of the teachers, their previous knowledge and experience in the use of computers, at the time of the use of this type of prototype in education.

5.1.1 Procedure

To reach this goal, at the end of each work session with DIDAKTOS, subjects were asked to write down, in a usage diary, their opinions concerning the following dimensions, taking into account their performance in the session and the intended task: perception of the ease of use (technical perspective); perception of the usefulness of the prototype (functional perspective) and perception of the degree of demand of the prototype for the proposed task (theoretical perspective).

The chosen dimensions of analysis took into account the relevant aspects of the use of the prototype for the task proposed, as well as relevant questions raised by researchers that had used similar prototypes, although with different objectives [4][5][6].

The analysis of the data obtained, presented in the figures below, is the result of the attribution of value 1 to a negative opinion and of value 2 to a positive opinion (except for the dimension "Degree of Demand", where an inverse system was applied).

It is also necessary to stress that the number of sessions for each experimental condition was different, corresponding, however, to an equal period of time working with the prototype (18 hours).

5.1.2 Preliminary results of the fluctuation of representations towards the prototype, per experimental condition

Figures 1 and 2 present the fluctuation of the representations towards the prototype of the subjects of the two experimental conditions (Exp and N-Exp), in the work sessions with the prototype.

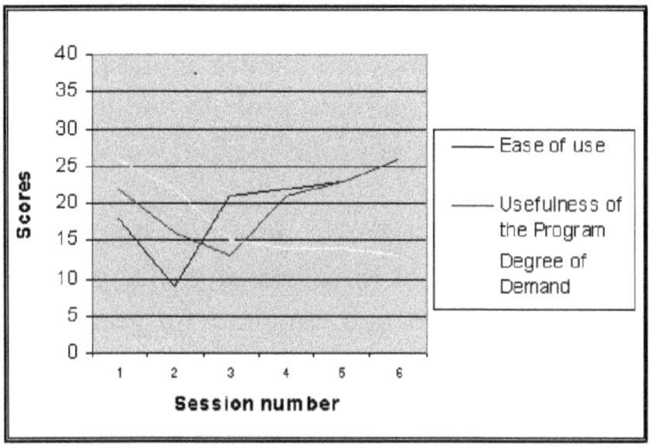

Figure 13-1. Fluctuation of the representations towards the prototype, per dimension of analysis, extracted from logbooks (Exp Group)

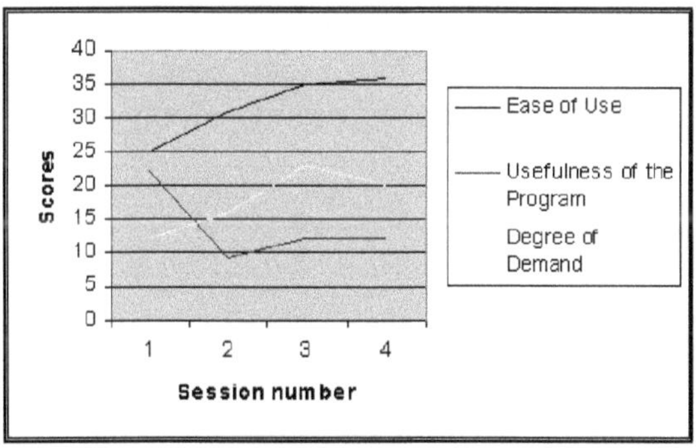

Figure 13-2. Fluctuation of the representations towards the prototype, per dimension of analysis, extracted from logbooks (N-Exp Group)

The figures permit us to conclude that different representations exist, per dimension of analysis and per condition. However, and from a mere exploratory analysis, the data allow us to state that there is a "borderline" session where a stabilization of the trends of progression can be observed in the dimensions under analysis, independently of the conditions (session 3, in the two conditions, if we make an exception of the values of the dimension "Usefulness of the Program" for the Exp condition). The Exp condition reveals a representation fluctuation towards the dimension "Usefulness of the Program" that follows, *roughly speaking*, the representations associated to "Ease of use". In our opinion the progression of these two representations presents a more normal configuration than the ones present in the N-Exp condition, where the curves of progression of the two dimensions do not coincide. In a mere speculative exercise, this can be evidence of a separation, in the context of use for action, of the two dimensions in the N-Exp condition, something that does not happen in the Exp condition. In other words, the subjects in the Exp condition probably do not distinguish the ease of use of the prototype from its possible usefulness, which possibly did not happen in the N-Exp condition.

The data presented allow us also to infer that there are curves of progression that differ in terms of the dimension "Degree of Demand" of the prototype between conditions (with a tendency for gradual attenuation in the Exp condition, that discloses a more delayed and tenuous trend in the N-Exp condition).

5.1.3 Preliminary results of the fluctuation of representations towards the prototype per Attitude towards Computers and Technology, in the Exp experimental condition

Figures 3 and 4 present the fluctuation of representations towards the prototype of the subjects of the Exp experimental condition, splitting the group according to the Attitudes towards Computers and Technology revealed by the subject.

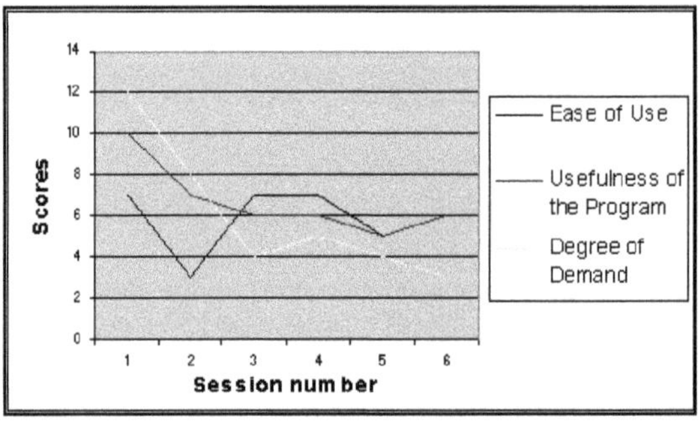

Figure 13-3. Fluctuation of representations towards the prototype, per dimension of analysis, extracted from logbooks, of the subjects of the Exp condition, with Negative Attitudes towards Computers and Technology

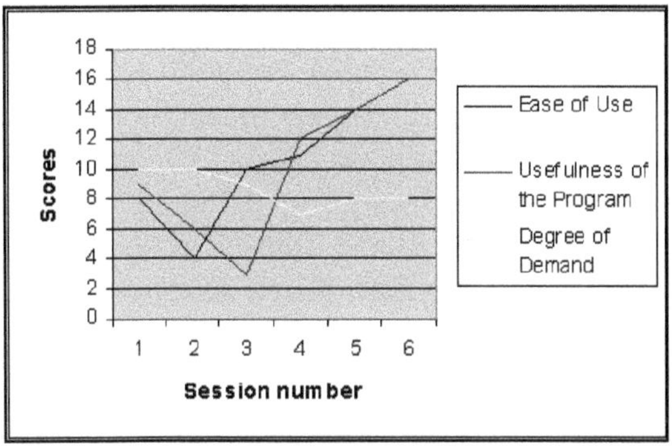

Figure 13-4. Fluctuation of representations towards the prototype, per dimension of analysis, extracted from logbooks, of the subjects of the Exp condition, with Positive Attitudes towards Computers and Technology

The data allow us to observe some trends. The subjects of the Exp condition with Positive Attitudes towards Computers and Technology obtain higher raw results and, generally, higher scores than the subjects of the same condition with Negative Attitudes towards Computers and Technology. An exception may be perhaps made in the case of the dimension "Degree of Demand" which reveals, in the subjects with Negative Attitudes towards Computers and Technology, lower and, therefore, more positive values. However, the progression of the representations, per session, in this dimension for this group of subjects, is somehow abrupt, possibly revealing some difficulty in the understanding of the task proposed and a somewhat delayed understanding of the underlying theoretical support of the prototype used. On the other hand, the values of this dimension in the group of subjects with Positive Attitudes towards Computers and Technology seem to reveal certain stability in the representations, which can mean a faster understanding of the theoretical perspective that supports the prototype.

As to the dimensions of analysis "Ease of Use" and "Usefulness of the Program", the subjects of the experimental condition with Positive Attitudes towards Computers and Technology reveal positive trends of progression from session to session, something that does not happen with the group of subjects from the condition that reveals Negative Attitudes towards Computers and Technology.

5.2 Future work

The analysis of the representations of the subjects towards the prototype is still incomplete. This task will be completed with the presentation of results of the fluctuation of the representations of the subjects with the split according to Epistemological Teaching Preferences and Attitudes towards Computers and Technology, in all the experimental conditions.

We must also emphasize that these data will be complemented with data of a qualitative nature, corresponding to pertinent opinions illustrative of perceived tendencies, produced by the subjects in the usage diaries, with the intention of valuing and materializing quantitative information, whenever justifiable.

ACKNOWLEDGEMENTS

The authors wish to thank the Portuguese Foundation for Science and Technology and POSI (Programa Operacional para a Sociedade da Informação) for the financial support for this project.

REFERENCES

1.]Fosnot, C. (1996). Construtivismo e Educação – Teoria, perspectivas e prática. Lisboa: Instituto Piaget, 1996.
2. Jonassen, D., Mayes, T., McAleese, R. (1993). A manifesto for a constructivist approach to technology in higher education. In T. Duffy, D. Jonassen & J. Lowyck (Eds.), *Designing constructivist learning environments*. Berlin, Heidelberg: Springer-Verlag.
3. Spiro, R., Coulson, R., Feltovich, P., Anderson, D. (1988). Cognitive flexibility theory: advanced knowledge acquisition in ill-structured domains. In V. Patel (ed.) *Tenth Annual Conference of the Cognitive Science Society*. Hillsdale, NJ: Lawrence Erlbaum, 375-383.
4. Moreira, A. (1996). *Desenvolvimento da flexibilidade cognitiva dos alunos-futuros professores: uma experiência na Didáctica do Inglês*. Dissertação de Doutoramento. Aveiro: Universidade de Aveiro.
5. Fitzgerald, G., Wilson, B., Semrau, L. (1996). Designing effective multimedia programs to enhance teacher problem solving skills and cognitive flexibility. In P. Carlson & F. Makedon (Eds.), *Proceedings of ED-Media 96*. Charlottesville, VA: AACE.

6. Carvalho, A. (1999). *Os Hipermédia em Contexto Educativo*. Braga: Instituto de Educação e Psicologia, Centro de Estudos em Educação e Psicologia.
7. Conklin, J. (1987). Hypertext: An introduction and survey. *IEEE Computer*, 20 (9), 17-41.
8. Leggett, J., Schnase, J., Kacmar, C. (1990). Hypertext for Learning. In D. Jonassen, H. Mandl (Eds), *Designing Hypermedia for learning*. Berlin, Heidelberg: Springer-Verlag.
9. Halasz, F., Schwartz, M. (1994). Model Hypermedia. *Communications of ACM*, 37 (2), 31-39.
10. Dede, C., Palumbo, D. (1991). Implications of hypermedia .for Cognition and Communication. *Association for Impact Assessment Bulletin* (9), 15-28.
11. Silva, B. (1999). Questionar os fundamentalismos tecnológicos: tecnofobia vs. tecnolatria in P. Dias e C. Freitas (eds.) *Desafios'99*. Braga: C.C. Nónio XXI.
12. Jonassen, D. (1988). Designing structured hypertext and structuring access to hypertext. *Educational Technology*, 28 (11), 13-16.
13.]Moreira, A., Almeida, P., Raposo, R. (2001). DIDAKTOS – *Didactic Instructional Design for the Acquisition of Knowledge and Transfer to Other Situations*. v.1.0 (beta), LCD, UIDTFF, Aveiro: Universidade de Aveiro.
14. [Spiro, R., Jehng, J. (1990). Cognitive flexibility, random access instruction, and hypertext: Theory and technology for the nonlinear and multi-dimensional traversal of complex subject matter. In D. Nix, R. Spiro, (Eds.) *The "Handy" Project. New Directions in Multimedia Instruction*. Hillsdale, NJ: Lawrence Erlbaum, 163-205.
15. Dias, P., Gomes, M., Correia, A. (1998). *Hipermédia e Educação*. Braga: Edições Casa do Professor.

Chapter 14

MOCHO

A Web Portal on Science and Scientific Culture

João C. Paiva[1], Luiza A. Costa and Carlos Fiolhais
Centre for Computational Physics of the University of Coimbra and [1]Department of Chemistry, Faculty of Sciences of the University of Porto

Abstract: "MOCHO" (www.mocho.pt) is the first Portuguese web portal on science and scientific culture. It is a project of the Centre for Computational Physics of the University of Coimbra, which is sponsored by the Portuguese programs "Nónio - 21st century" and "Ciência Viva". Students who are now attending primary and middle schools were born in the middle of the 80s and belong to the so-called *net generation* (or *zap generation*). They grew up in the digital era being, therefore, familiar with cell-phones, computers, Internet, etc. The challenge for them is to select information among the enormous amount which is available in the Internet. The offer of valuable scientific and pedagogical information which is made by "MOCHO" can be an important help for their work, both at school and at home. We describe the portal here.

Key words: Computer networks and education, hypermedia and multimedia, educational software.

1. INFORMATION TECHNOLOGIES AND THE 21st CENTURY SCHOOL

The 21st century students – The *net generation*

Sociologists, especially those working on marketing, have been studying and classifying the younger generations, trying to characterize the markets and their evolution. For that purpose they created expressions like *baby-boomers* (people born between 1946 and 1965) and, especially, *generations X* and *Y*. The *baby-boomers* are in power today, *generation X* (people born between 1966 and 1975) are the young adults who are just starting their

M. Llamas-Nistal et al. (eds.), Computers and Education. Towards a Lifelong Learning Society, 167–178.

professional life, and *generation Y* (people born between 1976 and 1985) are now attending universities. Kids attending the 21st century's primary and middle schools are known as *net generation*.

Although it is always risky to categorize large groups it is probably helpful to use the marketing language and perspective to describe the school population. Let us then describe the *net generation* [1].

It is formed by young people born in the middle of the 80s, the "under 18". They are often also referred to as *N-gen*, *e-generation*, *generation Z*, *zap generation*, *homo zappiens* [2, 3, 4]. Their main characteristics stem from the fact that they were born and raised in the digital era. Therefore, cell-phones, computers, the Internet, cable TV and play-stations are familiar for them. They would not know what to do without them and they cannot even imagine the world without them. For these kids computers and the Internet are as common as telephones and TV were for the *baby-boomers*. Quoting Don Tapscott, Canadian author of "Growing up Digital": "Today's kids are so bathed in bits that they think it is all part of the natural landscape. To them, the digital technology is no more intimidating than a VCR or a toaster."[1]

Some authors classify this group as materialistic, consumer addicted, ambitious, optimistic, idealistic, curious, etc. Their elements give too much importance to brands, fashion and looking. Most of them do not read printed text unless they are forced to and they only commit themselves to an activity if they think they will have fun with it [3, 5]. These results have to be looked at carefully, taking into account the differences between the American and the Portuguese societies. Nevertheless we believe that similar studies in Portugal would show similar results.

The *net generation* is used to action, *i.e.*, they organize their daily life in several activities, some of which simultaneous. They grow up doing multiple tasks and seizing every minute. They go to school almost since their birth, from kindergarten to high school, where they are now. They especially like to work in teams (although sometimes it may seem otherwise).

The best way to describe them is probably through the term *zap generation*. In fact, their life is a constant zapping – they go from channel to channel in front of the TV set, which they cannot handle without the remote control, and they chat at the same time in different computer chat rooms under different virtual identities. They use their cell phones to send text messages to their boyfriends/girlfriends, while they listen to their favorite rappers on MTV. Their keywords are selection, interactivity, and communication. They like to surf the Web searching for data they need for their homework. But for them it is difficult to select and organize the enormous amount of information that is nowadays available. For that purpose their technical skills are not enough: they simply lack experience. One of the goals of the school is precisely to provide that experience.

The 21st century society – The information society

The information society has become a sociological paradigm. The sheer notions of knowledge and wisdom have suffered a metamorphosis, being now related to the management and synthesis of information rather than to its acquisition or memorization [6].

Unlike in the industrial society, in today's information society «there are more and more workers for whom information is the only raw material and the only product. And as knowledge is becoming the capital of a developed economy, the centre of gravity keeps shifting to the knowledge worker.» [7]

In such a society, new products are appearing continuously. They demand new jobs which, in their turn, demand new skills. There are no jobs for life anymore; an individual may have several jobs during his lifetime and has to look for adequate training whenever needed.

Education will be a permanent activity. But that activity will no longer be restricted to the school.

The 21st century school

Schools cannot remain indifferent to what is happening around them, to the new challenges placed by society. They must adapt to the new possibilities offered by the information and communication technologies. While conveying the disciplinary subjects, either new or traditional, schools should respond to pupil's aspirations and necessities and also to the desires of the society at large.

The *net generation* considers the school more a meeting place with their peers than a learning place. They enjoy learning (in fact, curiosity is one of their main features) but they believe that they learn better if they use the new technologies.

In spite of their importance, the information technologies are not the magical answer to the main educational problems. But it is worth quoting Sherry Walton, member of the "STEP project" (an American program that trains teachers in using information and communication technologies in schools): "I am not convinced that computer technology is going to solve significant education problems. But, the kids are so motivated by computer usage and technology that it is ridiculous not to use the tools in meaningful and engaging ways." [8]

The 21st century teacher

Communication has always been a fundamental aspect of daily life. Due to new technologies, communication has become easier, faster, and more successful than ever. Some skeptics still make reserves about the use of technology in areas, such as the education, which are characterized by intensive human relations [9]. We can answer them emphasizing that computers will never replace people. On the other hand, computers are tools whose purpose is just to help people. Quoting Faramarz Amiri, who wrote several articles on the use of new technologies in education: "Computers may never replace (…) teachers but teachers who are computer–literate may replace those who are not".

It is a fact that the *net generation* created the *generation lap* instead of the traditional *generation gap* [2], that is, kids sort of "carry" adults, helping them to deal with their difficulties on information technologies. The digital proficiency of their students scares many teachers, who feel inferior because they cannot cope with them and fear they may lose their authority and prestige. But, reacting to that fear, they should be ready to profit from the technical help of their pupils.

The 21st century's teacher should be ready to learn continuously. This does not mean that he/she does not master his/her subjects or does not analyze the issues deeply. Teachers do not have to feel intimidated by technological novelties: they have to accept that the *zap generation* they are teaching is, in what concerns computers, some steps ahead.

The Internet – digital resources for teaching and learning

The Internet, the modern global information and communication network, is a resource whose future and consequences cannot be easily foreseen. It may support various activities going from daily activities to scientific and academic projects.

Education cannot help being influenced by the Internet. The Net allows more and better communication with old and new partners. Furthermore, qualities and values that can be acquired by using ICT at schools will certainly be reflected in the students' attitudes:

i – Sharing

Users with common interests can share projects and information through Internet pages.

ii – Collaboration

People living thousands of kilometers apart can carry out a diversity of common projects, either synchronous or asynchronous, discussing and working together through their Internet pages and especially through e-mail. This is what usually is referred to as "collaborative work".

iii – Solidarity

This is one of the most common present values in the Internet since its beginning. There are countless web sites promoting it.

iv – Discovery of «new worlds»

We can find in the Net information about practically anything. This is the best way of realizing that we are only a very small part of a much diverse world. This is also an opportunity of encouraging tolerance and respect for other people and ideas.

v – More and better information

The access to the endless source of information which is available in the Internet can only improve if the information is well organized, namely through web portals.

vi – Time sparing

Organized information at the touch of our fingers results in a large economy of time in comparison with the information in conventional libraries and archives. The Internet increases the quality of what is taught and the way it is taught. If schools refuse to commit to the new technologies, the gap between them and the society will widen.

Teachers, who are supposed to guide their students through the "information oceans", will never be dispensable. Their skills, their good sense and their enthusiasm will always be essential.

2. MOCHO – A WEB PORTAL ON SCIENCE AND SCIENTIFIC CULTURE

What is "MOCHO"

One of the Internet problems is related to one of its most praised characteristics: the huge amount of information may lead to the loss and dispersion of the inexperienced users. Organized information has therefore an enormous value.

"MOCHO" (www.mocho.pt), created in 2001 by the Centre for Computational Physics of the University of Coimbra, is the first Portuguese web portal on science and scientific culture (Figure 1). It is sponsored by the program "Ciência Viva" [11], created by the Portuguese Ministry of Science and Technology, and by the program "Nónio - 21st century" [12], organized by the Portuguese Ministry of Education.

Although "MOCHO" aims to develop and spread science and scientific culture to everybody it has as particular target the *zap generation*. It deals mainly with Physics, Chemistry and Mathematics because these so-called basic sciences lack more diffusion and support in Portugal, but also includes other sciences, trying to bridge the gap between exact and human sciences.

The portal is intended to have a great impact in the Portuguese-speaking pedagogic and scientific communities and beyond. Since it is supposed to help the youngsters who are looking for scientific information, it should be based on tools which are attractive to them.

Figure 14-1. "MOCHO" home page

A brief description of "MOCHO"

An important part of "MOCHO" is a collection of links with short descriptions. These links are organized in specific areas under topics and sub-topics. Users may choose to look at a given site by reading a critical appreciation accompanied by the indication of the site's language. The portal has a powerful and fast search engine (Figure 2), which makes the searches very easy.

On the left of "MOCHOS" homepage some links point to science sites made by the portal's authors (including all sites of "Omniciência" [10], an earlier project also sponsored by the program "Ciência Viva"). On the right we find some especially chosen science sites, being this list continuously updated.

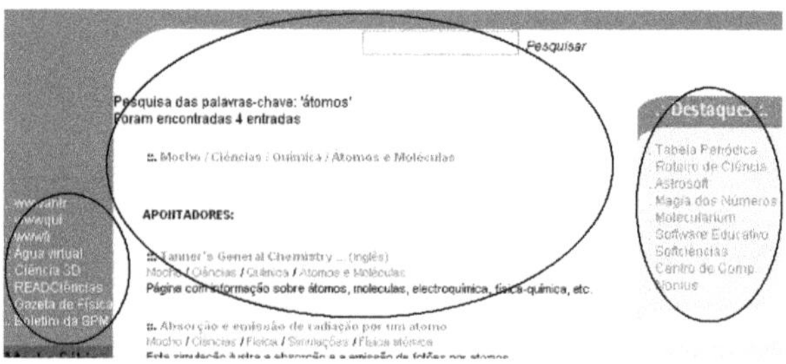

Figure 14-2. Search engine, local science pages and other highlights.

The users' most checked sites are automatically listed being the new additions easily shown. Every month a "site of the month" is announced under the name of "Mocho Sábio". Users (students, teachers, and other people interested on science) may use a specific interface to suggest links to be added to "MOCHO".

The results of periodic polls are published online.

Some technical issues

"MOCHO" was built using a modern PHP technology which shows several advantages:

- Fast and reliable search engine.
- Detector of broken links.
- Spelling checker.
- The addition of new links and comments as well as page rebuilding is done without the need for any html code editing.

A selected group of people, from different scientific areas, is allowed to add information using a username and a password. They should provide access to new valid and useful information.

Local information at "MOCHO"

"MOCHO" encompasses several digital resources:

A. Educational Software

"MOCHO" contains several computer programs on Physics, Chemistry and Mathematics topics, most of which can be free downloaded. That is, for instance, the case of "Le Chat" [13] (Figure 3). They were created by "Softciências", a project of the Portuguese Societies for Physics, Chemistry and Mathematics, which was established in the 90s with the support of the Ministry of Education.

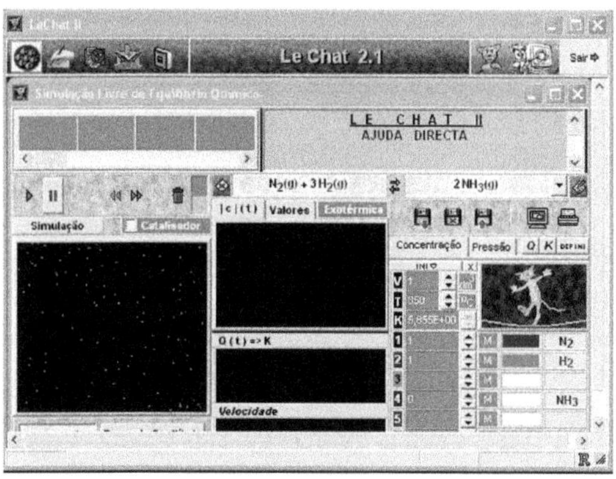

Figure 14-3. "Le Chat", a simulation on chemical equilibrium.

B. Science and Technology Guide

The "Science and Technology Guide", written by Armando Vieira and Carlos Fiolhais, is especially addressed to youngsters being its purpose to spread science resources such as grants, jobs, competitions, etc. It includes information about research centers, libraries, associations, books, digital materials, etc. It has been published as a book by "Ulmeiro" [14], with the sponsoring of "Ciência Viva", but the online version corrects some misprints and upgrades the information.

C. Online Periodic Table

"MOCHO" includes the Periodic Table of the elements, in both Portuguese and English. This conveys large information on the chemical elements, such as properties, applications, occurrences, history, graphics, etc. Among other images, it includes a gallery of about 600 minerals identifying their constituent chemical elements. It has been visited not only by Portuguese but also by many international visitors.

D. Nonius

"Nonius" is a site with more than 10 gigabytes of original information whose purpose is to help the teaching and learning of Mathematics. Its responsible is Jaime Carvalho e Silva, a professor of Mathematics at the University of Coimbra. It is a widely used resource for many Mathematics teachers.

E. Molecularium

This web site shows some molecular animations (Figure 4). It is original in what concerns the simulation techniques (Java) and pedagogical methodologies [15]. This page was built with the help of "Exploratório Infante D. Henrique", a science centre in Coimbra.

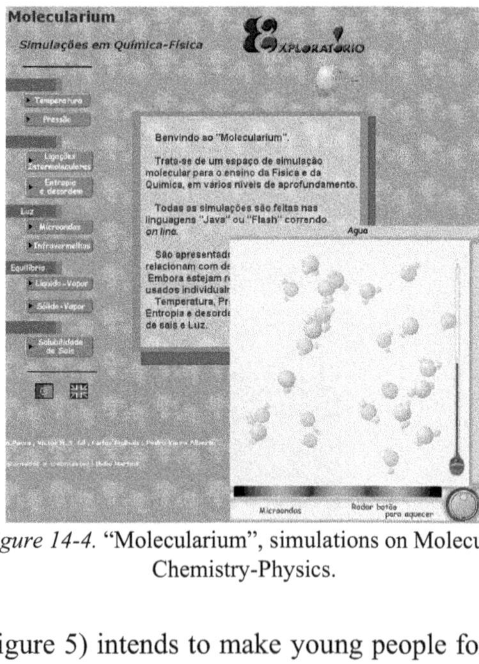

Figure 14-4. "Molecularium", simulations on Molecular Chemistry-Physics.

F. The Magic of Numbers

The Magic of Numbers (Figure 5) intends to make young people fond of Mathematics through the use of various games and challenges. All its modules can run online, so that they can be easily accessed. This project was written in "Flash 5" taking advantage of the potentialities of this language.

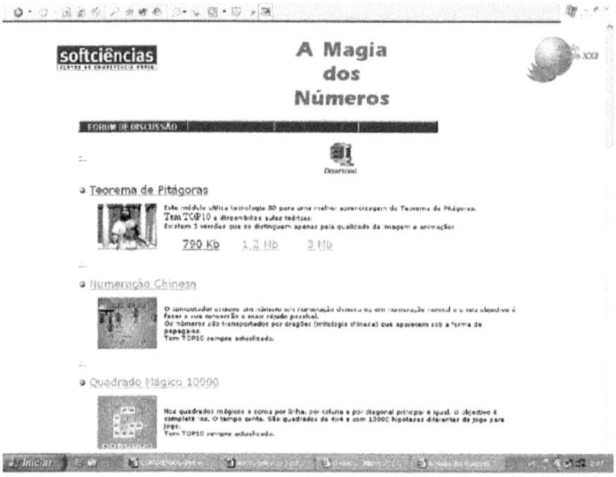

Figure 14-5. "The Magic of Numbers", a set of mathematical games.

3. MAIN PROGRESSES AND NEWEST ADDITIONS.

Treasure Hunt

The *Treasure Hunt* took place during "Netdays", a week promoted by the European Union to encourage the use of new technologies in schools. The 2002 edition took place between the 19th and the 23rd of November 2002 and was targeted to high-school students. Those students were supposed to answer some questions of Physics, Chemistry and Mathematics on the basis of the Internet. They were asked to include the URLs of the sites where they had found the answers. The Portuguese branch of Microsoft sponsored the event and offered prizes to the winners.

Discussion Forum

There are discussion forums where questions and answers can be posted in areas such as Anthropology, Astronomy, Physics, Mathematics and Chemistry. The answers of invited scientists were posted online.

4. THE IMPACT OF "MOCHO"

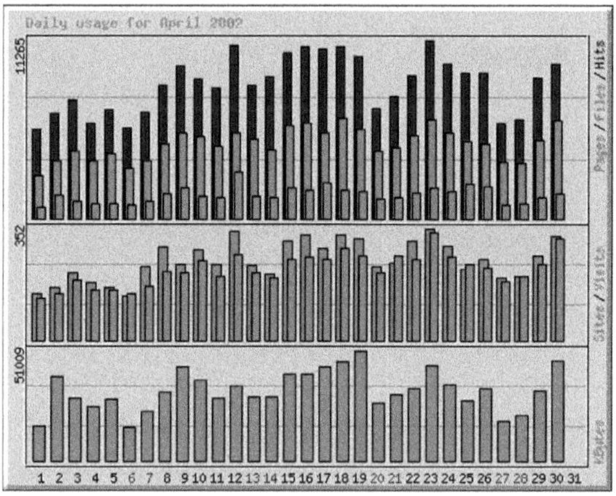

Figure 14-6. "MOCHO" daily statistics for April 2002.

We plan to evaluate systematically the impact of our web portal. The number of hits surpassed 70000 during the first eleven months, a fact which is not only revealing but encouraging. The contents of the portal have also been growing. Usage statistics for April 2002 can be found in Figure 6.

The country usage data (Figure 7) show an expressive percentage of Brazilians (13%). There are some noticeable percentages of users from other countries due to some bilingual sections like "Periodic Table" and "Molecularium".

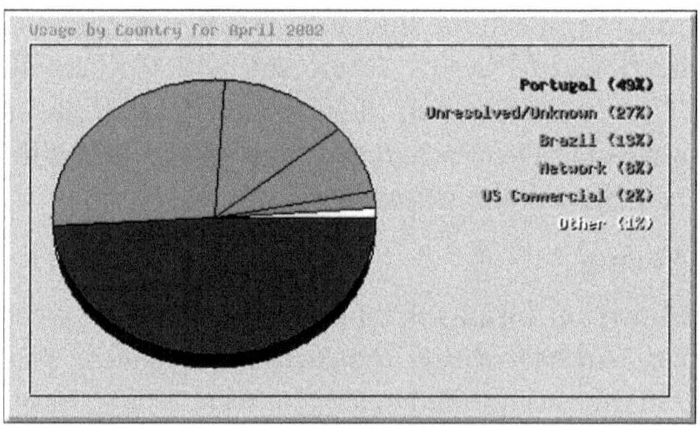

Figure 14-7. "MOCHO" users by country for April 2002

5. FUTURE DEVELOPMENTS

A web portal like "MOCHO" is a dynamic project, which should be continuously enlarged and enriched. We aim at improving it progressively, making it bigger and better. For that purpose, we intend to address the following issues in the near future:

A. Diffusion

The portal will be advertised in newspapers, magazines, radios, TV and educational meetings so that more people know it and take advantage of it.

B. New areas

New areas will be open, for instance Biology, Geology, Geography, etc. Humanities will also be covered although it has been difficult to find collaborators in that field.

C. Enlarge existing areas

We also plan to enlarge and improve the links and the critical appreciations within the existing areas and sub-areas. The evolution of "MOCHO" will comprise the growth of the local resources, as well as the creation of new ones. The portal will continue to include information from "Ciência Viva", the national agency for scientific culture.

D. Making contents available in other languages

Some contents are already available in English, but we intend to translate others to allow for a better visibility of the Portuguese activity in scientific education and science outreach.

E. Offline distribution

We are aware that the Internet is now and will be more in the future a privileged place for offering pedagogical materials, but the present bandwidth represents an obstacle. So we decided to publish a CD-ROM with all the "MOCHO" contents. This CD will be delivered, at no cost, to all Portuguese primary and middle schools, public and private.

F. Assessment

One of the main features of our project is evaluation. This will be carried out by researchers of the Faculty of Psychology and Educational Sciences of the University of Coimbra. In the first phase an online pool to teachers will be created. Some ongoing M.Sc. theses discuss the portal and evaluate some of its sections.

ACKNOWLEDGEMENTS

We thank all the people who made this project possible, starting with the two main sponsors, "Nónio - 21st century" and "Ciência Viva". We would like to thank specially Prof. Dr. Jaime Carvalho Silva, who has always collaborated with "MOCHO", and Miguel Marques, Gil Silva and Ilídio Martins, who were very active in the conception and maintenance of this portal since its very beginning. A special thank is also due to all teachers (and they are many!) who have been collaborating with us.

REFERENCES

1. D. Tapscott, "Growing Up Digital: the rise of the net generation", New York, McGraw-Hill, 1998.
2. D. Tapscott, "Growing Up Digital" [Online]. Available on 6/9/2002 at http://www.growingupdigital.com/.
3. IBM Global Industries:Education:PressReleases: Generation Z [Online]. Available on 6/9/2002 at http://www-1.ibm.com/industries/education/pressrelease/PRESSRELEASES _27106.html.
4. W. Veen, "New Teaching Methods for New Generations Wim Veen", [Online]. Available on 6/9/2002 at http://fc.noveum.his.se/Conferences/ps/nr2_zappiens.html.
5. C. Liu, "Faces of the new millennium: Generation Y" [Online]. Available on 6/9/2002 at http://pubweb.acns.nwu.edu/~eyc345/final.html.
6. "Livro Verde para a Sociedade da Informação", Missão para a Sociedade da Informação e Ministério da Ciência e Tecnologia [Online]. Available on 6/9/2002 at ftp://ftp.uarte.mct.pt/Docs/livroverde/livroverde.pdf.
7. Ministério da Educação – Departamento do Ensino Secundário, "O professor aprendiz – criar o futuro", Lisboa, 1995.
8. The STEP Project – Teams [Online]. Available on 6/9/2002 at http://step.evergreen.edu/teams/olympia_wa.html.
9. J. C. Paiva, "A Internet na Educação", Brotéria, 145, ps. 157-170, 1997.
10. C. Fiolhais and J. C. Paiva, "Omniciência – um CD-ROM do projecto Softciências", communication to the "IV Congresso RIBIE", Brasília, 1998 [Online]. Available on 6/9/2002 at http://solaris.niee.ufrgs.br/ribie98/TRABALHOS/223.PDF.
11. Ciência Viva – Ministério da Ciência e da Tecnologia [Online]. Available on 6/9/2002 at http://www.cienciaviva.mct.pt/home/.
12. .Programa Nónio Século XXI – Ministério da Educação [Online]. Available on 6/9/2002 at http://www.dapp.min-edu.pt/nonio/nonio.htm.
13. J. C. Paiva, V. M. S. Gil, and A. Ferrer Correia, "Le Chat: simulation in Chemical Equilibrium", Journal of Chemical Education 79, ps. 640-641, 2002.
14. A. Vieira and C. Fiolhais, "Roteiro de Ciência e Tecnologia". Lisboa. Ulmeiro, 2001.
15. J. Trindade, J. C. Paiva, and C. Fiolhais, "Visualizing molecules: on-line simulations and virtual reality", Europhysics News 32, ps. 14-15, 2001.

Chapter 15

EXPERIMENTAL FINDINGS WITH COLLABORATIVE WRITING WITHIN A PROJECT-BASED SCENARIO

Flávia Maria Santoro[1], Marcos R.S. Borges[2] and Neide dos Santos[3]
[1,2]Universidade Federal do Rio de Janeiro, [3]Unversidade do Estado do Rio de Janeiro

Abstract: The process definition is a key issue for the successful use of collaborative project-based learning environments. We built a cooperation model expressed by patterns in order to point out these ideas. In this paper, we describe the scenario chosen to evaluate the model: collaborative writing projects and EdiTex, a groupware tool to support them. We tested our ideas by using EdiTex in two case studies, with over 30 participants. The results were promising, pointing out to the relationship between the process design and the level of collaboration.

Key words: Computer-Supported Collaborative Learning, Collaborative Writing

1. INTRODUCTION

The definition of activities in a project-based collaborative learning environment is extremely important to determine the positive interdependence required to stimulate collaboration [1][2][3]. Teachers and students need flexible environments to support them in the use of the computing technology and to allow the configuration of different scenarios for collaborative projects. In spite of this, most CSCL environments neither provide mechanisms for the definition of the collaborative process, nor address all stages required in a project-based approach.

Previously, we proposed a Cooperation Model for project-based learning, presenting solutions for the definition of educational collaborative processes and their relation to learning theories, cultural aspects and background

M. Llamas-Nistal et al. (eds.), Computers and Education. Towards a Lifelong Learning Society, 179–190.

knowledge. Our approach was to express the main issues of the collaborative process in a conceptual patterns' system [4]. From this model, we developed an infrastructure for collaborative project-based learning environments [5]. The scenario chosen to evaluate the model was projects where groups of students had to write documents. Thus, they should define their flow of work in order to achieve the objectives and use appropriate tools to support them.

This paper presents EdiTex, an educational groupware for collaborative writing, implemented within this context. Our goal was not only to observe the act of writing collectively, but also to evidence the importance of modeling the process of collaborative writing in order to augment it and, consequently, enhance learning in a CSCL environment.

In Section 2, we briefly discuss the theoretical basis of project-based learning, which constitutes our work context. Section 3 describes the design and implementation of EdiTex. Section 4 presents the results obtained with the use of EdiTex in real educational settings. The conclusions and future assignments are outlined in Section 5.

2. PROJECT-BASED LEARNING

Project-based learning is not a new educational approach. The Project Method was designed to solve real-world problems by using a variety of instructional practices, including laboratory work. Rather than creating curriculum based upon the subjects, this method taught content through discovering solutions to real problems that occur in an individual's life [6].

The Project Method was reinforced by Dewey's ideas, for whom, education depended on action [7]. Knowledge and ideas emerged only from a situation in which learners had to draw them out of experiences that were meaningful and important to them. These situations had to occur in a social context, such as a classroom, where students gather and handle materials, creating a community of learners who build their knowledge together.

Learning through projects happens by means of interaction and articulation among distinct areas of knowledge. These connections are established as part of the students' daily knowledge, whose expectations, desires and interests are mobilized in the construction of scientific knowledge. It is up to the teacher to provoke the students' mindful of implicit concepts, interviewing at appropriate stages. Projects develop ability to 'learn how to learn', so that each one can reconstruct the knowledge, integrating contents and skills according to his universe of concepts, strategies and beliefs besides developing the ability to work in a team, making decisions, formulating and solving problems. Projects are typically carried out in the context of a group, and can be supported by CSCL area.

A project requires a certain amount of dedicated time to planning and management. For George and Leroux [8], a project should be structured in time and partitioned in successive stages. The careful planning of the activities is necessary to provide the project with a temporary structure. Previous experience can predict possible results of future steps, although these anticipations should be implemented and adjusted in agreement to the conditions of the real situation. Therefore, the definition of the activities and their execution allows the configuring of interaction and its products in the project. Furthermore, it allows the teacher, who is not used to submitting collaborative situations, to understand them and to help the apprentices.

Teachers should elaborate situations that stimulate the students to work in a collaborative way, by considering hypothetical solutions for proposed problems, discussing them, pondering them and arriving at the end product with awareness of the process accomplished. A process describes the group's strategy to reach to the final goal with the participation and contribution of all members. The transitions from individual to group tasks make each participant's performance clear. Processes that have already been followed can be a good reference for new groups. Therefore, the possibility to reuse, to refine and to work over past processes is considered as the group memory.

Based on our premise for collaborative project-based learning and the specifications given by the cooperation model [4], we proposed a collaborative writing scenario and implemented a groupware tool to support it. Next section presents EdiTex, including its requirements and design.

3. EDITEX: THE COLLABORATIVE WRITING IN AN EDUCATIONAL SCENARIO

In order to test the effectiveness of modeling the collaborative process, we created a particular project-based learning environment, tailored to writing activities. Projects generate specific outcomes, which involve a set of tasks that need supporting tools. The flow of tasks must provide the maintenance of the collaboration, the sense of responsibility in the group, the perception of the goal at each stage and high levels of interaction.

Projects are related to research, which always starts with a problematic proposition. In our particular case, students should learn a given theme within the context of a project. The proposed situation was the collaborative writing of a paper. The students must define a set of activities in order to carry out the project. There is not a standard process for a project; it depends on the group's profile and on the theme. Therefore, the environment must be flexible in order to supply the characteristics of any kind of project.

The writing of a collaborative document is a process of building knowledge through group interactions, where the apprentices must be encouraged to discuss the theme actively in such a way that both the individual and the group learning can be assured. The collaborative writing is a four-step process: a) brainstorming – survey of suggestions and ideas of each participant about the theme; b) planning and organization of ideas – the suggestions of each participant are stored, classified and organized, serving as a data base to posterior phases; c) composition – each participant edits a complete text or is responsible for one of its parts; d) review – texts edited by each participant are reviewed for the finalization of the document.

Some approaches can be adopted for setting up the Composition and Review phases: (i) each one of the participants writes a full version of the text and argues their ideas in order to reach a consensus; (ii) each one of the participants is responsible for writing a part of the document, using the ideas generated by everyone and a single text is composed joining the parts; (iii) the full text can be broken up in parts defined by the users, to be totally constructed at the same time for the whole group. Any approach must adopt a policy of annotations, comments and suggestions, in order to stimulate the interaction among the participants.

A collaborative writing tool must provide mechanisms for adding notations and commentaries in the document sections. All the members should have the possibility to visualize the complete document, to exchange messages and to discuss ideas on the document. We can observe that many of the available collaborative writing tools are not oriented to educational activities. Some do not incorporate mechanisms for annotations and comments or provide effective support for the interaction [9][10][11].

The tool for collaborative writing was designed for considering problems and solutions related to co-authorship in CSCL environments. A conceptual pattern [12] is the format adopted to describe the characteristics of the collaborative writing scenario and the tools' requirements to support it. A pattern presents a problem, a context and the solutions suggested. EdiTex was specified from the requirements met in two patterns: *Collaborative Writing of Documents Activity* and *Tool for Collaborative Writing*.

Pattern Name: Collaborative Writing of Documents Activity

Problem: How can a collaborative writing activity be carried out in a learning environment as part of a project development?

Context: Many projects developed within learning environments involve the co-authorship of documents as part of the activities.

Forces: The collaborative writing activity can contribute by stimulating the interaction, and by the sharing and construction of knowledge. It is necessary to define the rules of interdependence in the accomplishment of

the task in order to guarantee that it will be carried out in a collaborative way.
Solution: The activity must be described according to following criteria:
a) Objective: Students should acquire knowledge on the subject oh the document; they should interchange information in order to reach the objective; b) Roles: The writing task can involve some roles: coordinator, writer and publisher; c) Products: A document can contain texts, figures and graphics; d) Interdependence: It is a joint effort, therefore no part is presented separately by individuals of the group; e) Rules: each member of the group should be responsible for the document as a whole, being able to edit one or more of its parts individually. All members can contribute with suggestions and commentaries in all parts of the work; f) Support Tools: collaborative-writing editors should support all the described characteristics.
Known uses: Some CSCL environments implement the activity of collaborative writing. In some of them, collaborative writing is the central activity, and its main goal is the learning of writing texts [9][10][11]. In other environments, the collaborative writing is inserted in the context of some tasks to be passed on for the group.

Pattern Name: Tool for Collaborative Writing

Problem: What are the requirements for the implementation of a collaborative writing tool to support the learning process?
Context: A collaborative writing activity is usually present in project-based learning environments. Therefore, it is necessary to specify the requirements for the tool support in order to carry out the activity.
Forces: The collaborative activities proposed in the learning environments have some characteristics that should be supported by computational tools. Their requirements are related to the description of the task to be supported.
Solution: The solution is a list of requirements that can be implemented through collaborative writing functionalities: a) Edition: The user can edit the document either synchronously or asynchronously. The document must be structured through a format defined by the group. A participant is responsible for the parts of the document created by him. A mechanism for annotations and commentaries on the document's fragments must be available. b) Awareness: All members of the group must visualize the complete document, get information about a fragment and receive notifications about changes made in the document. c) Coordination: It must be possible to define roles, with different responsibilities. It must be possible to make interchangeable roles. d) Interaction: The participants must be able to communicate and interact through mechanisms provided by the tool. It must be possible to register the discussions. e) Document storage: It must be possible to store and access versions of the document with its annotations.

Known uses: The requirements specified in this pattern had been extracted from the main works in collaborative writing [9][10][11][13].

EdiTex was implemented considering the problems and solutions described. In EdiTex, a text is composed of fragments that can be of any type: words, paragraphs, phrases, sections or chapters. The group can define the level of detail of the fragments. Each fragment has an author and an identification number. Comments can be associated to each fragment. The main screen of the EdiTex has three work areas (Figure 1): a) *Edition Area*: private space where each user edits its fragments, before sharing it with the group; the content that is being edited is not visible for the other participants until the author 'sends' it to the group. b) *All Fragments*: allows the visualization of the full text; sometimes it is necessary to rearrange the fragments in order to get a coherent text; c) *Notes*: a notepad, where each user writes comments and annotations about a specific fragment.

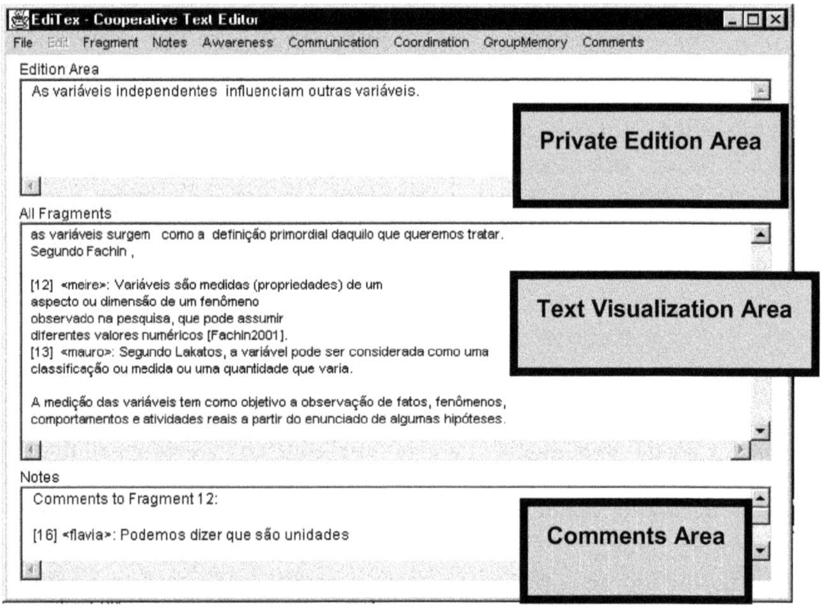

Figure 15- 1. EdiTex Main Interface

Following, the tool functionalities and forms of work are detailed.

a) Edition: The user edits a part of the document fragment, using the work area designed for this function. Each user owns parts of the document, which are entirely his responsibility, but he must be aware that each fragment will contribute to the final document. Each member can work in an asynchronous way, or together with the others in a synchronous way. The window for visualization of the full document is not editable. The user writes comments on fragments edited by other users, making suggestions, associated to the fragment identified by its number.

b) Awareness: The tool has a List of Users that shows who is logged on at that particular time. The mechanism allows users to know with whom they can interact in the collaborative writing task.

c) Interaction: Communication among the users can be done through chat or message exchange. Talks are stored and are made available for visualization.

The implementation of EdiTex was made specializing the framework provided by COPSE infrastructure detailed in [14]. The framework is a client server architecture that provides the basic services for communication, cooperation and awareness. The data model handled by it represents the data storage in a document composed of fragments and annotations.

4. EXPERIMENTAL FINDINDS WITH EDITEX

We would like to evaluate the evolution of the collaborative process in depth within a project development in our CSCL environment, so we defined a criterion concerned with the several aspects related to this subject. The criteria are summarized in four groups: Communication, Contribution, Coordination and Awareness, which represent the increasing levels of the collaborative process. In Table 1, we presented a synthesis of these criteria, used in our case studies, as a starting point for analysis and comparisons among the processes accomplished by the students in several cases.

Table 1. Criteria and Measure Units

Criteria	**Measure Units**
Communication (Interaction and participation)	Number of exchanged messages
	Nature of exchanged messages
Collective Knowledge Building (Contributions)	Number of contributions while constructing a collective product
	Quality of contribution in the construction of a collective product
	Construction/Inference on the contribution of other group members
Coordination (Concentration and organization)	Engagement within a process design
	Performance of the tasks
Awareness	Understanding of tasks and its relationship

4.1 First Case Study

The goal of the first case study was to evaluate the influence of a formal process to stimulate the collaboration in groups that learn a theme through the development of projects using a CSCL environment support.

The motivation for this study relied on a discipline called CSCW Laboratory [15] in post-graduation on Computer Science at UFRJ (The Federal University of Rio de Janeiro). The project was to write essays about two themes. Two different situations were proposed: (i) to accomplish the project without an explicit process defined, and, (ii) to accomplish the project with an explicit process configured. In the first case, the members of the groups elaborated texts in an ad-hoc manner, and, in the second one, the activities, relationship and products generated were well defined and known previously by the groups. Our goal was to compare the two situations.

The following variables were defined: group formation (control), proposed situation (control), number of contributions through messages and comments (dependent), quality of contributions (dependent), explicit collaborative process (independent), and CSCL environment (independent). The participants from the study were six post-graduation computer science students, who were selected by the teacher, taking the background and experience into consideration in order to balance the groups. Two groups of three students worked on similar projects; in the first case they did not define process and in the second one they outlined their process and pursued it. In both projects, it was defined a theme and a problem, and the groups had to investigate the subject and produce a textual rehearsal based on their discoveries. A bibliography was given as a starting point for the research.

In Group 1, personal communication problems among the participants occurred. These problems almost invalidated the comparisons between the two experiments. The group tried to specify a plan for its process in the second project; but, as they reported in the questionnaire, they did not follow it. The students used the collaborative tool to write the second paper, but they did not perform the planned work stages.

In the first project, Group 2 performed a very high degree of interaction, which became apparent to them. In spite of many messages without content, the discussions presented clear negotiation attempts. The low level of planning and coordination was also commented on.

Comparing the results obtained by the second group in the two projects, the participants discerned an increase in the collaboration level. They attributed this result to the explicit process design. It also could have happened due to the fact that people were already familiarized with EdiTex, and that they have used far more tool resources for discussions (through addition of comments). Thus, people had a feeling of improvement in the interactions and in the understanding of what they should do (the amount of messages also increased significantly). Many comments were associated to each part of the text and discussions were generated around these comments, which created a deeper relationship among the individual contributions.

In a normal situation, when the work is not monitored by the teacher, the participation of the group members is not explicit, the group disguises the lack of interaction and presents a job well-done by one (or by some) of the participants who takes all the responsibility. With the use of such environments, it is quite remote for this possibility to occur, because all the work is very explicit. Yet, the environment is a catalyst that takes the group to a collaboration state. The more a group understands the process, the higher is the collaboration level is. Apparently, Group 2 demonstrated this.

On the other hand, it was observed that the environment is not able to support all social situations. Group one's members were not able to communicate with themselves even when provided with all the CSCL mechanisms. As they affirmed, individual's commitment is fundamental; if it does not exist, it will never be possible to configure a collaboration process. The problems experienced by them can be related to the heterogeneous group composition, with people from different areas and in particular one of them with little experience in the use of computational tools.

However, an important conclusion can be reached. In the first project, Group 1 attained a result, and we can infer that this happened because it was much more similar to the traditional molds. At moment they had to define its interaction forms and improve the relationships within the project; it was not possible to go on. In this sense, we can affirm that the use of the environment addresses the work for a more interactive and explicit form, which is still not usual in our cultural context.

4.2 Second Case Study

The second case study involved twenty-two students learning Computers and Education, in Pedagogy under-graduation course at Gama Filho University (UGF) in Rio de Janeiro, all of them with little background knowledge in Computer Science. One of the proposed assignments in the context of the discipline was a project, where the students should discuss topics related to the introduction of computational resources as pedagogical support in schools and write a proposal for it. The experimental approach used here was a comparative case study.

The class was divided in six groups, where three groups developed the project without previous planning of the activities, and the other three, with a defined process. In both cases they used EdiTex to support them. We wanted to compare the results of the two types of work; moreover, to study the degree of collaboration accomplished in the project. The same measure units of the previous study were used. A low number of messages were exchanged among all group members, due to the fact that they all had basically communicated through the text over its fragments. For the generation of the final version, they eliminated the coordination, discussion and negotiation parts. The teacher tracked this implicit exchange of messages within the text. EdiTex allows you to extract the indexes (subjective) from relationship among the individual contributions, verifying the commented contributions, the suggestions and modifications made by members of the group to the other people's work.

All the groups used the voice as a communication resource, which did not constitute a problem for, because all the interactions took place inside of the laboratory and with the teacher, who was also an observer, registering the most important events manually. For example, in spite of Group four's considerations in having a good collaborative process, it was noticed that its members were confused in performing the tasks, who were aided by the teacher on several occasions simply because of the lack of experience they had in the field of technology, however, having defined quite an explicit process helped them substantially.

This study indicated that the explicit process design could really stimulate the collaboration in project-based learning environments, because, in general, the groups that defined their work processes had better results in collaboration. Even so, many factors interfere in the results and these cannot be widespread but just applied to similar cases. One of the most interesting aspects observed is groupware tool usage, which was different from everything they had ever tried before. This was already enough to establish a collaborative state in all groups. People were accustomed to group work in a traditional manner with a division of tasks; they had to change the way they work. Another observation is the lack of experience in the definition of the work processes and moreover, the inability of evaluating the process was a constant in the groups. Thus, the use of this type of environment should necessarily go through an adaptation phase and that the initial experiments will be full of uncertainties and lessons to be learned.

4.3 General Results

The general results show that the group's composition, the nature of the task, the collaboration context and the infrastructure for communication are key points for successful collaboration in groupware. In all case studies, the tasks performed were similar; all of them involving the collective production of texts, despite the work processes having been different. The groups were composed of people with similar academic background, and even though, we observed great differences in work dynamics. Individual characteristics have a strong influence; therefore the environments must offer conditions of stimuli, as well as exploit individual's successful work.

Now it is important to carry on our research in order to achieve, as much as possible, a generalization of the results achieved. A characteristic of the formative evaluation, such as the one used in our work, that is, in less authentic studies, from the point of view of a theory validation, can bring valuable preliminary results. In spite of the size limitation of the accomplished studies, many problems were discovered and can be applied in future experiences.

5. CONCLUSIONS

We strongly believe that the modeling of the aspects involved in the project-based learning process, such as collaborative writing, is a key point for the successful use of CSCL environments. To test our ideas on the improvement of the collaborative process, we built EdiTex, a groupware application that provides support to processes of collaborative writing. Then, we analyzed the use of EdiTex collaborative capacities in two case studies. We verified that the group composition, the task nature, the cooperation context and the infrastructure for communication are key points for successful collaboration. In all the case studies, the tasks had been sufficiently similar; all of them involving the collective production of texts, despite the fact that work processes had been different. The groups were composed of people with similar academic background; nevertheless, great differences were noted on forms and dynamism of work. Individual characteristics have a strong influence; therefore the environments must offer conditions of stimuli, as well as exploit individual's successful work.

The results were very promising, clearly pointing out the relationship between the process design and the level of collaboration. The mechanisms implemented proved to address our main goals and configured real situations of developing a project and stimulating collaboration. Future projects are intended to carry on our research in order to achieve a generalization of the results achieved.

ACKNOWLEDGMENTS

Flávia M. Santoro is sponsored by FAPERJ (Fund. Carlos Chagas Filho de Amparo à Pesquisa do Estado do Rio de Janeiro): #E-26/152.116/2001.

REFERENCES

1. E. L. Tiessen, and D. R. Ward. "Developing a Technology of Use for Collaborative Project-Based Learning". In: *Proceedings of Computer Support for Collaborative Learning-CSCL'99,* EUA, 1999, pp.631-639.
2. T. Koschmann, "Dewey's Contribution to a Pattern of Problem-Based Learning Practice". In: *Proceedings of 1st European Computer-Supported Collaborative Learning Conference,* Holland, 2001, pp.17-22.
3. [G. Bourguin and A. Derycke, "Integrating the CSCL Activities into Virtual Campuses: Foundations of a New Infrastructure for Distributed Collective Activities". In: *Proceedings of the 1st European Conference on Computer-Supported Collaborative Learning – EuroCSCL'01,* Holland, 2001, pp.123-130.
4. F. M. Santoro, M. R. Borges, and N. Santos, 'Cooperation Model for Learning: A System of Patterns'. In: *Proceedings of the Conference on Educational Multimedia, Hypermedia and Telecommunication,* Canada, 2000. (in CD ROM)
5. F. M. Santoro, M. R. Borges, and N. Santos, "Learning through Collaborative Projects: The Architecture of an Environment". *International Journal of Computer Applications in Technology,* 16 (2/3), 2003, pp.127-141.
6. W.H. Kilpatrick. *Foundations of Method: Informal Talks on Teaching.* New York: Macmillan, 1926.
7. J. Dewey. *Democracy and Education.* New York: Free Press, 1966.
8. S. George, P. Leroux. "Project-Based Learning as a Basis for a CSCL Environment: an Example in Educational Robotics". In: *Proceedings of 1st European Computer-Supported Collaborative Learning Conference – EuroCSCL'01*, Holland, 2001, pp.269-276.
9. D. Decouchant, A.M.M Enríquez, E.M. González. "AllianceWeb: Cooperative Authoring on the WWW". In: *IEEE Press Proceedings of the 5th International Workshop on Groupware – CRIWG'99*, Mexico, 1999, pp.286-295.
10. Y. Tanikawa, M. Suzuki, H. Kato. "A Synchronous Collaborative Editing System for Learning to Write". In: *Proceedings of Computer Support for Collaborative Learning Conference – CSCL'99*, USA, 1999, pp.621-630.
11. O.M. González, M.J. Verdú, Y.A. Dimitriadis, C.A. Osuna, C.A. Iglesias, J. López. "PENCACOLAS: Groupware for Learning". In: *Proceedings of 3rd.International Workshop on Groupware*, Spain, 1997, pp.71-80.
12. J.O. Coplien. "Pattern Languages for Organizations and Process". *Object Magazine*, 4 (4), 1994, pp.46-51.
13. M. Koch, J. Koch. "Using Component Technology for Group Editors- The Iris Group Environment". In: *Proceedings of OOGP Workshop, European Computer-Supported Cooperative Work Conference - ECSCW'97*, UK, 1997, pp.44-49.
14. M.S. Dias. "COPSE - Cooperative Project Software Environment" (*in Portuguese*). M.Sc. Thesis, COPPE/UFRJ, Rio de Janeiro, Brazil, 1998.
15. R.M. Araujo, F.M. Santoro, M.R.S. Borges. "The CSCW Lab for Groupware Evaluation". In: *LNCS Groupware: Design, Implementation, and Use. Proceedings of 8th International Workshop on Groupware – CRIWG'02*, Chile, 2002, pp.222-231.

Chapter 16

VIRTUAL OBJECTS: AN APPROACH TO BUILDING LEARNING OBJECTS IN ARCHAEOLOGY

A. Fernández-Valmayor, M. Guinea*, M. Jiménez#, A. Navarro, A. Sarasa
Dpto. Sistemas Informáticos y Programación: {valmayor, anavarro, asarasa}@sip.ucm.es
Dpto. de Historia de América II: guinea@ghis.ucm.es
#*Grupo de Ingeniería del Software e Inteligencia Artificial: mjimenez@lola.sip.ucm.es*
Universidad Complutense de Madrid – Spain

Abstract: This article describes the first stages of an educational project aimed at converting the archaeological and ethnographical objects of the Departamento de Historia de América II: Antropología de América, of the Universidad Complutense de Madrid into digitalised educational resources that may be accessed by teachers, students and visitors alike. To create these educational resources, the concept of virtual object has been developed. This is a concept that is similar to that of learning object but is of a more generic nature, allowing us to use it to group together all the information about the real objects used by archaeologists. To demonstrate the viability of the virtual object concept a web site has been set up with hypermedia access for both the use and maintenance of the educational resources.

Key words: Virtual object, learning object, web technologies, archaeology, hypermedia

1. INTRODUCTION

The *Chasqui* project, jointly developed by the Departamentos of *Historia de América II: Antropología de América y Sistemas Informáticos y Programación* of the Universidad Complutense de Madrid, aims to convert the archaeological and ethnographical material available in the former of the two departments into educational resources. To construct these educational resources, the concept of *virtual object* has been developed: a digital object that can be used to group together all the information related to a specific

M. Llamas-Nistal et al. (eds.), Computers and Education. Towards a Lifelong Learning Society, 191–202.

archaeological or ethnographical object. Then, using basic virtual objects, other more elaborate educational resources can be constructed and integrated, together with other virtual objects, into a web environment that can be used for both teaching and research.

For its research work and teaching, the Departamento de Historia de América II has a museum and a laboratory with over two thousand archaeological and ethnographical objects from various American cultures. These objects have been donated or are the result of research projects carried out by the department. They are at varying stages of the process of identification, classification and analysis and are used as comparative and support material in practical training. The most abundant archaeological material is ceramic, but there is also a significant amount of objects made from stone, metal and shell. The ethnographical collection also contains objects of wood, feathers, string, leather and animal shells. Within the field of environmental archaeology, the laboratory has an interesting comparative malacological collection (over one hundred species) from the bio-geographical region of Panama, as well as a more limited collection of animal bones from the tropical rainforests. The Departamento de Historia de América II also has a wide range of documentary resources (collections of graphic material and documents): field logs, excavation diaries, slides, profiles, analyses, etc.). Up to now, access to all of this material was only possible through physically visiting this department. Although the study *in situ* of archaeological remains is most gratifying for both the student-researcher and any other interested party, the key issue from the scientific-educational point of view is the information that can be deduced from the object in question: its age, origin, size, material, etc. The relations the student is able to establish between the different archaeological remains is also of fundamental importance, including the construction of a model or an objective description of the culture that created and used this object. For this reason, the challenge of this project is to provide all students and researchers with access to all of this material without loss to its information potential.

To assist in the work of the researcher and teacher, we have developed an application capable of processing all the aforementioned information that uses the concept of virtual object as a guide. Due to the specificity and the nature of the information that may be associated with a virtual object, a basic requirement of our system is that the researchers must be able to introduce data into the system directly and continually, since they are the only ones actually qualified to carry out this task. Furthermore, it must be borne in mind that completing the study of an archaeological object and establishing its relations with other objects is a constant and laborious process that is never completely finalised.

There are other two requirements in the system. First, introducing and querying information must be as straightforward as possible. Second, it must be possible to do so from any computer on the network. Since the main disadvantage of an approach based on objective processing of the data associated with archaeological objects is that the individual does not have a direct perception of the objects that is interacting with, the system must have an intuitive hypermedia access with high-quality graphics.

Unlike other computer projects applied to teaching, this project does not focus on the definition of a methodology for the creation of teaching units, or on the specification of their possible characteristics: student adaptability, pedagogical strategies or the representation of the basic concepts of the reference domain [1], [2]. The major aim of this project can be considered as being complementary to those projects because its main goal is to enrich the bases on which different teaching methodologies may later be based. In other words, the aim of this project is to create an environment with basic computerised educational resources upon which other more complex educational resources may be constructed, such as courses or teaching units.

The approach used in this project was inspired by the learning object concept promoted by initiatives such as ADL (*Advanced Distributed Learning*) [3], [4] and IEEE/LTSC (*Learning Technology Standards Committee*) [5]. Under the name of SCORM (*Sharable Content Object Reference Model*), ADL proposes a specification that is applicable to the construction of complex learning objects (which may be structured as a module or as a course) from other more simple objects, down to the most basic learning objects (atomic). In our case, we have preferred to limit ourselves to a concrete application domain: the teaching of archaeology as it is carried out in the Departamento de Historia de América II, and we use this context as a starting point for developing concrete teaching experiences. The kernel of the system consists of a relational database in which the fundamental entity is the virtual object. Furthermore, and seeking to obtaining a standard method for the classification of information, and to being able to establish all the relations required between virtual objects, each virtual object is described by means of a metadata model based on the LOM (Learning Object Metadata) proposal [4], [6].

On the other hand, to design the hypermedia interface that provides access to the educational resources we use our own design model, *Pipe* [7]. In this way, an intermediate representation between the requirements specification and the application is obtained.

In this article, the construction process of the application, the different educational standards and the design model used are described. Finally the results obtained, together with the conclusions and future work are included.

2. EXISTING TECHNOLOGIES

Our application is based on technologies related to the definition of education standards for the development of distributed teaching systems and other technologies related to hypermedia engineering.

2.1 Educational standards

The ADL initiative and in particular the specification proposed in SCORM were the main reference in the conception of this project. Other initiatives that were used as a reference include ARIADNE [8], IEEE/LTSC [5] and IMS [6].

SCORM defines a *content aggregation model* that must be pedagogically neutral. The content aggregation model proposed by SCORM is made up of three elements: the *content model*, the *metadata* and the *packaging model*. The content model, in turn, is made up of three elements: *assets* (the most basic content), *Sharable Content Objects*, SCOs, which is a set of assets that can be executed within the teaching system environment, and *content aggregation*, which are structures that are capable of organising different learning resources to form a coherent teaching unit (it could be said that an aggregation structure defines a taxonomy for a set of learning resources).

As presented in this paper, the concepts of virtual object and educational resource used in our system to organise archaeological information may be considered as a pragmatic approach to the content and metadata model proposed by SCORM.

On the other side, the development of teaching platforms based on the concept of learning object attempts to solve many of the practical difficulties that have traditionally afflicted the development of computer-based courses and teaching systems and has a fundamentally pragmatic focus that is motivated by the type of institutions behind these initiatives [5], [6].

The problems that can arise from teaching systems based on the learning object approach can basically be summarised by the fact that they tend towards a learning process excessively pragmatic and simplistic, based on the presentation of information, simple simulations and tests (in many cases, very close to behaviourist concepts). This feature, to a certain extent, may be considered as a regression to the initial (and highly criticised) computer-based teaching [9].

The approach presented in this work is greatly influenced by the aforementioned concept of learning object [5], [10]. However, it is adapted to a specific domain and the work schemes that impose an oversimplification of the learning process have been removed. Consequently, where possible, the same materials used by the professionals of the area (in our case, archaeologists) are used. These objects are placed at the disposal of students, bearing in mind that the said objects are not only for use in a teaching environment, but that they are also aimed at assisting the professional work of the researcher (archaeologist, historian, etc.) and for use in other, broader contexts, such as the cultural diffusion of research work (in our case, in the fields of archaeology, anthropology and history).

As previously mentioned, the organisation and classification (indexing) of learning objects with a standardised metadata model has been one of the activities that have occupied most of the time of the different organisations taking part in the task of standardising and developing web-based teaching [11]. The work carried out by IMS, IEEE/LTSC and SCORM has consolidated the LOM proposal as the main reference for classifying digitalised educational resources and placing them at the disposal of the web-user community. Thus, the structured focus of the definition of meta-information (LOM metadata model) implies that the describers that jointly make up a conventional and standardised description of an educational resource are grouped together in significant categories. The basic scheme is made up of nine categories [6].

On the other hand, there are different groups, such as Dublin Core [12] and ARIADNE, which have mapped out their metadata schemes to LOM (which has a less exhaustive level of detail).

The use of LOM in our context present some difficulties because the researchers (archaeologists) do not use the digitalized objects (learning objects) that LOM seeks to classify exhaustively as primary objects in his or her work, but rather he or she uses the archaeological artifacts that have been retrieved from digs (e.g. arrowheads, ceramic vases, decorative objects, musical instruments, etc.) Furthermore, the archaeologist also uses more conceptual objects, such as wells or excavated structures, field logs, plans and reports on the process of the dig, material analysis results, etc.

This situation led us to consider the introduction of the concept of virtual *object*, which is the computerised object that represents the real object with which the professional of the area works, and which, in turn, can be made up of other virtual objects. Initially, the virtual objects are not comparable with learning objects, but rather they belong to a broader concept. However, the virtual objects that are described by means of LOM are the basis for the construction of real learning objects (such as practical or theoretical modules) that will use the materials with which the researcher works as a base.

This concept of the virtual object offers a series of advantages in the development of web-based teaching environments which are currently being explored through the construction of a series of prototypes that, in principle, have enabled us to homogeneously process those which we might consider purely educational resources (virtual objects) and the more professional resources used by the archaeologist. This creates interactions (synergy) between the teaching and research activities whose early results have been found to be very satisfactory.

2.2 Hypermedia engineering

As data access is made through a hypermedia interface, we have chosen to use a hypermedia design model to characterise the design of this component of the system. Although in principle the existence of a database led us to consider the use of models such as RMDM [13] or approaches such as WebML [14], we finally rejected this option. The reason is quite simple: the philosophy behind the use of these models is based on the existence of relations between the different entities of the model as the basis for the hyperlinks. The problem lies in that the relations of our database support the existing connections between the different components of virtual objects, but have no value from the hypermedia point of view. We therefore investigated other possibilities. Models such as OOHDM [15] or Labyrinth [16] were too powerful for our needs and their excessive performance produced undesirable situations (e.g. the lack of default browsing semantics). On the other hand, the other systems studied [17] were too simple for our purposes (e.g. very basic user interfaces). We therefore chose to use our hypermedia representation system, Pipe, as it seemed to be the most balanced and suitable option.

The Pipe model [7], [17] is based on the separation of content and their link relationships (*content graph*) of the user interface and the interpretation of the content relationships (*navigational schema* and *canalisation functions*). Both features, and the relations existing between both, are supported by visual notation. Furthermore, the Pipe model has a representation in XML [18] format. The description of the hypermedia application using this format is interpreted by a Java application (*Automatic Prototypes Generator, APG*), which is responsible for the rapid generation of prototypes. The following section shows an example of the application of our model.

3. SYSTEM DEVELOPMENT

3.1 Web Development

One important requirement of our system is that researchers must be able to continually update the information grouped around the virtual objects and from any location with a computer that has access to the network. From the student's point of view (or that of any other kind of user), the possibility of accessing the virtual objects (whether for teaching purposes or otherwise) from any point connected to the network is also important. The current solution to this type of requirement involves the use of a web environment: a client-server architecture based on a standard browser and HTTP. This type of architecture has two very different parts. On the one hand are the processes carried out on the client's side: a standard browser that interprets a document and interacts with the user through HTML and JavaScript. On the other are the processes implemented on the server that manages and processes the data shown to the user through different languages and/or database management systems, such as, and in our case, PHP [19] and MySql [20].

The development of the first prototypes of our system, demonstrated that mixing the code that was to be run on the client with the code that was to be run on the server in the same document caused different management and maintenance problems:

- Significant coupling between HTML and PHP. When incorporating anything more than a simple description of the interface within the pages (e.g. obtaining or modifying information about the virtual objects, processing user permission), the code became too complex.
- Difficulties in the development and debugging of the code. In general, each page may contain a code that is run on the server and a code that is run on the client. This can lead to confusion of one with the other and make it difficult to monitor the flow of the application, which in turn complicates debugging (the errors on a page may be due to crashes in the HTML code, in the JavaScript code or in the PHP code, which are also similar in syntax).
- Difficulty in incrementally modifying the data model. Changes in the data model (e.g. in the definition of the virtual objects) led to changes in almost all the application.

To solve these problems, we decided to use an architecture that was based on the *Model-View-Controller* 2, MVC 2 [21]. With this set-up, when the user carries out an action on the interface on the client side (web browser), originating a new request to the server, it is processed by the controller. Depending on the request it receives, the controller can make a modification to the data model and re-route to the appropriate page. From this page, the status of the data model can be consulted in order to complete the response and the result is sent to the client; this concludes the operation cycle.

Fig. 1 shows an application screenshot corresponding to the management of virtual objects.

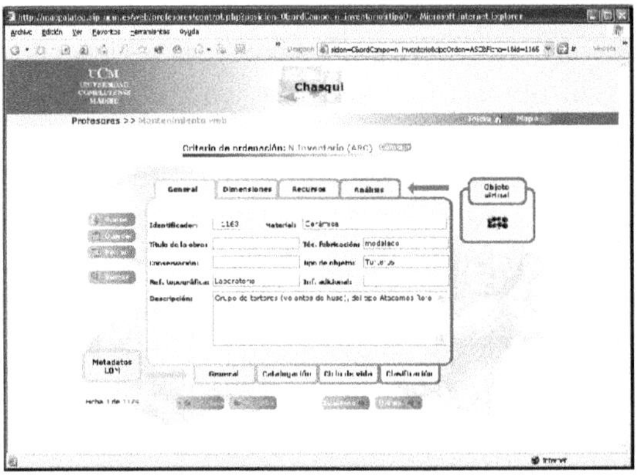

Figure 16-1. Application screenshot

3.2 Hypermedia design

The Pipe model is based on separating content from links and separating contents and links from the graphic interface. At content level, there is an introductory text that provides access to the content of the application. This content is a laboratory, a museum and an area dedicated to system management. In turn, the content of the laboratory and the museum link up with the different descriptions that are extracted dynamically from the system database. Moreover, this content is linked to descriptions from three projects: Esmeraldas, Incapirca and Chinchero. The content structure is similar. They all have a description of the projects, making it possible to extract different information dynamically from the database. Fig. 2 shows the application content graph. In this figure we have eliminated some accessory contents that are not source or destination of any link.

The graphic interface is made up of several screens, which correspond to each of the parts into which we have divided the resources (resources, laboratory, museum, application management and the three projects). Apart from the area dedicated to application management, the other screens are very similar. These include a panel showing the main text and another showing the content extracted from the database. Moreover, they include other panels for showing information that is not linked at content level.

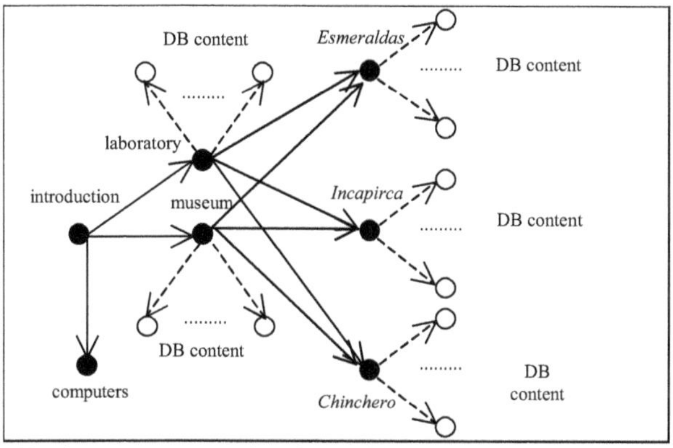

*Figure 16-2.*Application content graph. The solid circles represent static content, and the empty circles represent dynamic content. The solid lines represent static links, and the dotted lines represent dynamic links.

Thus, Fig. 3 shows the design of the screen corresponding to the Esmeraldas Project, together with its relation to the content graph.

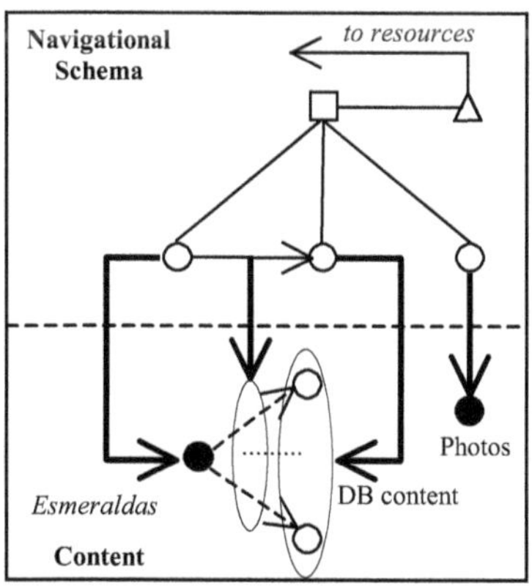

Figure 16-3. Navigational schema and its relation with the content graph. The bold lines show the allocation of content and content links to the elements of the browsing diagram. In the navigational schema, the square represents a window, the circles represent panes inside this window, and the triangle represents a button that gives access to another window. The arrow represents navigational relationships among the panes of the window.

The Pipe model has an associated Java application, APG, which enables the rapid generation of prototypes based on XML coding of the browsing scheme and a representation of content in XML format. Fig. 4 (a) shows the XML browsing scheme equivalent to Fig. 3, and Fig. 4 (b) shows the prototype generated.

```
<?xml version="1.0" encoding="ISO-8859-1"?>
<!DOCTYPE aplicacion SYSTEM "aplicacion.dtd">
<aplicacion id="ap1">
          <ventana id="v1">
                    <nombre>Ventana1</nombre>
                    <panel id="p1.1">
                              <contenidoPanel>
          <contenidoDefecto>/contenidos/foto</contenidoDefecto>
                              </contenidoPanel>
                    </panel>
                    <panel id="p1.2">
                              <contenidoPanel>
          <contenido>/contenidos/BD</contenido>
                              </contenidoPanel>
                    </panel>
                    <panel id="p1.3">
                              <contenidoPanel>
          <contenidoDefecto>/contenidos/texto</contenidoDefecto>
                              </contenidoPanel>
                    </panel>
          </ventana>
</aplicacion>
```

(a)

(b)

Figure 16-4. (a) XML coding of the browsing scheme. (b) Prototype generated. The extraction of content from the database is currently performed manually.

4. CONCLUSIONS AND FUTURE WORK

It is evident that new technologies represent important progress in expanding pedagogical capacities in learning environments. On this occasion, we have developed a system capable of showing a considerable number of archaeological resources to a wide audience, which up to now were only available to a small group of people.

To develop this system, we used numerous concepts from what has come to be known as *e-learning*, but we adapted their application in favour of a more pragmatic approach. The result is the virtual object, influenced by current standards, but modified to our needs. This virtual object has served as the basis for architecture suitable for rapid prototyping and development; this architecture also sufficiently fulfils the requirements that were initially expressed by the archaeologists. All of this has been achieved without being totally detached from the change in orientation currently taking place in educational technologies. On the contrary, its greatest disadvantage is to be found in that it has not been developed in complete accordance with the said standards.

On the other hand, the hypermedia component we are developing benefits from a well-defined design backed by rapid prototyping techniques that are, in fact, extremely valuable for the development of a hypermedia application.

Future work includes the adaptation of virtual objects to be in complete accordance with educational standards, together with the completion of the hypermedia interface, which is currently under development. We are also working on the integration of relational technology with the Pipe model and the automatic prototype generation mechanism.

ACKNOWLEDGEMENTS

This work was financed by the *Comité Español de Ciencia y Tecnología* (Spanish Committee for Science and Technology) (TIC2000-0737-C03-01).

REFERENCES

1. R. Carro, E. Pulido, P. Rodríguez, "Dynamic Generation of Adaptive Internet-Based Courses". Journal of Network and Computer Applications. Academic Press. http://www.idealibrary.com .Vol. 22. November 1.999, pp.249-257
2. Rodríguez-Artacho, M., Verdejo, F., Mayorga, J.I., and Calero, Y. "Using a high-level language to describe and create web-based learning scenarios". In Proceedings of the IEEE Frontiers in Education Conference (FIE99), San Juan, Puerto Rico. IEE Society. 1999.
3. J.D. Fletcher, Philip Dodds, "All About ADL", Learning Circuits. http://www.learningcircuits.org/
4. Advanced Distributed Learning Initiative. Sharable Courseware Object Reference Model (SCORM). http://www.adlnet.org/
5. IEEE Learning Technology Standards Committee (IEEE LTSC) Learning Object Metadata(LOM).http://ltsc.ieee.org/wg12/
6. IMS Global Learning Consortium. http://www.imsproject.org/SpecAction.cfm
7. A. Navarro, B. Fernández, A. Fernández-Valmayor,, J.L. Sierra, "Formal-Driven Conceptualization and Prototyping of Hypermedia Applications". FASE 2002 Grenoble, 6-14 April, 2002. LNCS (Vol. 2306), Springer-Verlag, Berlin, 2002.
8. ARIADNE http://ariadne.unil.ch/
9. Wenger, E. Artificial Intelligence and tutoring systems. Morgan Kaufmmann Publishers, Los Altos, 1987.
10. Sun Microsystems-Education and Research White Papers. "E-learning Application Infrastructure". http://www.sun.com/products-n-solutions/edu/elearning/
11. Sun Microsystems-Education and Research White Papers. "E-learning Interoperability Standards". http://www.sun.com/products-n-solutions/edu/elearning/

12. Dublin Core Metadata Initiative. : http://dublincore.org/
13. T. Isakowitz, E.A. Stohr, P. Balasubramanian , "RMM: a methodology of structured hypermedia design". Communications of the ACM 38 (8), 34-43, 1995.
14. S. Ceri, P. Fraternali, A. Bongio, "Web Modeling Language (WebML): a modeling language for designing Web sites". Records of the 9th International World Wide Web Conference. Amsterdam, 15-19 May, 2000.
15. D. schwabe, G. Rossi, S.D.J. Barbosa, "systematic Hypermedia Application Design witho OOHDM". In Proceedings Hypertext 96, Washington, 1996.
16. P. Díaz, I. Aedo, F. Panetsos. "Modeling the dynamic behaviour of hipermedia applications". IEEE TOSE, 27 (6), 550-572, 2001.
17. A. Navarro, "Conceptualización, prototipado y proceso de aplicaciones hipermedia". Doctoral Thesis. Dept. of Information Systems and Programming. Universidad Complutense de Madrid. 2002.
18. W3C Extensible Markup Language XML). http://www.w3.org/XML/
19. PHP. http://www.php.net/
20. MySql. http://www.mysql.com/
21. G. Seshadri, "Understanding JavaServer Pages Model 2 Architecture. Exploring the MVC design pattern". http://www.javaworld.com/javaworld/jw-12-1999/

Chapter 17

A TECHNOLOGY FOR BUILDING WEB-BASED LABORATORIES FOR TEACHING ELECTRONICS

Harvey Giraldo Arboleda[1], Mauricio Alvarez Mesa[2] and José Edinson Aedo Cobo[1]

Department of Electronic Engeneering. Antioquia University[1]. Calle 67 No. 53-108, Medellín Colombia.E-mail: joseaedo@udea.edu.co. Universidad Politécnica de Cataluña[2]. España

Abstract: In countries with educative coverage difficulties, it becomes necessary to develop and use new technologies that allow expanding education supply for a larger group of the population. In engineering field, one of the difficulties to fulfill this objective is the high cost of training and practice laboratories. In relation to electronic engineering, a way for having a large number of laboratories could be to develop WEB- based laboratories, available at any time, in such a way that even the less difficult experimental practices could be carried out by students, without physically visiting laboratories. This paper presents the development of a hardware-software system to integrate a basic electronic laboratory on the WEB. This laboratory has a WEB interface that allows carry out experiments using simple electronic circuits, remotely varying its parameters and obtain circuits output signal measures. With the construction of this laboratory prototype, students could carry out practices involving diodes, field effect transistors, bipolar transistors and small signal amplifier. The methodology developed in this work can be easily extended to other types of laboratories and to industrial applications.

Key words: Web-based laboratories, Java Servlets

INTRODUCTION

One of the problems Colombian Public Universities face at the moment is the need for increasing education coverage with a restricted budget.

M. Llamas-Nistal et al. (eds.), Computers and Education. Towards a Lifelong Learning Society, 203–214.

Especially in engineering field, this problem has become more serious due to requirements for appropriate laboratories, which are very important in engineering education. On the other hand, the last reform in the program of studies in the University of Antioquia intends an immersion of students, in the engineering practical world, from the first terms, which shows the need for having more resources for experimenting.

A solution to these demands could be the incorporation of new technologies for implementing laboratories [1], which will allow a major efficiency in their use. Inside this trend, there are the so-called "WEB- based laboratories," which have lately had a great development, specially in control system field[2-4]. Nevertheless, the development of WEB-based laboratories has been almost non-existent, in the field of analog electronics.

In this paper, a novel strategy for implementing WEB- based laboratories for teaching basic analog electronics is presented. Based on this strategy, a hardware-software system was developed which allows the connection of the laboratory to the WEB. The laboratory consists of a set of measurement and signal generation equipment connected through a local network. The laboratory also has a set of devices and electronic systems used to establish experiment schemas. Interconnections of these devices are made through analog CMOS transmission gates. Therefore, experiments can be programmed from commands remotely sent.

A user could have access to the laboratory by a WEB page. In this page, a user can choose the experiment, establishing instruments he/she will use, the circuit schema to be tested, the kind of polarization apply on the circuits, the frequency and type of electrical signals that he/she wants to apply to the circuit. A user can also establish which measures will be carried out and which instruments should be connected to obtain them. Results of an experiment are sent back to the user through another WEB page dynamically generated. This page includes graphs and tables with the values of measured output signals in the circuits under test. Students hereby are physically carrying out experiences, and the measurement is done in the circuits with real devices. The remote laboratory also allows the student perform different kinds of experiences by changing parameters of the experiment.

The software system was developed using Java Servlets and Java Server Pages(JSP) as basic technologies for the server side dynamic WEB applications development[9-10], in contrast to CGIs (Common Gateway Interface) that is less efficient, less secure, and less portable [9].

Servlets establish an interface mechanism for executing server applications under a user's requests. JSP allows adequately separating the WEB page design from the server WEB programming, since it allows mixing both static HTML and dynamical contents generated by Servlets. For the system development, two servers were used: a Linux machine running

Apache WEB server integrated with Tomcat Servlet container and a MS-Windows machine connected to the laboratory.

This article has several sections: Section 2, presents a description of the general architecture of remote laboratory. Section 3 presents the structure of the software developed in Java. Section 4 describes the hardware architecture of the laboratory. Section 5 shows the design of an integrated circuit developed in order to expand the laboratory capabilities having some experimental practices using custom integrated electronics. Results of the first prototype WEB-based laboratory are described in section 6. Finally, the section 7 presents the conclusions and future work.

GENERAL ESTRUCTURE OF WEB-BASED LABORATORY

This laboratory (instruments and circuits) is connected to the University local network through a server called laboratory server which provides specific HTTP services for equipment handling. This server receives connections from another server that has access to the WEB. This last server stores the main pages of the laboratory (Its address is http://microe.udea.edu.co/labvirtual). This architecture was adopted for security, so the laboratory server cannot be directly accessed. Figure 1 shows the distribution of used servers.

At the beginning, the laboratory is oriented toward analog electronics practices. Instruments used in it are connected to the network using GPIB interface. Devices and electronic circuits used to carry out experiences can be set in a specific configuration using a microcontroller which is managed through the serial interface of the laboratory server. This microcontroller establishes a connection among the devices commanding analog CMOS switches.

The laboratory server is connected through university local network to the main server which has a WEB connection. In both servers, the Jakarta Tomcat software and Apache WEB server which allows the execution of Servlets and offers WEB basic services, have been installed. Section 3 describes, with more details, the connection strategy and the software structure developed in this work

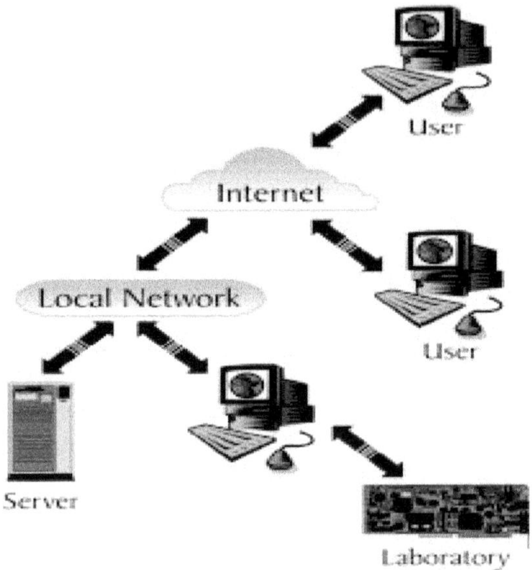

Figure 17-1. Connection to Internet of the Remote Laboratory

SOFTWARE ESTRUCTURE

The software for handling the laboratory is divided in two main parts: The first one was developed for users' access control to the laboratory and for running on the WEB server. The second one was developed for instruments and equipment control. This last part is executed in the laboratory server.

– Access control system

This system consists of the laboratory main page, which provides access to Servlet in order to control the laboratory usage by authorizing or denying its access, according to equipment availability. When a user is authorized to execute a remote experiment, he/she receives a WEB page with the list of available experiments. This list includes: Small Signal Amplifier, the MOSFET characterization, the diode characterization and the BJT characterization. On this page, the user selects the experiment he/she wishes to carry out and the server sends back to him a WEB page with configuration parameters form of the corresponding experiment. Some of these parameters are: Type of wave (sine, square, triangular, etc), signal frequency in Hertz, resistance values in the circuit, and polarization voltages of the active components. When the user clicks on the measure button, the parameters chosen are sent to a JSP (It was built having a different one for each experiment). The JSP processes the parameters and verifies if they are valid for the experiment chosen and then it returns a page containing data and graphs with experiment results. In order to generate this page, the JSP calls a corresponding instrument control Servlet, which uses configuration parameters for executing the experiment.

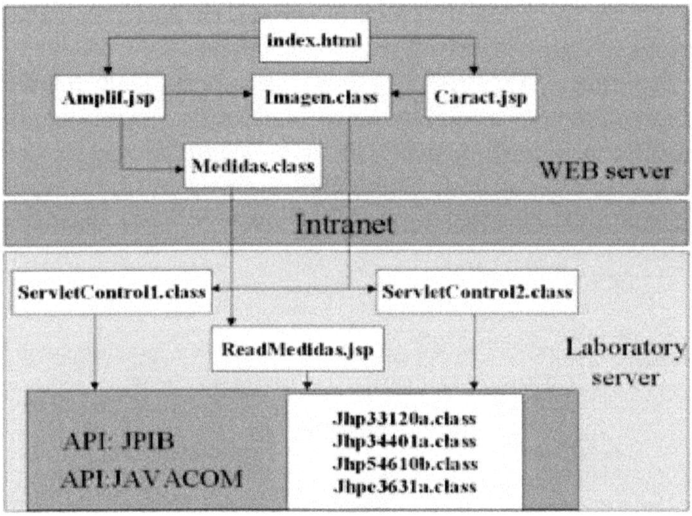

Figure 17-2. Estructure of the Software

The access Servlet and the experiment JSPs are located in the WEB server. The instrument control Servlet is located in the laboratory server. Communication between both servers is done by HTTP through the local network [7-8]. Figure 2 shows the relation between WEB pages, Servlets and JSPs.

According to this connection scheme, two electronic systems were used: the first one contains the microcontroller and is connected to the server through a serial interface; this system controls the instruments. The second one is used for instrument control and is connected to the server bus. Figure 3 shows the distribution of these two electronic systems.

– Instruments Control

To execute basic electronic experiments, several instruments are required such as: a digital oscilloscope, a programmable signal generator, and also some programmable current and voltage sources.

The control of these instruments is made using a GPIB interface what allows interconnect them in a network with a PC control (laboratory server). The communication between control servlet and the instruments are made through a GPIB port driver, which has been developed in Java. By means of this driver, the instrument is shaped according to parameters chosen by the user. Each experiment has a control Servlet, which calls the drivers of required instruments. Control Servlet processes, shaping commands of each instrument receive answers about requested actions.

Each experiment requires its own instruments and interconnection schema; consequently, a commutation electrical system handled by a microcontroller was implemented. This microcontroller receives commands through a server's serial port. Commands are sent by the control Servlet. This interface was developed using the API of Java communications: JavaComm.

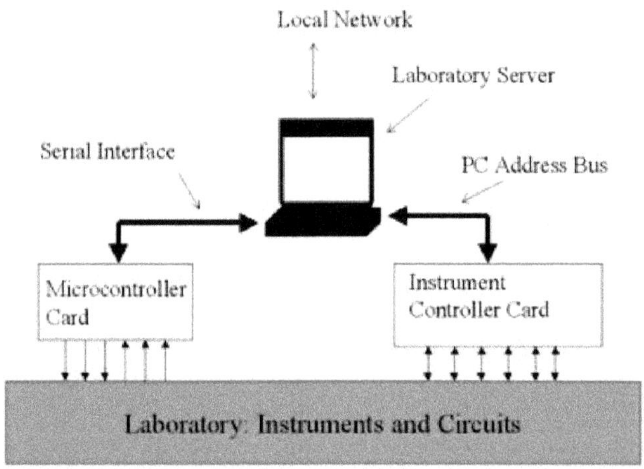

Figure 173. Connection of the Electronics System for Controlling and Configuring of Circuits

HARWARE STRUCTURE

From the hardware point of view, the remote laboratory includes: measure instruments, signal generators, and power sources, devices and circuits used to shape experiments and a microcontroller, which is responsible for generating commands to shape the experimental schema.

Measure instruments and multimeter are typical instruments found in any basic laboratory of electronics. Instruments used in this work have a GPIB interface, which makes it possible to connect them to the GPIB network and to the laboratory server.

The oscilloscope and the multimeter are used to carry out electrical measures on the circuit under test. The power supply is used to bias the circuits. The DC voltage of the sources can be established remotely by the user. The signal generator permits to carry out experiments with small-signal amplifiers. This generator can generate several forms of electrical signal with different amplitude and frequency from a few hertz to 15 MHz. Also, the programming of this instrument can be remotely established by the user.

In this work, the 68HC08GP32 was selected due to its great number of I/O ports, which is used to control different circuit shaping. To perform the circuit shaping analog switches which can be commanded by digital signals were used. These analog switches make the circuit connection or disconnection to the instruments, according to commands sent by the microcontroller. In figure 4, the distribution of two experiments: a simple MOS amplifier circuit and the MOSFET characterization is shown, as an example. R1 and R2 are variable resistance and their value is established by a sequence of digital pulses. According to figure 4, if the experiment with the amplifier is chosen, the microcontroller sends the digital commands for closing analog switches S1, S2, S4 and S5. These switches connect the signal generator, the supply source and oscilloscope channels to the input and output nodes of the MOS amplifier. The microcontroller sends a train of digital pulses to establish the value of the polarization resistance (R1) and load resistance (R2). These resistances can vary from 1 to 100 KOhms. Resistance values are remotely defined by the user. Once, the experiment is shaped, and then measure instruments and signal sources are programmed through GPIB interface. Each instrument has its own address. The program that controls the instruments was written in Java. Similarly, for a MOS transistor characterization, also shown in the figure 4, the procedure consists on closing the S3, S6 analog switches to connect the polarization sources. In this experiment the user chooses the voltage ranks, apply for both polarization sources, so the Java program automatically shapes the instruments in order to apply voltage sequences to the transistor drain and transistor gate according with voltage ranges. The source-drain current (I_{DS}) is measured through a voltage resistance, using the multimeter. Once the voltage (V_{DS}) and current (I_{DS}) data are obtained, the graph of I_{DS} - V_{DS} characteristics is built. Java program is executed in the laboratory server and the user receives the graphic of characteristics. The first laboratory prototype has experimental schemas for diode characterization, BJT and MOSFET characterization, and small signal MOS amplifier. All these schemas use discrete devices.

In order to expand experimental schemas for teaching integrated electronics, it was designed a chip (integrated circuit) with some basic circuits that can be selected to carry out different experiments. In Section V, this IC is described.

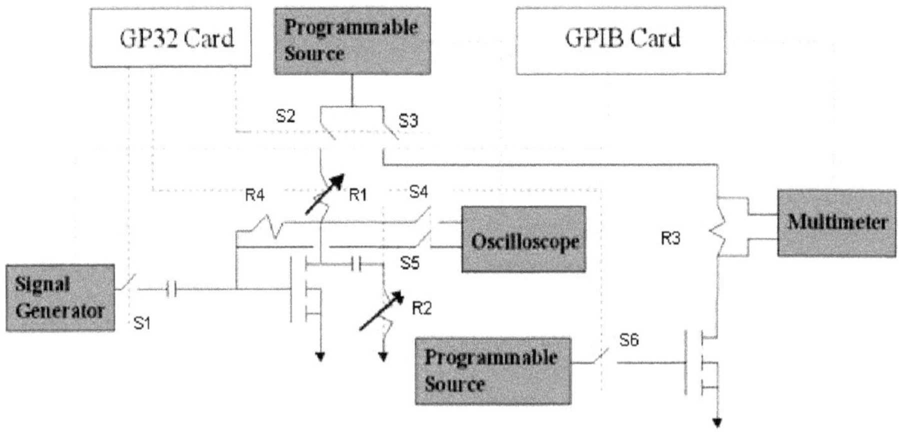

Figure 17-4. Configuration of two experiments: a) Simple small-signal MOS amplifier. b) MOSFET characterization.

CIRCUITAL SCHEMAS FOR THE INTEGRATED ELECTRONIC TEACHING

In order to integrate, into the laboratory, experiences using designed circuits described in the physical representation, an integrated circuit (IC) was conceived and designed, which becomes a way of getting the required experimentation and analysis for teaching the design process of a signal amplifier using MOS technology[6].

Using this methodology some basic circuit blocks have been implemented which can be used for the students in order to execute different experiences having all information about parameters technology, layout, and design considerations used in the manufacturing of IC.

Based on this strategy, some differential amplifiers with common source and source follower configuration were designed and implemented. Additionally, other subsystems like ring oscillators, analog switches, a first order switched capacitive filter, and some different size transistors were designed. The IC offers the possibility of experiencing each one of subsystems.

All designed circuits -which constitute the IC- were implemented considering that they will be tested using a remote Internet access scheme. The integrated circuit architecture is strongly programmable allowing choosing a subsystem to be used by switching some pins of the circuit. In this way, it is possible to establish a remote connection between measure instruments and the required subsystem.

Similarly, it is possible to change the gain of different amplifiers allowing; for example, in the voltage amplification step gains from 15 dB to 38 dB, according to the connected charge and also according to the variation of frequency response [11].

Figure 5 shows the layout of IC designed. The IC was designed utilizing CADENCE software using a 0.6 microns DLM CMOS process. The chip size is 2 x 2 square millimeters and, currently, it is being manufactured by AMS through MPC (multi project chip) services from TIMA laboratory in France.

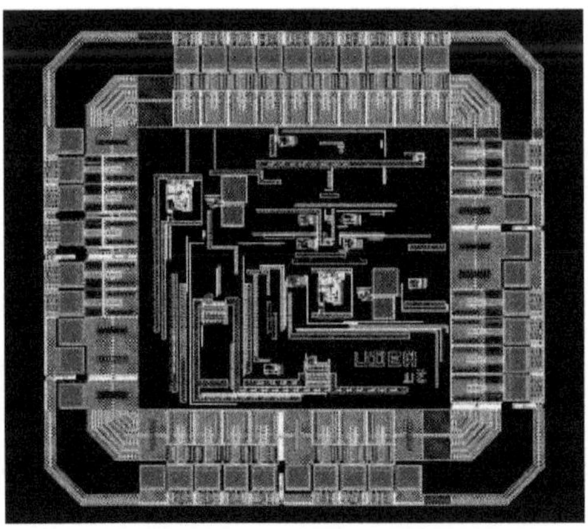

Figure 17-5. Layout of the IC

RESULTS

A prototype laboratory has been built in order to evaluate its performance in an Electronic Engineering program. In this first version, the laboratory has a simple interface where the user selects the practice to develop and establishes the parameters that he/she wishes to use in his/her experiment.

From there, the experiment begins giving a click in the button of measuring. In figure 6, the WEB page corresponding to the characterization of a MOSFET transistor, is showed. Once the program for characterization of the transistor is executed, the result information is sent to the user. In figure 7, it appears an example of characterization results.

Nowadays the system is under evaluation by the students of Semiconductors course of Electronic Engineering. Basic practices of device characterization and small signal amplifiers have been realized in a remote way. Practices with more complex systems will be carried out visiting the real laboratory.

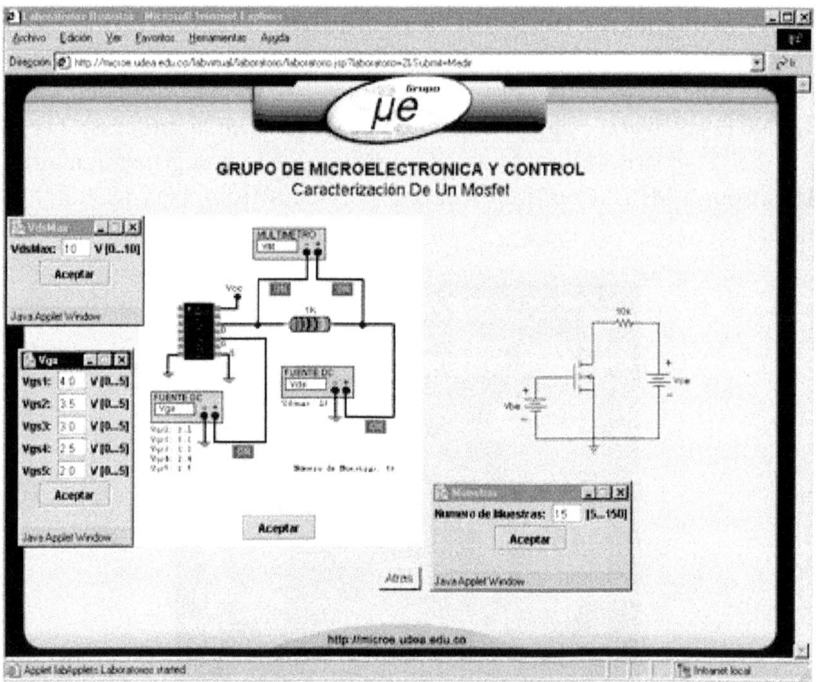

Figure 17-6. WEB Page of the MOSFET Characterization

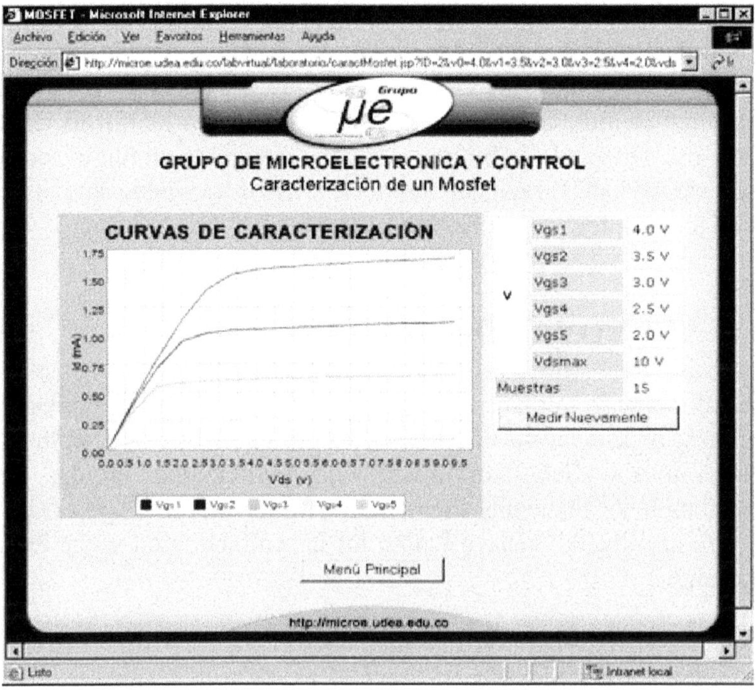

Figure 17-7. Results of the MOSFET Characterization

CONCLUSIONS

In this work, a new strategy for connecting basic electronic laboratories to the WEB services was conceived and implemented. Its development system includes hardware and software components. Both components were developed allowing establish a laboratory using basic circuits oriented to test analog electronics. The system performance evaluation has showed its efficiency to optimize the access to hardware resources, more specifically for executing the simplest experiments. That because the system allows a valuable time reduction required by students, to execute this type of experiences and, additionally because the laboratory is available 24 hours by day.

From a design point of view the remote laboratory software was developed using an object oriented methodology based on the Java programming language, which makes it portable and facilitates its application to other experimental schemas. Software part includes server programming, Servlets and JSPs. The communication system uses the serial port (API JavaComm) and the instrument communication software uses the GPIB interface (GPIB API). Hereby the developed software uses only one programming language (JAVA) which allows a greater integration of different applications, besides the portability between platforms and WEB servers is also obtained. As future works, the integrated circuit conceived for this purpose and the graphical interface will be available and it will be improved looking for a friendlier laboratory.

ACKNOWLEDGEMENTS

The authors wish to thank Colciencias and CODI for their support for the development of this work. Equally we would like to thank Carolina Mora, Marcela Zuluaga, Sebastian Izasa who participated in the Servlets implementation for managing the instruments and in the graphical interface design. We also thank Gustavo Patiño for his collaboration in the integrated circuit design.

REFERENCES

1. C. C. Ko, B. M. Chen, J. Chen, Y. Zhuang and K. Chen, Tan, “Development of a Web-based laboratory for control Experiments on a couple Tank apparatus” IEEE Trans. on Education Vol. 44, No.1, February 2001, pp. 76–86.
2. C.C. Ko, B. M. Chen, S. H. Chen, V. Ramakrishnan, R. Chen, S. Y. Hu and Y. Zhuang, “A large scale web-based virtual oscilloscope laboratory experiment”, Inst. Elect. Eng. Sci. Edu. J., vol. 9, no. 2, pp.69-76., 2000.
3. M Shor and Bhandari, “Access to an instructional control laboratory experiment through the Word Wide Web”, in Proc. 1998 Amer. Contr. Conf., Philadelphia, PA., pp. 1319-1325.1998.
4. “Web-based virtual laboratory, Nat. Univ. Singapore”, http://vlab.ee.nus.edu.sg/vlab
5. MC68HC08GP32 Technical data. HCMOS Microcontroller Unit. Motorola Semiconductor Product Sector.
6. D. J. Comer and D. T. Comer. U. “Teaching MOS Integrated Circuit Amplifier Design to Undergraduate”, IEEE Trans. On Education, vol. 44, pp. 232 –238, August. 2001.
7. Reuven MLerner, “Server-Side Java with Jakarta-Tomcat”. Linux Journal. April 2001. http://www.linuxjournal.com/article.php?sid=4576
8. Petr Sorfa, “Using and Writing Java Servlets”, Linux Journal, January 2002. http://www.linuxjournal.com/article.php?sid=4819
9. Marty Hall. “Servlets y Java Server Pages”. Guía Práctica. Pearson Educación. México 2001.
10. Herber Schildt. “Java 2. Manual de referencia”. MacGraw Hill. Madrid 2001.
11. G. A. Patiño y J. E. Aedo, "Implementación de un circuito integrado orientado a la enseñanza del proceso de diseño de circuitos analógicos básicos con tecnología CMOS". EITI-2002, Universidad Nacional de Colombia, ISBN 958-9352-55-3, Sept. 2002.

Chapter 18

A TOOL FOR THE CREATION OF WEBSITES BY CHILDREN BASED ON EDUCATION THROUGH PROJECTS

André Luís Alice Raabe, Rudimar S. Dazzi, Anita M. R. Fernandes, Simone Criminácio
Grupo de Desenvolvimento de Software Educacional - Ciência da Computação - CTTMar - Universidade do Vale do Itajaí - SC - Brazil

Abstract: This article presents KidWeb – a website construction tool for children, which is aimed at assisting activities carried out with children in the third and fourth grades of Elementary School, based on Education through Projects. It addresses the studies already carried out in this area, analyses of the interfaces of HTML Editors and authoring tools for children. It also explores the way in which this software program operates and offers perspectives on its use in the school context.

Key words: WEB-based tools and resources, Educational Software, Teaching through Projects

1. INTRODUCTION

Nowadays, the computer has become a reality in schools, serving as a tool that enables the child to become involved in educational experiences, in which the process of acquiring knowledge is not only theoretical, but also practical.

Analyzing the activities carried out in Elementary Schools that work with Education through Projects, it was observed that in the majority of activities, the children are encouraged to develop a final product. This is generally in the form of a document, image or composition created using the computer.

M. Llamas-Nistal et al. (eds.), Computers and Education. Towards a Lifelong Learning Society, 215–226.

Often, however, the software used to support these activities is not appropriate to the context and language of the child.

In view of this fact, KidWeb was developed. It is an authoring tool designed to assist children in the creation of multimedia compositions in the form of websites. With this in mind, it sought to develop an interface that was more appropriate to the reality of the child.

This article is divided as follows: Item II presents the theoretical concepts related to Education Through Projects and the Generating Themes and describes the visits made to the schools that work with this teaching method; item III presents the search for indicators for constructing the KidWeb interface; item IV gives a description of KidWeb; item V presents KidWeb within the context of Education Through Projects; and item VI gives some Final Considerations.

2. EDUCATION THROUGH PROJECTS

In Education through Projects, cognitive, emotional and social aspects are present in the construction of knowledge, and are put into practice by means of previously prepared activities, in which learning is more than a simple act of memorization and teaching does not mean simply passing on ready-made content [1]. The practice of Education Through Projects aims to improve on the general trends in Education and includes, among others, the following characteristics:

a) The student becomes the subject of his own learning, not merely an executer of activities, but more of a co-participant;
b) The search for information by the students is merely guided by the teacher who does not provide any ready answers;
c) The classroom practices go beyond a static, decontextualized vision in that they are supported by reality; by the knowledge baggage that the students bring with them and by what they really want to discover, no longer being dependant only on the choices made by the adults.

The creation and practice of projects in schools should not leave out the disciplinary contents but rather, should give them added dynamism, enriching them and linking the process of learning these contents with the current reality [2]. When working with projects, the contact the children have with the disciplinary contents is not abstract or theoretical. On the contrary, the search for solutions to the questions proposed in the project leads to a need to learn and in this process; the students are faced with the disciplinary contents, which come to be seen as valuable cultural tools for understanding reality.

The project in Education through Projects is comprised of four phases:

1. Selecting the Generating Theme;
2. Gathering Information;
3. Organizing the Information;
4. Displaying the Information.

In the first phase, the student, together with his colleagues and teachers, selects a generating theme for the project. The theme may be suggested by a single student, by the teacher or by a group of students. The important point is that this choice involves everybody and becomes the choice of everybody.

A theme is called a generating theme because whatever the nature of its scope, like the activity it leads to, it contains the possibility of spilling over into other such themes which, in turn, lead to new tasks to be taken up [3].

Once the theme has been selected, the work continues with students gathering information from different kinds of sources, such as conversations or interviews with various informants, outings or visits, bibliographic research, Internet research and drawings, among others.

In the third phase of the project, Organizing the Information, the student determines the final direction his project will take, which may be in the form of a poster, a newspaper, a cartoon-style comic strip, poetry, etc., and organizes the material to be presented. It is important that during this phase, different types of sources are used to present the various viewpoints.

In the final phase, Displaying the Information Collected, the student displays the final product in the school to his colleagues, teachers and parents.

2.1 Education Through Projects in Practice

With the aim of confirming the validity and relevance of constructing the tool, visits were made to two municipal schools that work with Education through Projects, attended by children from early childhood through to the end of Elementary Education. These schools also assisted in the definition of indicators for the construction of KidWeb.

One of the concerns that was perceived is the attempt to ensure that the educational proposals are up-to-date and that they offer children a wide range and variety of experiences. With this in mind, the schools base themselves on the Quality of Life Project, which proposes the creation of a curricula divided into weeks, including themes such as "Environment week", Good manners week" and "Elections week", according to commemorative dates and events and the interests of the students. The teachers design the curricular and interdisplinary activities, including them in the proposed theme.

In the vast majority of activities carried out, the final product is a display of the information collected and organized by the students. This is normally in the form of posters or computer-generated documents using software programs such as Word, Paint and Kidpix.

The schools visited have Computer Laboratories for the carrying out of projects that are integrated with the classroom activities, according to the context of each week and using the computer as another tool for assisting in the children's cognitive development.

The schools expressed a need for software to support these activities in Elementary Education and plan to integrate the Internet with the classroom disciplines, offering the student yet another source for research and project development.

In view of these issues, it was confirmed that the construction of KidWeb could contribute to the carrying out of activities related to Education Through Projects, since these activities usually generate a final project in the form of a document. The creation of these documents using an HTML editor, designed according to the characteristics of the child and the nature of the activities, is a tool which can help to develop cognitive skills, changing children's ideas about the Internet and enabling wider access to the activities developed in the classroom.

3. THE SEARCH FOR INDICATORS FOR THE INTERFACE

The interface should function as bridge between the child and the system [4]. The first step in planning the interface is to identify the ages of the children for whom the project is aimed, since it is extremely important to take into consideration the type of user and his characteristics in order to ensure that his requirements are met. It was established, together with the specialists of the schools visited, that the most suitable age group for KidWeb would be students in their 3rd and 4th grades of Elementary Education.

In order to determine the indicators for the development of the software functions, the HTML Editor *Microsoft FrontPage Express* was analyzed. Also, the authoring software *Fine Artist* was analyzed as it is an authoring tool aimed at children, and the HTML editor for children *HotDog Junior*, which works with the same age group as KidWeb.

3.1 *Analysis of the MS-FrontPage Express Software*

FrontPage is a software program designed for the MS-Windows Platform, which enables the construction and editing of Websites in HTML format. The main screen, where the pages are prepared, is comprised of basic icons, a standard toolbar and formatting toolbar, the buttons on these toolbars represent the most frequently used commands.

Creating an HTML page using FrontPage is similar to creating a document using a text editor. Thus, it is not necessary to have special knowledge of HTML. Editing is done visually, and the corresponding code is generated automatically.

It includes all the most common resources for composing electronic documents, such as cutting, copying, pasting, returning, formatting font, inserting images, formatting background color and so on.

To facilitate the organization of the texts and images of a Web page, FrontPage enables the use of tables which display, like a spreadsheet, lines and columns into which text can be typed; Both images and texts can be used as hyperlinks, which link to another Web page, image or table when clicked on by the visitor.

3.2 Analysis of the Fine Artist Tool

This tool was chosen because of its suitability for the target public of the proposed project. It has icons that are appropriate to the reality of the children, providing them with an authoring environment. The Fine Artist tool enables the child to create comic strips, animated images, posters and stickers.

The environment also has tools aimed at teaching artistic techniques, such as notions of dimension in the creation of a design [5]. Also, the child's imaginative capacity can be shown by adding sounds and animated images to their work, or by the use of ready-made figures. It also enables the practice of writing, whereby the child can construct words that can then be linked to sounds and visual effects, with the addition of colors.

Fine Artist may, at first, confuse the child, due to its wide variety of resources; however its intuitive and user-friendly interface makes it easy to use. Some interesting features are highlighted, such as:

1. The use of icons which are visually appealing to the child public;
2. The linking of sounds to words: the users can use the sounds available on the environment, or record new ones to link to the words [5];
3. The edition of images from the tool's archive;
4. Each student creates a directory with his or her name, where works created using the environment are saved.

3.3 Analysis of HotDog Junior

Hotdog Junior is an HTML editor for children which has an interface in English. The software has its own character (a dog), who presents the editing functions.

The software is comprised of a menu with fairly large buttons for choosing, building, visualizing and saving an HTML document.

The child can create a page visually, select the background color and add items such as images, texts, links etc.

Texts are typed in a special text box and for formatting the text, a dialog box opens with a series of options from which the child selects the letter style, color and text alignment.

To add images, a dialog box is opened where the child can select the desired image. The selected items are distributed on the page according to the order in which they are inserted by the child. The child can then visualize the page and save it.

4. DESCRIPTION OF KIDWEB

In order to develop an educational software project, it is necessary to address the technical and teaching aspects. The choice of taxonomy is important for determining the main characteristics of the software and giving direction to the modeling and implementation process. KidWeb fits within the modality of an authoring tool, since it enables the student to explore a wide range of cognitive skills while exercising his creativity.

It was decided to provide four templates of pre-prepared pages with specific places for inserting the title, texts, images and links, as it was believed this would make it easier for the child to create the page, which is an important characteristic of software programs developed for this public. Figure 1 illustrates the selection screen for one of the templates.

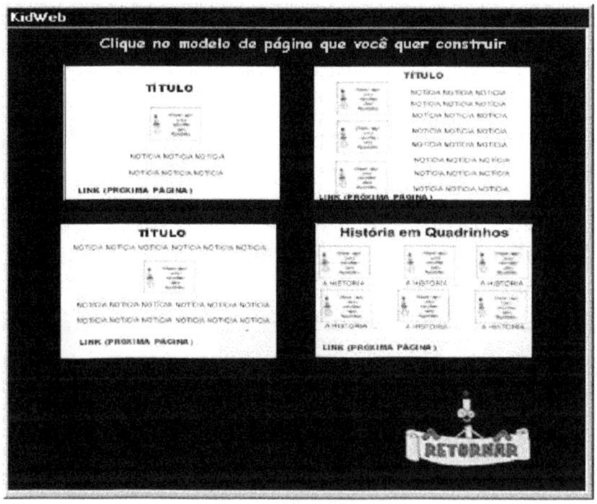

Figure 18-1. Selection screen of a template.

The functions defined for the editor were based on the FrontPage program. They are: “Format Paragraph”, “Cut”, “Copy”, “Paste”, “Change Background Color”, “Save”, “Print”, “Visualize page” and “Help”. These were chosen as they are the most basic tasks used in creation of websites.

Through an analysis of HotDog Junior, it was observed that it is important for the program to have its own character, which the child can identify. The character Izinho (I for Internet) was therefore created, which is predominantly yellow and fairly large, so as to facilitate clicking with the mouse. The figure was created bearing in mind the age range for which the software was designed. The character can be seen in detail in Figure 2 below.

Figure 18-2. Character Izinho of KidWeb.

The main screen where the page is put together is comprised of an editing area, surrounded by icons. This enables the student to see the icons clearly, and gives the general impression of an uncluttered, pleasant environment.

The software performs basic functions, such as: creating a new HTML document, based on the template selected, saving this document, inserting images, text and hyperlinks, and formatting. Figure 3 shows the KidWeb interface with a template for creating a comic-strip.

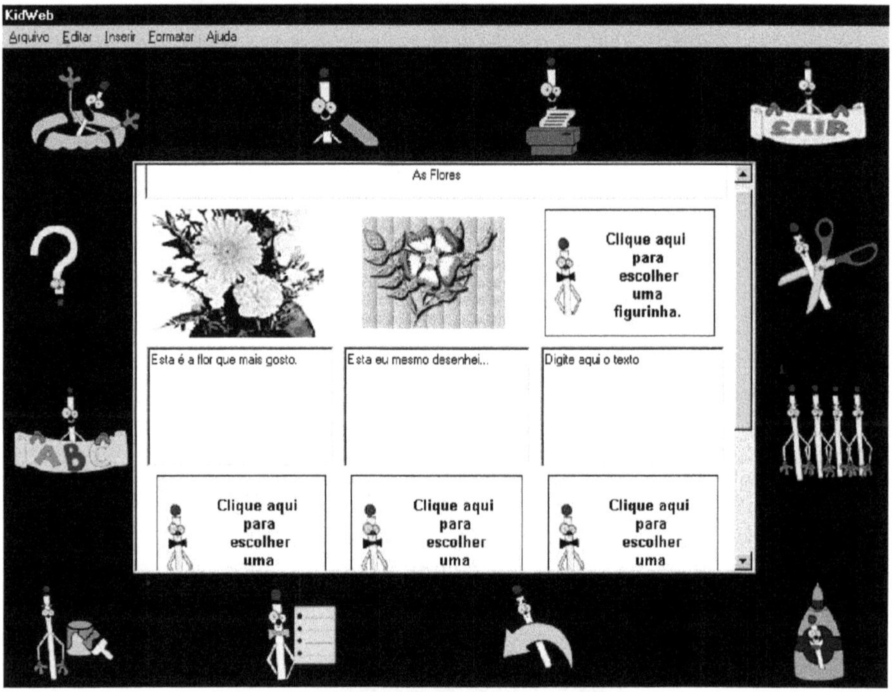

Figure 18-3. KidWeb Interface.

The child creates the page in whatever way he wishes, since the formatting of the letters, background colors and image are inserted according to his imagination. The page can be visualized using the KidWeb visualizer. Figure 4 demonstrates a page designed using KidWeb.

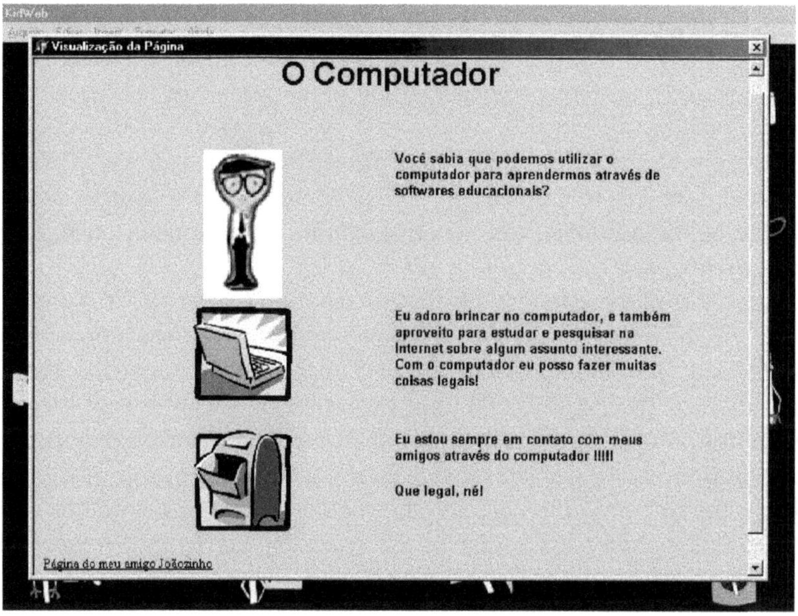

Figure 18-4. Page designed using Kid Web.

The child does not need any prior knowledge of HTML in order to use KidWeb, since it is a visual software program. In other words, the HTML code is generated automatically as the page is being built.

KidWeb enables the teacher to select the standard file in which the software will search for image archives. Thus, archives of images related to the Generating Theme selected can be built up. The file in which the HTML documents are saved may also be selected, and if it is a shared file of the school's local network, this can facilitate the task of combining the works produced by the children into a digital dossier, which can be displayed over the Internet to other children, parents, coordinators etc.

A module still has not been built for automatic publication of pages on the Internet, and the FTP procedure still needs to be carried out.

5. KIDWEB AND EDUCATION THROUGH PROJECTS

The relation between KidWeb and Education through Projects becomes clearer when each stage is analyzed in isolation. In the Gathering Information phase, the child and teacher can collect or create (using software such as Paint) an archive of images and make them available for their colleagues to create their websites. For this, KidWeb provides the option of a standard file in which images are sought. This file can be shared among the various users, and may vary according to the wishes of the teacher or the generating theme.

In the Organizing the Information phase, the child can use KidWeb to organize the project in the form of a website, using the templates provided. This may be an individual text, poetry, a comic-strip, a newsletter, a report of an interview, etc.

In the final phase, Displaying the Information Collected, it is important that the child is able to divulge his work and is given the opportunity to communicate it. The dossiers are an important strategy for the final organization of the projects. Within this context, KidWeb will serve as a doorway for publishing the projects on the Internet and a new opportunity to use a tool for building websites that is totally geared towards children.

Thus, the use of computers in educational institutions, initially seen as just a complementary discipline in the students' curriculum, comes to be viewed as a powerful learning tool within the pedagogical context.

6. FINAL CONSIDERATIONS

Education Through Projects was a primary motivating factor for this work, since the characteristics of the tasks carried out and the support provided by the software tools indicated the possibility of using an authoring tool for the Internet, an HTML web page editor.

It is recognized, however, that this tool is not restricted to activities relating to Education through Projects, as it can also be used in conjunction with other teaching approaches, or without any specific context.

The involvement of the education specialists of the schools visited enabled us to discover another potential use of the tool, which is related to knowledge of the techniques of building websites. This can bring, as a positive consequence, a change of perspective on the part of the child, towards the information available on the Internet, so that he becomes no longer merely a consumer, but a producer of information.

Another positive factor is that it facilitates access to the works produced by students in the schools, enabling them to be seen by parents, colleagues in other schools, or even online communities for children, such as Kidlink [6].

Furthermore, the Internet enables the child a more direct contact with the world, which meets another present need: direct experience as a learning modality that is more propitious for developing creative problem-solving skills [7].

It is believed that KidWeb could become a highly useful tool for children, acting as motivating tool in the teaching/learning process in schools. The use of KidWeb in learning activities in schools is already being carried out and will be explored in future works.

REFERENCES

1. Vieira, Fábia Magali Santos. (23 June 2000) Pedagogia de Projetos [Online]. Available at: http://www.connect.com.Br/ntemg/pedagp.htm
2. Oliveira, R. Informática Educativa: dos Planos e Discursos à Sala de Aula. Campinas: SP, Papirus, 1997.
3. Freira, Paulo. Pedagogia do Oprimido. Editora Paz e Terra, Rio de Janeiro, 1987.
4. Marucci, R.A. Projeto de Interface e Multimídia para Crianças. Workshop de Informática na Escola, Congresso Nacional da Sociedade Brasileira de Computação (National Congress of the Brazilian Computing Society), annals p. 759-770, Rio de Janeiro, 1999.
5. Boff, Elisa. Giraffa, Lúcia M.M. Criação de Histórias em Quadrinhos de forma cooperativa na Web. Simpósio Catarinense de Computação, annals p. 639-649, Itajaí – 2000.
6. Lucena, Marisa. Comunidades Dinâmicas para aprendizado na Internet. Revista Brasileira de Informática na Educação No. 2. April 1998.
7. Sobral, Adail. Internet na escola – O que é, como se faz. São Paulo: Edições Loyola, 1999.

Chapter 19

INTERACTION ANALYSIS FOR FORMATIVE EVALUATION IN CSCL

Alejandra Martínez[1], Yannis Dimitriadis[2] and Pablo de la Fuente[1]
[1]*Dpt. of Computer Science, University of Valladolid, Valladolid, Spain*

[2]*Dpt. of Signal Theory, Telecomunications and Telematics Engineering, University of Valladolid, Valladolid, Spain*

Abstract: The development of methods and tools that support formative evaluation in Computer Supported Collaborative Learning (CSCL) is a strategic research subject for the improvement of this area, which is still in an incipient status. According to the current learning theories, the evaluation of collaborative learning has to be based on the study of interactions within their context, the integration of different perspectives, and the adoption of an interpretative research paradigm. The use of computers has been considered as an opportunity for evaluation, due to its storage and processing capabilities, but it also adds new questions to the traditional challenges of collaborative learning research. We present our vision on this problem, focusing on the issues related to the automatic support to the representation and analysis of collaboration. We have modelled them by means of the *extended cycle of collaboration management,* which has been proposed as an adaptation of a previous one that was oriented to systems that scaffold collaboration. We describe its main characteristics, and then we focus on the first phase of the cycle: The automatic collection of information about interaction, for whose support we have proposed a generic model of collaborative action, which is briefly introduced in the paper.

Key words: Formative evaluation support, interaction modelling, CSCL, XML.

M. Llamas-Nistal et al. (eds.), Computers and Education. Towards a Lifelong Learning Society, 227–238.

1. INTRODUCTION

The area of Computer Supported Collaborative Learning (CSCL) is a recent research paradigm in educational software, based on the application of computer networks to collaborative learning processes. From a theoretical perspective, CSCL is based on social theories on learning [1,2] that emphasise the role of social interaction in the construction of knowledge. The development of CSCL systems is very complex, due to its interdisciplinary nature, the diversity of actors implied in the process, and the variety of aspects that must be considered: learning improvement, school organization, software design, distributed systems, human-computer interaction, etc. After the initial years of the paradigm, when the main efforts were oriented towards the design of innovative CSCL systems, it is now necessary to focus on their evaluation, in order to detect appropriate lines of research and development that might contribute to enrich the field. Given the nature of the area, these evaluation processes are complex, and can be oriented to any of the aforementioned issues.

During the nineties, the evolution of theories on collaborative learning led the researchers to consider interactions as the main unit of analysis, which thus became the basis for the study of collaboration [3]. More recently, the situated learning approach has highlighted the intrinsic relationship between socio-cultural context, social interaction and human cognition, and proposes the use of an interpretative paradigm for the study of learning process in contrast with the traditional methods [4]. This vision is accepted nowadays by the scientific community, but it poses many challenges, both in the definition of theoretical models able to integrate all the desired analytical perspectives (social, interactive and individual), and in the proposal of methodological tools for the support of an interpretative approach for evaluation [5].

Our interest in these problems is due to our current work in the refinement of the DELFOS framework. DELFOS ("a Description of a tele-Educational Layered-Framework Oriented to Learning Situations") [6] was defined in order to support the design of CSCL applications. We are working in the refinement of the issues related to the *formative evaluation* of the applications, of the learning processes supported by the tools defined in the framework, and of the framework itself. This has led us to *identify the problems* that CSCL poses to the support of evaluation, and to propose a generic *model of the process of evaluation support*, on which we have based the revision of the existing proposals related to this problem in the literature [7]. As a result of this revision, we have proposed a mixed method of evaluation that integrates automatic analysis processes in an overall interpretative evaluation framework. The tools that support these automatic processes aim at increasing the efficiency of the normally demanding interpretative evaluation procedures, in order to enable the teachers to carry out the formative evaluation processes as part of their normal activity in the classroom. These analysis tools have also to be generic and flexible in order to facilitate their application in different CSCL situations. We have proposed a computational model for the representation of collaborative action that supports the aforementioned requirements of efficiency, generality and flexibility. The mixed method and the model for the representation of action have been thoroughly described respectively in [8] and [9]. In this paper we aim at providing an overview of the problem of the support to formative evaluation in CSCL, pointing out what we think are the main issues that must be taken into account.

The paper has the following structure: after this introduction, the section two presents the context and implications of the general problem of evaluation support in CSCL. Then, the section three focuses on the description of the model of the evaluation support process we have proposed: the extended cycle of collaboration management. The section four outlines our proposal of a computational representation of collaborative action based on XML. The paper finishes with the main conclusions drawn from our experience in this area, and the open lines of research.

2. FORMATIVE EVALUATION IN CSCL

In this section we will present our vision about evaluation as a formative process based on an interpretative research paradigm that leads to the use of qualitative methods for evaluation, and the problems posed when this vision is applied to the CSCL domain.

Evaluation is a very wide term that can pursue different goals and refer to a large number of aspects. In our work we focus on *formative evaluation processes*, which can be understood as those that help to gain insight into some aspect of reality with the aim of improving it. Evaluation conceived as such is performed continuously along the *learning process*, which becomes the main objective of evaluation. Formative evaluation can be considered as a form of research that aims at achieving practical goals, and therefore, is influenced by the research paradigm that is adopted. We distinguish between two main research paradigms: the positivist and the interpretative. The former considers knowledge as something objective, which can be "discovered" through studies that seek scientific rigor as the main quality criterion, which results in a decrease in the meaningfulness of the case. The latter considers that knowledge is built in interaction with the environment, and it is based on the study of real experiences in all its complexity, and with methodologies that place a high value on the participation of the members of the community [10]. As mentioned beforehand, CSCL is based on theories of learning that emphasise its situated nature so that evaluation cannot avoid the social and cultural context on which the learning processes take place [1]. The interpretative approach to evaluation is closer to this perspective than the positivist one, and thus, it is the vision we have adopted in our work. This option yields a number of consequences, namely: the preference for the study of *real scenarios* (learning taking place in curriculum based experiences) as opposed to experimental situations, the study of the *process* as a main part of the evaluation, an inductive style for the evaluation designs, and the adoption of *ethnographic methods* for the collection and analysis of the data. These methods include the observation of the activity throughout a long period of time, interviews to the participants, video and audio recording, etc. [11]. The use of these ethnographic methods in computer-based environments offers new opportunities for research, such as the possibility of setting up new learning situations, and the use of the computer as a new tool for the collection and analysis of data. However, computer support to ethnographic research poses new problems, too. We consider the following ones to be the most important:

- *Access to the sources of data.* The access to the field is a known problem in ethnographic research, and the evaluation designs defined under this perspective consider explicitly how to face them [11]. In the case of studies based on automatically collected data, it will be necessary to solve the technical problems related to data access, such as the need of getting the appropriate rights from the system administrator to access the system logs. The tools will have to include specific functions to collect interactions, which should be *independent* of the code of the CSCL applications in order to provide modular solutions, and *transparent* to the users so that they do not interfere in the learning processes.
- *Management of large quantities of data with low semantic value.* The computer provides the possibility of storing all the actions performed by the users with little or no effort. This can lead to a saturation of data with no meaningful value, impossible to process either automatically or manually. Thus, it is necessary to face the problem of the internal representation of the data so that it can support the analysis process.
- *New types of interaction.* The introduction of computer networks promotes new forms of interaction, and with them, new challenges for research in collaborative learning. Crook [12] distinguishes between interactions *in front* of the computer (small groups that work on the same computer); *through* the computer (communication or actions performed mediated by the network); and *around* the computer (interactions that take place at classrooms where work is supported by computers). Table I

presents the relationship among different aspects that must be taken into account in an evaluation process and the possible data sources that can be used in an ethnographic study, showing which of them are the most appropriate data sources for each one of the different aspects. Examining the table, it can be seen that the data collected by the system are the only source appropriate for the study of the interactions that occur through the computer, and thus, they play an important role in the evaluation of CSCL experiences. Additionally, data collected automatically can be used, in a complementary mode with other data sources, for the study of the interactions in front of the computer and the students' attitudes. The table also shows that the global evaluation process has to consider a number of sources of data and evaluation issues. Therefore, the integration of all these issues should be a main objective in the design of evaluation processes of quality.

Table 19-1. Levels of suitability of different sources of data for the study of a number of aspects that can be included in the evaluation of a CSCL environment. **Notation:** ✓: the method is very appropriate, ~: the method is not totally suited to the aspect; –: the source of data is not suitable for studying the corresponding evaluation aspect.

	System events	Audio, Video, Observations	Post-hoc comments	Interviews	Questionnaires
Int. in front of the computer	~	✓	-	-	-
Int. through the computer	✓	~	-	-	-
Int. around the computer	-	~	✓	~	~
Int. outside the classroom	-	-	-	✓	✓
Opinions	-	-	✓	✓	✓
Attitudes	~	~	✓	✓	~

- *Presentation of results.* A known problem in qualitative research is the large volume of data that have to be managed, which, as mentioned above, is usually increased with the use of computers. In order to perform evaluation and make it possible in real situations, it is necessary to reduce this volume and show the results to the evaluator in an intuitive manner. The use of graphical methods of visualisation can help to achieve these objectives, and the computer can be a convenient tool for the production of these graphical representations.
- *Ethical and privacy issues.* As in every research process, the participants of the experience have to be informed of the fact that they are being observed, of what is the scope of these observations and of what are the objectives of the study. They have to be given the possibility of auto-excluding themselves from the evaluation. In order to provide for these

issues, the systems that support evaluation should include specific functions, such as filtering the data of those persons that do not want to be observed or converting the data related to identity in order to increase privacy.

- *Study of the impact of the introduction of the technological system*. Last, but not least important, the introduction of computers for the support of collaborative learning implies the need of studying the impact of these media on the learning processes and on the overall culture of the classroom.

Therefore, the adoption of an interpretative paradigm leads to the use of ethnographic methods of research for carrying out the evaluation. We have seen that the computer yields new opportunities to support these methods but it also presents new requirements. In order to give an answer to these challenges, an integrated evaluation system is required, where data coming from the computer can be combined with others taken from traditional ethnographic sources of data. Our group has proposed a mixed evaluation method that faces these requirements [8]. Here, we will focus on the issues related to the automatic support to the analysis of collaboration. We have based the study of this problem on the definition of a generic model of the evaluation support process, which is presented in the next section.

3. THE EXTENDED CYCLE OF COLLABORATION MANAGEMENT

In this section, we describe the *extended cycle of collaboration management,* which we have proposed as a generic model for the systems that perform analysis of interactions in order to support collaboration. This extended cycle has its origin in our effort to adapt the *cycle of collaboration management* proposed in [13] to the scope of the systems that support evaluation. The original *cycle of collaboration management* focused on the systems that aim at providing on-line support for the collaborative learning processes. We will refer to them as *scaffolding systems*, as opposed to the *evaluation support systems,* that are the ones on which we are focusing in this paper. In spite of the fact that both processes (scaffolding and evaluation) share the need of performing analysis of interactions in order to build a model of the state of collaboration, the differences between their final objectives led us to propose an extension to the original model, in order to focus on the specific issues of evaluation.

What are the differences between scaffolding and evaluation? From our point of view, the main ones are the *moment* on which the intervention takes place, and the need of *ideal models* of collaboration. Regarding the moment of the intervention, scaffolding has stronger restrictions than evaluation, as it has to be done in "real time", during the learning activity, so that the corrections can be applied by the learners in order to improve the learning process. On the other hand, evaluation is usually performed when the activity being evaluated (or a part of it) has finished. Therefore, scaffolding will need to implement some sort of predictive modelling, while this is not the case with evaluation. Regarding the need of an ideal model of interaction, scaffolding, due to its objective of providing advice to the students, needs an ideal model on which to base these instruction decisions. This does not happen in evaluation, a more exploratory process that has as a major objective the understanding of the processes themselves.

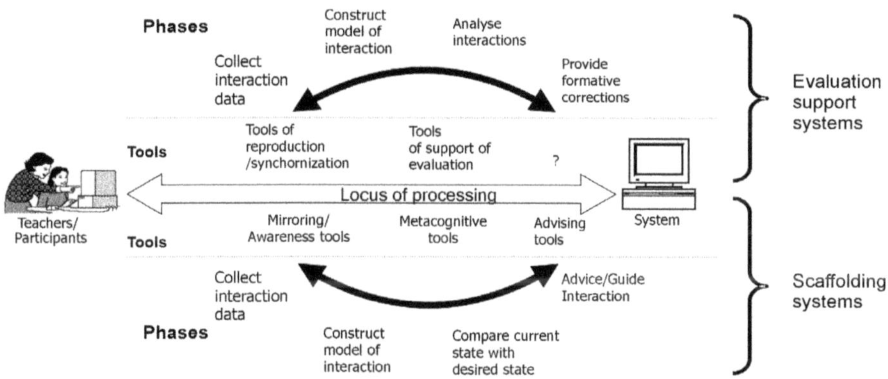

Figure 19-1. The extended cycle of collaboration management. The upper part shows the functions and tools oriented to support evaluation, while the scaffolding systems are shown in the bottom part, which is adapted from [13]. The figure shows the similarities and differences between the two types of systems, and the types of tools that support both processes according to the level of computational support of the processes.

Figure 1 shows the extended cycle of collaboration management, including the different phases that compose the two processes:

- *Collection of interaction data.* It is the first step in both processes, and it is basic for the posterior analysis. The kind of data that is collected, and more specifically, their semantic value, granularity and level of abstraction are fundamental for supporting a good quality analysis. It is necessary to note that, besides the data collected from the computer, both scaffolding and evaluation can be supported by other data collected from the environment. In this phase, the main problems refer to the access to the data and their representation in computational format.
- *Modelling the interaction state.* This phase consists of the steps performed in order to transform the collected raw data into a set of indicators that reflect a model of the interaction. These indicators provide

information about the state of the collaboration. The main difference between scaffolding and evaluation at this point is that in the former the models are built while the collaboration is taking place, and therefore they can need to predict a number of aspects about the collaborative processes, which is not the case in evaluation.

- *Analysis: Diagnosis vs. understanding*. In this third phase, the model of interaction is analysed with different purposes that depend on the particular cycle being considered. In scaffolding, the model is compared with an ideal model of interaction (implicit or explicit) in order to detect possible mismatches that will lead to some kind of advice to the learners. In evaluation, the main objective is to show the results of the analysis to allow the evaluator to understand the process in an efficient manner.
- *Feedback: Corrections vs. refinement*. In scaffolding, the result of the process takes the form of a set of advises or correcting actions which, according to the analysis, could bring the state of collaboration closer to the desired state. Evaluation has a wider scope, and can be oriented to suggest changes on many different issues such as the setting up of the situation, the scheduling of the activities, the attitudes of the participants, etc.

Besides the description of the phases, the cycle of collaboration management allows to classify the collaboration analysis tools, according to the level to which they provide automatic support. In the case of scaffolding, it is possible to distinguish between mirroring, metacognitive and advising tools [13]. Regarding the systems oriented to evaluation, we distinguish between *reproduction tools* and *evaluation support tools*. The former take the data collected from the computer and show them with no intermediate processing, as if it had been video-recorded. On the contrary, the *evaluation support tools* are able to extract indexes that can be shown to the evaluator, who will combine them with other sources of data and methods of analysis, in order to extract the formative corrections that will feed again the collaborative learning process. Finally, as it can be observed in the figure, there is a question mark at the last phase of the evaluation support cycle. This place would correspond to systems that were able to provide the teacher or the student with formative corrections about the studied processes. Therefore, this would be a sort of expert system oriented to evaluation, that given a set of inputs (not all of them necessarily provided by the computer), proposes a series of changes to the environment, based on some kind of knowledge about CSCL systems. We do not think that such a kind of system is possible, especially if we recall the issues that arise from the adoption of an interpretative paradigm, although it can be considered as an open line of research, which we have denoted by a question mark (?).

Based on the discussion presented in this section, it can be concluded that the systems that support evaluation present features that distinguish them from the systems that scaffold collaboration, and therefore it makes sense to consider them separately. However, in practice, this distinction is not so clear, and many aspects of the tools oriented to scaffolding will apply to evaluation support ones and vice versa. For example, the metacognitive tools and the evaluation support tools perform the same kind of activities. We refer to the two types of tools as *interaction analysis support tools*. As it has been discussed, the definition of an appropriate model for the representation of the data they collect about collaboration is basic for the support of all the phases that theses systems perform. The next section will briefly discuss our proposals related to this aspect.

4. AUTOMATIC DATA COLLECTION AND MODELING

The first phase of the process of collaboration management relies on an appropriate data representation, able to support the rest of the phases that take place in the extended cycle. To achieve this objective, the representation of the actions performed by the participants has to meet the following criteria: it has to be *generic* to be able to integrate the different sources, *flexible* so that it can be adapted to different analytical perspectives, and represented at an appropriate *level of abstraction*, so that it can be processed either manually or computationally. Finally, it has to be expressed explicitly in a standard language in order to promote *interoperability*.

Existing proposals for interaction modelling do not meet all these requirements. Either they are constrained to a single source of data, or they do not make explicit the representation format they use. Some systems rely on dialog analysis, usually based on some form of pre-codification performed by the participants, like EPSILON [14]. Others base the analysis on actions performed on structured shared workspaces, like the system proposed in [15], which presents interesting opportunities for research, but is restricted to these structured interfaces. Moreover, none of these proposals offers an interoperable solution based on an explicit and standard representation of the interactions.

As an answer to the absence of a model for the representation of collaborative action that met the desired requirements, we have proposed an XML-based representation of collaboration action. We have chosen XML [16] as it is a widely accepted standard that provides a common and understandable representation of the vocabulary, and can help to improve reusability, modularity and interoperability of the applications. The two main problems we have faced at defining the model are the need of modelling the *context* of the collaborative situations, and the need to provide a generic model able to represent the different types of interactions that take place in different collaborative situations.

Regarding *context*, although research in CSCL currently agrees on the need of considering *context* when interpreting human action, it is an open issue how this is to be done, and what elements should be considered when modelling it, especially from a computational perspective. Apart from very few exceptions, the model of context is usually performed ad-hoc, according to the particular needs of the situation being evaluated. As an alternative, we have proposed the use of the concepts of the DELFOS framework for the description of context in the model of collaborative learning.

The second aspect we have faced in our proposal is to provide a generic and operational *taxonomy for the representation of collaborative action*. As mentioned beforehand, existing approaches focus on the representation of a single feature of the interaction, which hinders the desired integration of different sources of data that are diverse in origin and in nature. We aim at integrating dialog and action, as well as automatic and manually collected data in a common structure, by means of a new classification that focuses on the agents that take part in interactions. This way, the proposal distinguishes between *direct*, *indirect* and *participation-oriented* interactions. They are further defined in their elements. The main advantage of this approach is that it easily accommodates to the data collected in each system for each type of interaction.

The validation of the model has been performed by its application to three different case studies [7]. These cases have shown that the model is valid for the representation of interactions coming from distinct data sources, like face-to-face interactions; answers to sociometric questionnaires; indirect actions performed through a document sharing workspace, as well as through a structured interface workspace consisting on a puzzle game for kindergarten children. Our experience in the use of the model shows that it has been expressive enough for situations of distinct characteristics, and that it is a powerful tool for supporting our mixed approach to evaluation, providing an important increase of efficiency in its procedures [8].

5. CONCLUSIONS AND FURTHER WORK

In order to contribute to the problem of evaluation support in CSCL, our group has proposed a mixed evaluation method and a model for the representation of action in CSCL. In this paper we have introduced some of the issues that have been considered in order to define these two proposals.

The adoption of a situated learning perspective for the study of CSCL leads to the need of assuming an interpretative paradigm for evaluation. This leads to a number of challenges, which have been identified and discussed in this paper. Focusing on the automatic support to evaluation, we have defined the extended cycle of collaboration support, which models all the systems that perform analysis of interactions in order to support collaboration, either in order to intervene in the processes (scaffolding) or in order to understand the processes in depth (evaluation). By defining the extended cycle, we provide conceptual framework that points out the specific issues related to evaluation as opposed to scaffolding, while we also highlight the similarities between the two processes.

We have proposed an XML-based representation of collaborative action, independent of the analytical approach, adaptable to different scenarios, and suitable for the representation of data coming from different sources, including field work as well as automatically collected data. One long-term objective of our group is to provide a component-based architecture where different modules can be plugged-in in order to fulfil the functions needed in CSCL situations, yielding the desired benefits of reusability. The model of collaborative action we have proposed and introduced in this paper can be used in order to design a set of generic, flexible and interoperable *storing components*. These components could provide interaction data suitable to be processed by different *analysis components*. We are currently working towards the integration of the model in a component-based system for CSCL [17], which will eventually lead to this modular and reusable solution. We encourage other members of the scientific community to use the model we propose in order to refine it and increase its generality.

ACKNOWLEDGEMENTS

The authors want to thank to all the members and collaborators of the Transdisciplinary group EMIC of the University of Valladolid for their contributions. The work presented in this chapter has been partially supported by the Spanish Ministry of Science and Technology (projects TIC2000-1054 and TIC-2002-04258-C03-02), the autonomous government of Castilla y León (project VA 117/01) and by Ediciones Don Bosco (Edebé).

REFERENCES

1. T. Koschmann, "Paradigms shift and instructional technology", in *CSCL: Theory and Practice of an Emerging Paradigm*, T. Koschmann, Ed., pp. 1-23. Lawrence Erlbaum Associates, N.J, 1996.
2. P. Dillenbourg, "Introduction; What do you mean by "Collaborative Learning"?", en *Collaborative Learning. Cognitive and Computational Approaches*, Pierre Dillenbourg, Ed., pp. 1-19. Elsevier Science Ltd., Oxford, 1999.
3. P. Dillenbourg, M. Baker, A. Blaye, and C. O'Malley, "The evolution of research on collaborative learning", in *Learning in Humans and Machines. Towards an Interdisciplinary Learning Science*, H. Spada and P. Reinmann, Eds. Elsevier Science, Oxford, first edition, 1995.
4. J.G. Greeno, "The situativity of knowing, learning and research", *American Psychologist*, vol. 53, pp. 5-17, 1998.
5. B.G. Wilson and K.M. Myers, Theoretical Foundations of Learning Environments, chapter, *Situated cognition in Theoretical and Practical Context*, pp. 57-88, Lawrence Erlbaum Associates, N.J., 2000.
6. C.A. Osuna and Y.A. Dimitriadis, "A framework for the development of educational collaborative applications based on social constructivism", in *Proceedings of CYTED RITOS International Workshop on Groupware, CRIWG '99*, Cancún, Quintana Roo, pp. 71-80, IEEE Computer Society Press, 1999.
7. A. Martínez. "A model and a method for the computational support of evaluation in CSCL" (in Spanish), unpublished PhD Dissertation, University of Valladolid, Valladolid, 2003.
8. A. Martínez, Y. Dimitriadis, B. Rubia, E. Gómez, P. de la Fuente, "Combining qualitative and social network analysis for the study of social aspects of collaborative learning", accepted in *Computers and Education*, special issue on Documenting Collaborative Interactions, 2003.
9. A. Martínez, Y. Dimitriadis and P. de la Fuente, "Towards a standard XML-representation of collaborative action", in *Procs. of CSCL 2003,* Bergen, 2003.
10. G. Rodríguez Gómez, J. Gil Flores, and E. García Jiménez, *Qualitative research methodology,* (in Spanish), Ediciones Aljibe, Málaga, 1999.
11. J.P. Goetz and M.D. LeCompte, *Ethnography and qualitative design in educational research*, Academic Press, Orlando, FL, 1984.
12. C. Crook, *Computers and the collaborative experience of learning*, Routeledge, London, 1994.
13. P. Jermann, A. Soller, and M. Muehlenbrock, "From mirroring to guiding: a review of the state of the art technology or supporting collaborative learning," in *Proceedings of EuroCSCL 2001.,* pp. 324-331, Maastricht MacLuhan Institute, Maastricht, 2001
14. A. Soller. "Modelling the process of collaborative learning", in *Proceedings of the International Workshop on New Technologies in Collaborative Learning,* Awaji-Yumebutai, 2001.
15. M. Mühlenbrock, *Action-Based Collaboration Analysis for Group Learning*, IOS Press, Amsterdam, 2001.
16. *Extensible Markup Language (XML)*, 2000, http://www.w3. org/XML/.
17. Y. Dimitriadis, J.A. Asensio, J. Toquero, L. Estébanez, T.A. Martínez and A. Martínez, "Towards a software component based system for the domain of Computer Supported Collaborative Learning (CSCL)" (in Spanish), in *Proceedings of Symposium on Informatics and Telecommunications,* SIT 2002, Sevilla, 2002.

Chapter 20

THE USE OF INFORMATION AND COMMUNICATION TECHNOLOGIES BY PORTUGUESE TEACHERS

The ICT

Jacinta Paiva, João C. Paiva[1] and Carlos Fiolhais

Centre for Computational Physics, University of Coimbra, and [1]Department of Chemistry, Faculty of Sciences, University of Porto

Abstract: We present a study made in Portugal, in 2001/2002, on the use of Information and Communication Technologies (ICT) by teachers of all teaching levels (except high education), in both public and private schools. It was an initiative of the Ministry of Education ("Nonio – 21st Century" program), which was carried out by the Competence Centre "Softsciences" and the Centre for Computational Physics of the University of Coimbra. Some of the conclusions of this study, that has collected data from 19337 teachers, are the following: the majority of Portuguese teachers own a PC and approximately half of them use it in several activities, though their use of computers with students is limited. Primary school teachers use often the PC in their schools, though, probably, in an incipient way. The self-training of teachers in ICT is quite common. The Internet is more used by 3rd cycle (last part of middle school) and high school teachers, being most of its users male and young. These and other conclusions should be taken into account in a strategy towards incrementing a better use of new technologies in schools. The whole study is available in: http://nautilus.fid.uc.pt/cec/estudo

Keywords: Use of computers in education.

1. INTRODUCTION

In the last few years, many steps have been undertaken in equipping Portuguese schools with hardware and software and in teacher training for the use of these equipments. However, there is still a long way to go till the

M. Llamas-Nistal et al. (eds.), Computers and Education. Towards a Lifelong Learning Society, 239–250.

Information and Communication Technologies (ICT) become integrated in a transversal way in the curriculum, coming up in schools in a planned and systematic way and not spontaneously and sporadically [1].

We have assumed that the use of this kind of technologies in education represents an advantage for teachers. The challenges of educational change are clear but not easy to overcome [2]. To follow national and European policies [3] it is necessary to know quantitatively the teachers' practices on their use of computers for the benefit of themselves and their students. This is the main aim of a study promoted by the Ministry of Education ("Nonio – 21st Century" program) and carried out by the Competence Centre "Softsciences" and the Centre for Computational Physics of the University of Coimbra. We made an inquiry, in the academic year 2001/2002, to 26707 Portuguese teachers, from 2499 schools of all levels (except high education), public as well as private. The answers were collected between December 2001 and April 2002. The statistical data arose from the analysis of 19337 questionnaires, *i.e.,* 72.4% of the total inquired. In 2000/2001, a pre-study, done in a small sample, allowed to improve the methodology [4].

We present here a brief description of the study, as well as a summary of its objectives, results, analysis and conclusions. We made a selection of tables and graphics, which may be more interesting to the educational community.

It is never too much to stress the importance of measuring and evaluating in order to select tools and methods that may lead to educational progress [5]. This study, which is a sequence of other surveys done by the Portuguese Ministry of Education [6, 7], namely studies on equipment in schools, portrays the situation in April 2002. We hope it may originate further progress on the ground.

2. IMPORTANCE AND ADVANTAGES OF ICT

Nowadays a school which does not have computers risks to become obsolete. As Adell [8] says: "The information and communication technologies are not any longer a didactic tool for teachers and students … they are in the world where the youth we teach are growing."

Considering ICT it is possible to talk about two contexts:

- The personal context, *i.e.*, the way teachers and students use computers individually (not linked by a pedagogical relationship);

- The educational context, including not only the class environment, where subjects are being taught, but also pedagogical relationships out of class.

In the personal context, the advantages of computers include time saving in routine tasks (tests, worksheets, homework, etc.), facility in researching specific topics, possibilities of distance training/learning, exchange of practices and experiences, etc. In the educational context we should refer to the differentiated interaction that a teacher can establish with his/her students using specific software, on-line search done by students and e-mail communication [9] to receive/send homework, etc.

Table 1 indicates some ICT uses in education, some of the activities that students can make with them and possible contexts.

In spite of the enthusiasm that usually accompanies the pedagogical use of ICT, we should say that they are not the elixir for all the troubles schools suffer!

Table 20-1. Applications, activities and contexts of ICT use in teaching/learning

Applications	Activities	Contexts
Word Processor (*Word*, *Publisher*, etc.)	Text and editing	Homework
Graphic/Drawing programmes	Graphic/Artistic activities	Project work
Spread sheet (*Excel*, *SPSS*, etc.)	Organizing information	Reinforcement classes
Multimedia/ CD-ROM	Information search	Support to disabled students
E-mail	Communication and interchange	Clubs/ associations
Internet (Web)	Information search	Homework
Pedagogical *Software*	Simulations /Games	Pedagogical support
Data acquisition Software	Scientific data research and treatment	Laboratory classes

3. STUDY

A. DESCRIPTION

The base of this study is a questionnaire aimed to know the real uses of ICT in personal and educational contexts by Portuguese teachers in 2001/2002. An exhaustive observation of a sample [10] was performed, being the results generalized to the whole population.

B. AIMS

We tried to obtain as much data as possible. However, if there are too many aims it is difficult to display and discuss the results. Furthermore, the aims must be precise in order to avoid ambiguities.

We have then defined the following goals:

→To know qualitatively and quantitatively what is the computing equipment that teachers own.

→To know about teachers training in the use of ICT.

→To relate the previous objectives with gender, age, professional situation, initial training, and teaching levels.

→Quantify and qualify teachers who use ICT in their practice.

→Quantify and qualify ICT use in educational context.

→Infer the reasons for not using ICT in educational context.

→Recognise the ICT aspects in which teachers feel to need more training.

→Look for the possibilities of incrementing ICT use in educational context.

→Generalise the results to the whole universe.

→Define or redefine other aims for further studies.

C. UNIVERSE

The universe to which we have generalised conclusions is the totality of Portuguese teachers in 2001/2002.

4. SOME RESULTS

Some Features of Portuguese Teachers

Our teachers sample reflects the national reality, shown in Table 2.

Table 20-2. Number of schools, teachers and students in Portugal, for all teaching levels except high education (data from the Ministry of Education, for 2000/2001)

Type of school	Nº of schools	%	Nº of teachers	%	Nº of students	%
JI	5683	34.52	11920	7.02	192532	11.20
EB1	8343	50.68	31963	18.83	417790	24.30
EB1,2	7	0.04	259	0.15	2037	0.12
EB1/JI	32	0.19	440	0.26	6436	0.37
EB2	30	0.18	1310	0.77	9920	0.58
EB2,3	596	3.62	45108	26.57	383929	22.33
EB2,3/ES	82	0.50	6396	3.77	51486	2.99
EB3	4	0.02	160	0.09	1426	0.08
EBI	48	0.29	2506	1.48	20683	1.20
EBI/JI	20	0.12	1125	0.66	8950	0.52
EBM	365	2.22	800	0.47	5927	0.34
EP	203	1.23	6486	3.82	29435	1.71
ES	66	0.40	8171	4.81	70353	4.09
ES/EB3	324	1.97	38434	22.64	334904	19.48
ESA	3	0.02	412	0.24	2157	0.13
Others	357	3.99	14267	8.40	181362	10.55
Total	**16463**	**100**	**169757**	**100**	**1719327**	**100**

Note: In the first column we use the following notation: A – Artistic; E – School; B – Basic; JI – Kindergarden; S – Secondary (high school); I – Integrated; M – Mediatized; P – Professional; numbers 1, 2 e 3 refer to first, second and third cycles of basic school (EB) respectively.

The majority of the sample is made up by women (76%).

The most represented range of age is 36-45 (34%) while the least represented is that made up by people more than 56 years old (Fig.1).

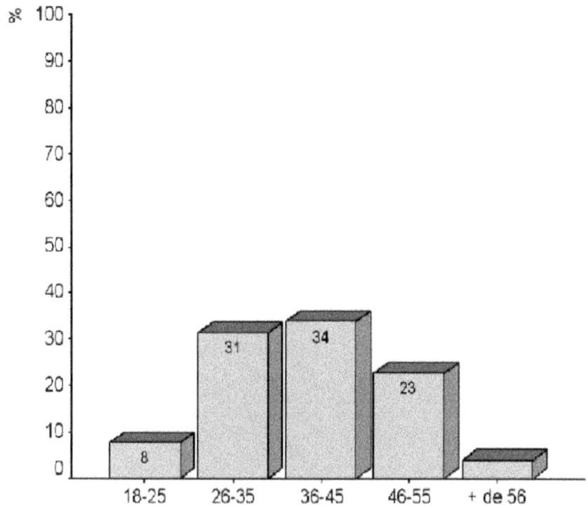

Figure 20-1. Distribution of teachers of sample by age

The majority (about 90%) of teachers had initial teacher training. More than half of the teachers of our sample had done their initial teacher training at a university.

Results for some questions

The majority of teachers (88%) own a PC and simple peripherals (Fig. 2).

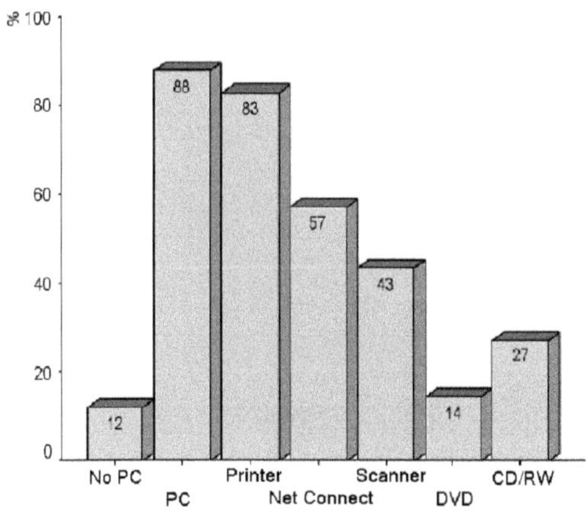

Figure 20-2. Personal computing equipment of the teachers.

About half of the teachers had self-learning in ICT (Fig. 3).

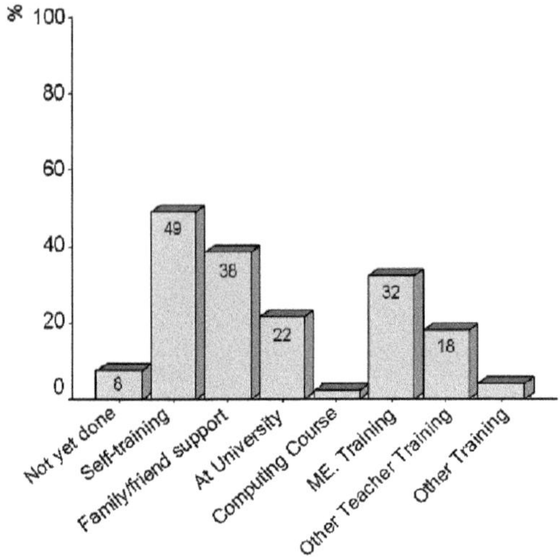

Figure 20-3. Distribution according to teachers training in ICT.

Almost half of the teachers use quite often the PC but 31% only uses the *Word* application. About 65% of teachers use the Internet. Only 29% use the Internet at school but half of the teachers use it at home.

Less than half of the teachers use e-mail, mainly just to communicate with friends. It is insignificant the use of e-mail from teachers to students (Fig. 4).

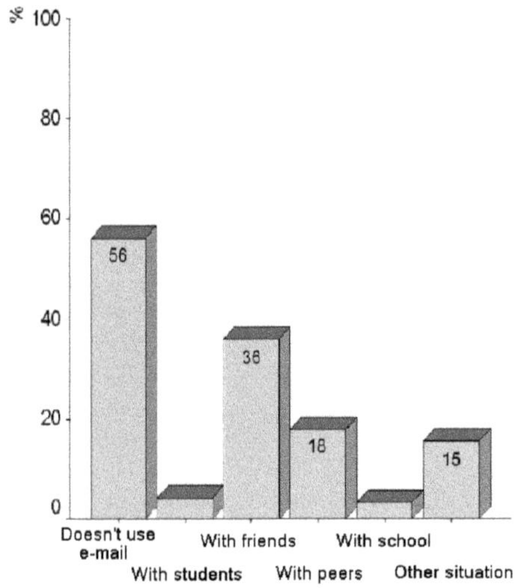

Figure 20-4. How teachers of our sample communicate by e-mail.

Only a quarter of all teachers use the PC with students, in or outside classroom.

From the 26% of teachers who use the PC with students, 42% belong to the 1st cycle (primary) and 24% to the 3rd cycle of basic and secondary (Fig. 5).

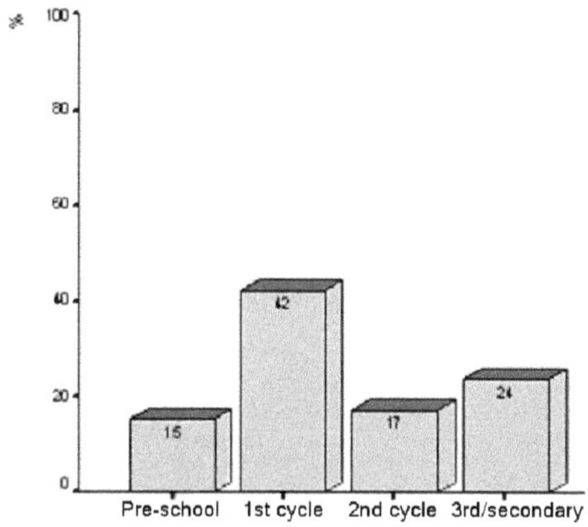

Figure 20-5. Distribution of teachers who use computers in educational context by levels of teaching.

The ICT application most used by students, when teachers use a PC in class, is the word processor. Pedagogical software, for example, is used less frequently.

The larger obstacles to the use of ICT, from the point of view of teachers, are the lack of resources, mainly technical but also human resources. (Fig. 6)

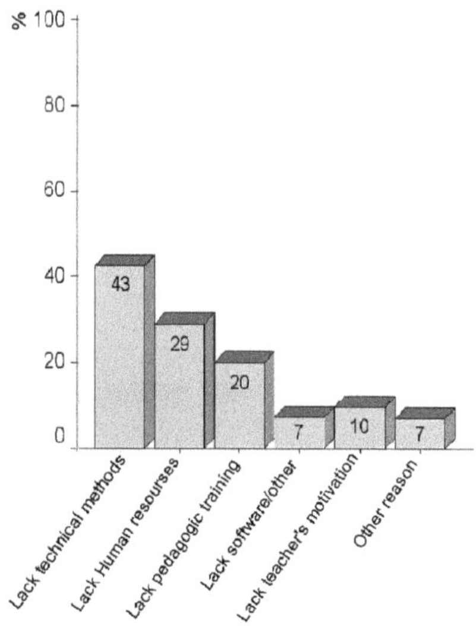

Figure 20-6. Distribution of teachers by obstacles to the use of ICT.

5. ANALYSIS AND CROSSING OF SOME VARIABLES

We present in the following some relations between variables, explaining the main ideas that come out.

Simple relation between parameters:

Teachers of the 3rd cycle and secondary use more their PCs to accomplish several private tasks (Fig. 7).

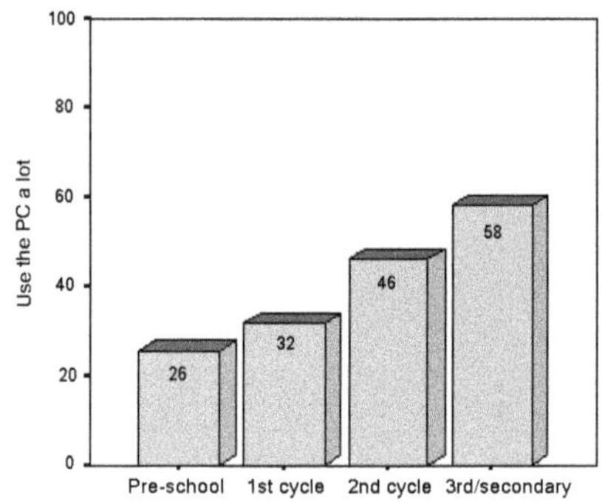

Figure 20-7. Distribution of the way teachers use computers for private purposes by teaching levels.

The majority of teachers who use the PC for performing several tasks had initial training at a university (41.7%).

The Internet is more used by teachers, for private and pedagogical purposes, as the teaching level goes up (Fig. 8).

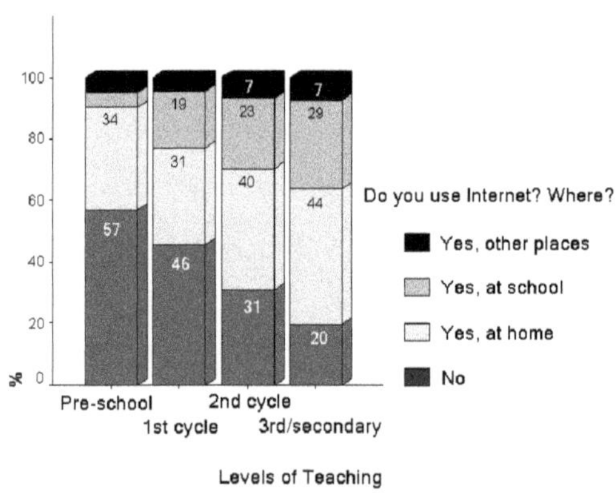

Figure 20-8. Distribution of the way teachers use the Internet by teaching levels.

The word processor is the application students most use, mainly in the 1st and 2nd cycle of basic teaching (Fig. 9), when teachers use computers with their students.

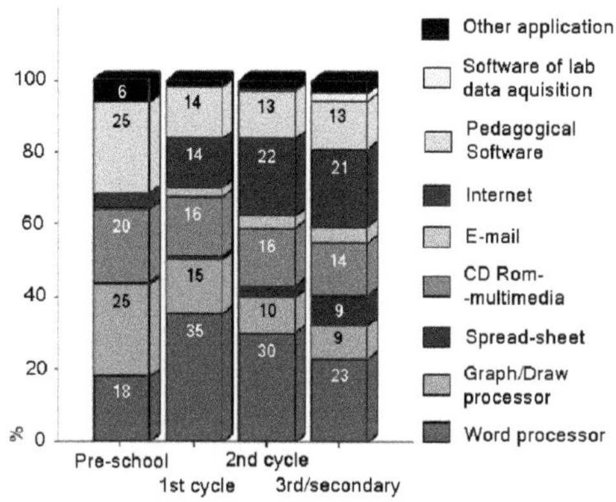

Figure 20-9. Distribution of ICT applications used by students according to the school levels.

6. SOME TRENDS SHOWN BY MULTIVARIED FACTORIAL ANALYSIS

We now present a multivariate factorial analysis of some questions, obtained through the use of the *SPSS* programme. This type of analysis produces qualitative graphics that allow recognising relations between variables. Such relations are particularly interesting in this kind of studies. These graphics should be interpreted looking for the proximity of marks describing the different variables in study.

Fig. 10 shows an example of multivariate factorial analysis. It displays the correlations between the answers to the questions: “Do you use the computer in classroom activities?”, “How many hours a week do you work in computer?” and “Do you use quite often the computer?”, when associated to the teaching levels. The low number of working hours at a computer is intimately related to its non-use to perform several tasks. We can also read that the teachers of 3rd cycle and secondary are those who are nearer a longer use of the computer for private purposes.

● "Do you use the PC in classroom?"

■ "How many hours a week do you work in computer?"

▲ "Do you use quite often the computer?"

◆ "What levels do you teach?"

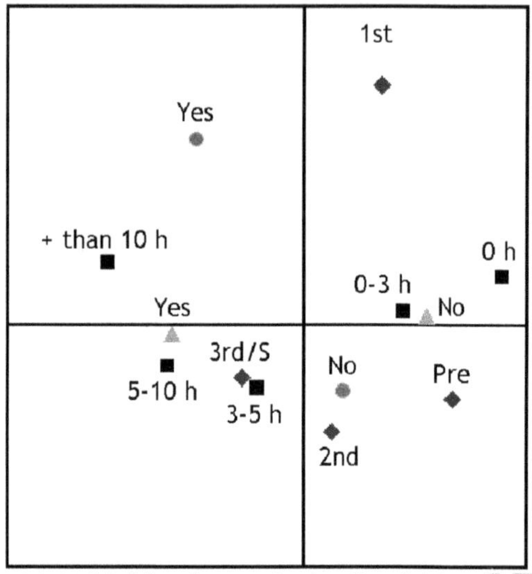

Figure 20-10. Multivariate analysis of variables: ● ■ ▲ ◆

CONCLUSIONS

We summarize here the main conclusions of our study:

- Teachers are mainly women (they are almost exclusive in pre-school teaching), followed by the 1st cycle (primary school). More than half (65%) of the teachers are between 26 and 45 years old. Most teachers from the 1st cycle are between 36 and 45 years old and the range 18-35 years old is more represented in 3rd cycle and secondary schools.

- Initial training for more than half of the teachers took place at a university and more than 89% of the teachers had a teacher training period.

- The computing equipments of teachers are many and varied. 88% of the teachers own a PC against 39% of Portuguese who owned that equipment in 2001. 57% of the teachers are connected to the Internet against 30% of Portuguese in 2001 [11].

- Although for most teachers (91%) the computer is a personal tool, its general use depends on the gender, age, initial training and teaching levels. Thus, male younger teachers had their computer training at the university and use more often the PC for a general purpose in 3rd cycle and secondary schools.

- Portuguese teachers quite often use the Internet and particularly e-mail (65% and 44% respectively), this use being more associated to younger male teachers. Surfing the Internet is mainly done by teachers at home. The e-mail, in particular, is mostly used by teachers of 3rd cycle and secondary. We would like to highlight that electronic communication between teachers and students is quite rare.

- 81% of teachers use the computer to prepare classes (except in the pre-school teaching). 94% of these do it for worksheets and/or tests and 54% use the Internet to make searches on the subject they teach.
- Self-learning and the attendance of courses promoted by the Ministry of Education are the two main ways teachers had their computer training.
- 26% of the teachers use the computer at their school in direct interaction with students in and out of the classroom. 26% of these users are teachers of the 1st cycle (42%), followed by teachers of 3rd cycle and secondary (24%).
- The major ICT applications used in direct interaction with students are the word processor, Internet search and also specific software to perform ludic/pedagogical activities.
- Almost all teachers, without distinction of age and levels taught, need and wish to have training in ICT applications.
- Teachers have, in general, more positive than negative attitudes towards ICT. However, many female teachers show negative attitudes. The two main obstacles for integrating ICT in schools are the lack of technical means and human resources.

The whole study which formed the basis for this article is available at http://www.dapp.min-edu.pt/nonio/pdf/utilizacao_tic_profs.pdf (in Portuguese), where several links to other works on ICT in Portugal and in Europe can be found. Other data including detailed graphical analysis are available at http://nautilus.fis.uc.pt/cec/estudo.

ACKNOWLEDGEMENTS

We acknowledge the support of the program "Nonio 21st Century" of the Ministry of Education. We were also supported by the Competence Centre "Softsciences" and the Center for Computational Physics of the University of Coimbra. We also would like to thank all Portuguese teachers who have collaborated in our study.

REFERENCES

1. S. Awbrey – Successfully integrating new technologies into the higher education curriculum. *Education Technology Review.* 7 (1996) 17.

2. N. Davis – Teacher Education and Information Technology: challenges for teacher education. *Journal of Information Technology for Teacher Education.* 8: 1 (1999) 3.
3. *Sociedade da Informação – Livro Verde para a Sociedade da Informação em Portugal.* Missão para a Sociedade da Informação, Lisboa, Graforim, 1997. http://www.missao-si.mct.pt
4. Jacinta Paiva - *As Tecnologias de Informação e Comunicação no Ensino: o caso particular da Antropologia,* Master thesis, Departamento de Antropologia da Universidade de Coimbra, Coimbra, 2001. http://nautilus.fis.uc.pt/wwwantr/tm/
5. H. Perraton – Choosing Technologies for Education. *Journal of Educational Media.* 25: 1 (2000) 31.
6. *Nónio – Alguns números sobre as tecnologias de informação e comunicação na educação* – Programa Nónio - Século XXI, 2001. http://www.dapp.min-edu.pt/nonio/nonio.htm
7. J. Ponte and L. Serrazina – *As novas tecnologias na formação inicial de professores.* Lisboa. Ministério da Educação, DAPP, 1998.
8. J. Adell – Tendencias en educación en la sociedad de lás tecnologias de la información. *EDUTEC, Revista Electrónica de Tecnologia Educativa.* 7 (1997). http://www.uib.es/depart/gte/revelec7.html
9. T. Hoel and S. Gudmundsdottir – The REFLECT Project in Norway: interactive pedagogy using email. *Journal of Information Technology for Teacher Education.* 8 (1) (1999) 89-110.
10. Instituto Nacional de Estatística – *Manual de Procedimentos da Produção Estatística,* 1997.
11. J. Mata – *Sociedade de Informação: Principais indicadores estatísticos* – Observatório da Ciência e da Tecnologia, Ministério da Ciência e da Tecnologia, 2002

Chapter 21

INTERACTIVE ENVIRONMENT FOR TEACHING DESCRIPTIVE GEOMETRY

Francisco Morgado [1,2] (morgadof@iol.pt), Pedro Almeida [1]

[1] *Escola Superior de Tecnologia de Viseu. Instituto Superior Politécnico de Viseu 3504- 510 VISEU PORTUGAL;* [2] *IT – Networks and Multimedia Group Dept. Informatics Univ. Beira Interior 6200 – 001 COVILHÃ PORTUGAL*

Abstract: A computer assisted environment in Descriptive Geometry is specified and developed. The program includes an interactive tool which permits the user the direct manipulation of the objects present in Descriptive Geometry. The environment developed has an object oriented architecture (OO), entirely developed in C++ and in a graphic library OpenGL. This way, the support to direct manipulation and to a non ambiguous representation is obtained. The environment was conceived as a set of sections that perform each of the requested functionalities. Each module can easily be put in a parametric form, allowing its application in teaching other similar areas of subject. In this work, the use of the computer shows how it becomes possible that all the cycle of teaching/learning Descriptive Geometry can be more effective; the student can obtain knowledge as fast as he wants and can become aware of some situations that in a ordinary classroom e would not be able to see. This way, we tried to contribute to something as "Knowledge is no inertly received, but actively built!"

Key words: Descriptive Geometry, teaching/learning, computer assisted teaching, Object Orientation, Represent, Visualize

M. Llamas-Nistal et al. (eds.), Computers and Education. Towards a Lifelong Learning Society, 251–262.

1. INTRODUCTION

The construction of educational environments for teaching and learning has motivated most different strategies, having, many of them, the computer's support. It is a tool of multiple applications. Considering a school as a laboratory where interactions are created and developed between those who are a part of the education process and society in general, the general opinion is the characteristics of the environments allow the integration of the learning process, between teachers and students approaching them to school.

The use of Computer Assisted tools in teaching Descriptive Geometry is defended as a mean to enhance and make more productive the cycle of teaching/learning [1].

The development of object oriented applications is also defended, because in future, its modification and extensibility are easier to perform, making them universal [2][3].

2. HISTORY AND APLICATION OF GEOMETRY

The student "...must develop the organization of thinking process by searching strategies to solve problems, and with the acquired knowledge should solve new situations..." [4].

2.1 Descriptive Geometry

Descriptive Geometry belongs to the area of Mathematics, has a thinking mechanism that begins in a small number of concepts, and trough deduction arrives to the final solution of the problem.

2.2 The source

Since the first Architecture works, it became necessary to materialize the initial idea trough drawings as a way to approach the effective construction. If that work became a master peace, that need was even more real. Thus, the first drawings were discovered by the artists of that time [5] and are truly excellent in the skill and intelligence used in their conception.

Performing a careful study of such drawings, Monge (séc. XVIII) concluded that all of them were based in a certain number of principles which became the basis Descriptive Geometry. He also saw [5] that all the problems placed in those drawings (the structure of the construction) were geometrical, and were solved with projections.

2.3 The Definition

Descriptive geometry is the science that studies all the metric proprieties of geometric figures using projections systematically.

Descriptive Geometry is therefore one of the branches of Mathematics. Thus is a creation of the human spirit where each thought comes as a consequence of the previous, being easy to concretize by means of a graphic or the materialization in space. All this led Monge to the statement: "Who knows how to represent the point, the straight line and the plane, knows all the Descriptive Geometry". The conclusion is that with a small sum of knowledge and with a logic and methodical study, one can arrive to the solution of all the problems is Descriptive Geometry.

2.4 The Purpose

Descriptive Geometry is a science which was born as a need which studies the way to proceed when cutting a stone (afterwards, to the wood cut, and recently to iron), to form vaults, stairs, lintels or other constructive "devices". These are not more than the old "drawings" after being properly geometrized. In order to have a proper knowledge of these "devices", the knowledge of Descriptive Geometry must be acquired first. One of the purposes is its application in Design and plastic Arts.

2.5 Actual Use

After some time, the initial concept of Descriptive Geometry lost most of its significance because faster and cheaper processes of construction were developed. But there are more applications of Descriptive Geometry. It is used in the field of Mathematics as a student's course and mind development, either in theoretical speculation, or in its practical application to the fields of Engineering, Architecture and Design.

To make judgment of the actual utility of Descriptive Geometry, one must remember that in a single plane we can represent all the machines, bridges, mines, buildings of all kind, and so on. All the aspects needed to comprehend and execute these structures are included in that plane. Descriptive Geometry is also an important auxiliary in the practical concept of models created by the designer.

2.6 Teaching Descriptive Geometry in our Schools

Descriptive Geometry is a course where the abstraction capability and the creation of new situations by the student have great acceptation; this fact is an important factor of the student's success in this area. The initial process of teaching Descriptive Geometry based in some simple definitions, which are the basis of all the knowledge.

The difficulty of the student is to know and become comfortable with these definitions. After passing this initial stage, new concepts are no longer difficult to them.

A graphic is presented (from the author's experience and of some teachers of Descriptive Geometry) and shows the level of difficulty of the student when studying Descriptive Geometry.

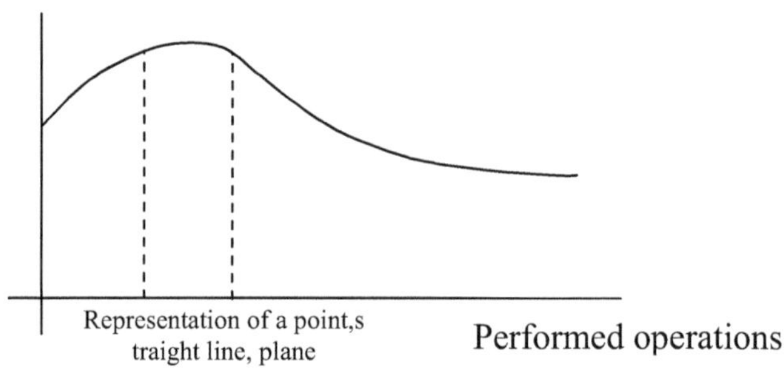

Figure 1: Relation between subject/difficulty of the student

The most important phase in the acquisition of knowledge in Descriptive Geometry is the initial one. For all this, one can resume what's been said in the following way: **Descriptive Geometry** = **Simple concepts** + **Operations** [6]

Operations = Σ(Simple operations in a correct sequence)

2.7 Conclusions

For all that's been said, becomes very important to support the student at an initial stage, so that the comprehension of the next subject is based in the previous.

This way, the construction of an environment that puts the teacher and the student "talking" to each other becomes very important. This conversation can enrich the student, and the teacher is an entity that aids the student in his investigations; this way, knowledge is acquired in a constructive and deductive way.

3. PROBLEM DEFINITION

The problem we propose to solve is to allow Descriptive Geometry to be taught using the computer and get the best performance form students.

The program is intended to perform a theoretical exposition of Descriptive Geometry and to solve the exercises needed to consolidate the theoretical exposition. However, problem specification must be all-purpose, so it can be easy to use more then once the basic structure of the developed application to other problems in Descriptive Geometry.

The program allows the teacher's definition of a problem, and also student's solution. The problem is then corrected by the teacher. It also must give the student the opportunity to check his own evaluation, in order to learn by correcting his errors.

The application to develop must contain the following components:

- Present concepts to retain;
- Write a problem in Descriptive Geometry by the teacher or the student;
- Allow students to solve the problem;
- Step by step correction by the teacher.

4. DEVELOPMENT

The development of the work as a general scheme was followed, which allows us the presentation of a modular architecture, flexible, and easily expansible. Functional modules of the system are identified and their functionalities are described.

General Scheme

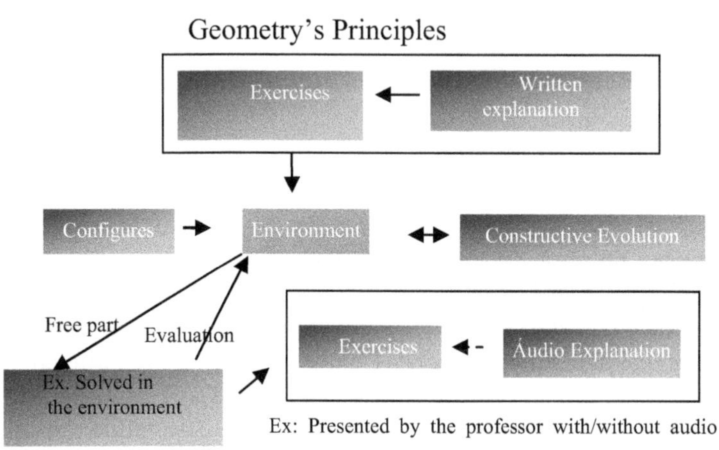

4.1 Configuration Module

This module is responsible for the configuration of the environment, allowing the user to change the configuration given by default. Some functionalities of this module may not be very relevant when thinking of the purpose of the program, however the possibility of changing the visual image of the environment is present, in a way to captivate the user to its use. As an example of these functionalities, we have Change light colour, Background colour.

Other configurations are more important in the environment, such as: projection lines thickness, points, ray, time interval used in animations.

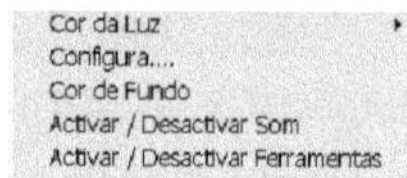

4.2 Exercises presented by the professor Module

In this module, the teacher is given the opportunity to solve exercises, in order to help the student with Descriptive Geometry. The teacher can also add an audio explanation of the process to obtain the solution. This way the student solves the exercise and at the same time, he listens to the process used to obtain the solution.

4.3 Module of exercise's evaluation

This Module allows the teacher to follow the student when he is trying to solve a problem. After solving a problem, the student can save it in a file to be delivered to the teacher. When correcting an exercise, the teacher can simply see the solution obtained by the student, or he can check all the steps used to arrive to the solution.

4.4 Descriptive Geometry's Basic Principles

With the purpose of offering the user a context similar to a classroom, the functionality **Basic principles** as programmed. This functionality allows the user to study the fundamental concepts in Descriptive Geometry, by presenting examples of the theoretical exposition.

In Basic Principles [

] theoretical concepts of each subject are presented: Point Representation, Straight Line, Plane, Intersections, Change of planes, Rebatimentos, etc..., These examples can be Simple (only with one step) or complex (with a sequence of steps) and can be controlled by the user, allowing him to go forward or backwards, depending on his capability of understanding [Figure 21-3]. They also have a written explanation of how the procedures were applied, and also the concepts used to each procedure.

This way, the student can learn taking the time he needs, making the learning process constructive, because the student controls what and how fast he learns.

The purpose of this module is to give the student some basic knowledge in order to solve other exercises. Therefore this module allows the student to see how the solution is obtained in an interactive procedure. That is not easily done in a book.

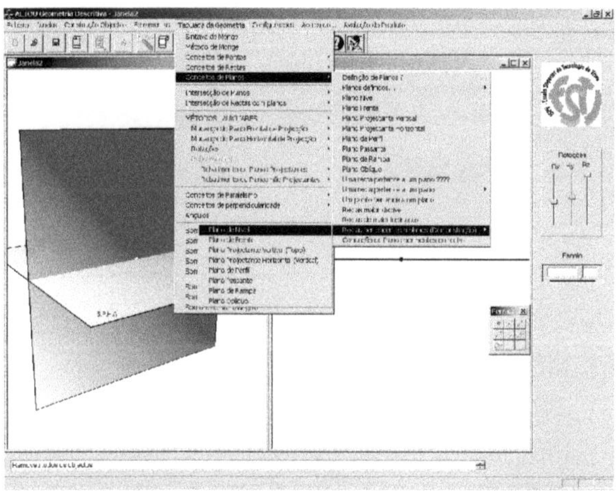

Figure 21-2: Descriptive Geometry's basic principles

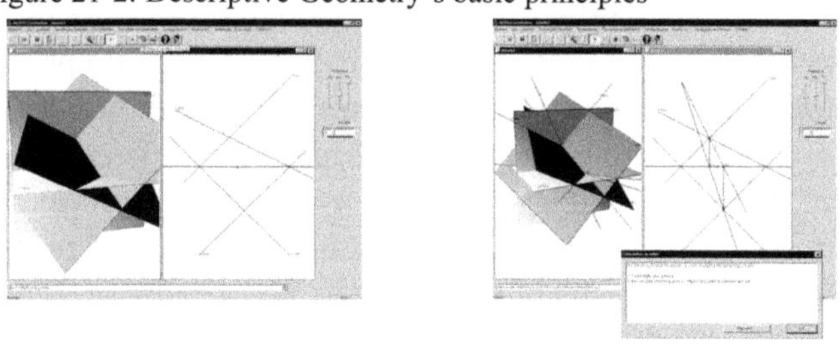

Figure 21-3: Forward/Backwards (Exercise: Intersection between two planes)

4.5 Free Part

After the study of Basic Principles, the user can create an infinite number of new situations, once there is a free part which allows the construction of points, Line segments, straight lines, planes, pyramids and cylinders.

The construction of objects can be carried out trough the introduction of data using the mouse or the keyboard.

After constructing those objects, several functionalities are offered which allow the construction of new objects, such as: we can choose a point and a straight line, and ask the system to build a new straight line parallel to the previous and containing the selected point.

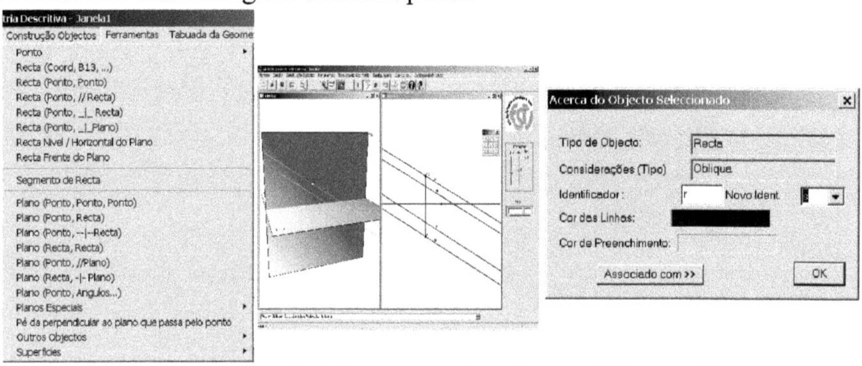

Figure 21-4: Basic principles, constructing objects, edit/change objects

We can edit/change the objects. This way we have access to their data. There is also available the information that lets us know if the object belongs to any of the objects with superior dimension present in the drawing; for example, if the edited object is a point, it tells if that object is in a straight line or a plane present in the drawing. If the object is a straight line the system verifies if it belongs to a plane present in the drawing. The construction of objects is carried out in 2D. The 3D representation is used by the user in order to be able to visualize the exercise he is constructing.

In 3D representation, the user is able to: *Rotate (along the 3 axes (XX, YY, ZZ))Zoom (In/out); Call the animation process(transition between 3D and 2D; Place/Remove the projections/traces; Place/Remove invisibility; Activate object's transparency; Paint; Etc.*

With some frequency, students tend to repeat identifiers. This makes the comprehension of the exercise more complex. The system allows an alert to the user to that fault.

We think the most important is to conceive a system which allows the

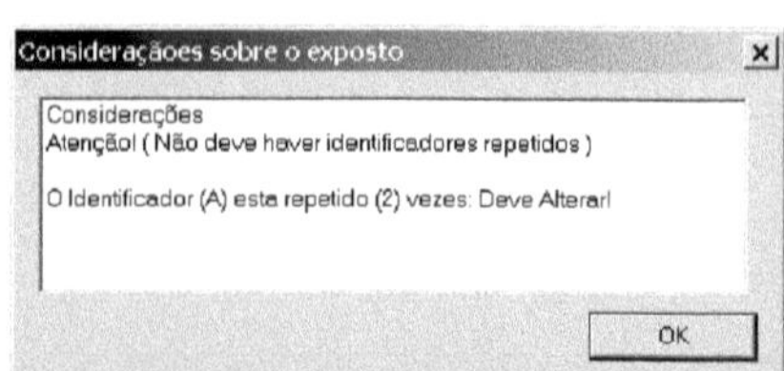

student to make mistakes, but indicates the error, rather than a system that admits no faults. This may leave the question: "... but why can't I place the same identifier!?...".

5. CONTRIBUTION OF FUTURE USERS

Our intention is to provide the user the possibility of contribution to the improvement (trough time) in future versions. Therefore it is possible to send comments/suggestions to the authors of the program. It is only necessary to fill the following dialog box, which is a part of the program.

We believe it is important that future users may contribute to the improvement of the product. They are the purpose of the program. In order to make future versions more sensitive to the user, the identification whether he is a student or a teacher becomes relevant. The interest for Descriptive Geometry is also an important factor.

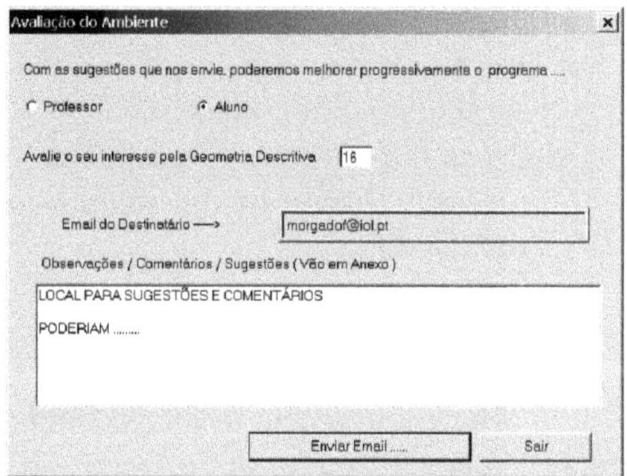

6. DEVELOPMENT PLATFORM

AEIOU - Geometria Descritiva was developed using Visual C++ 6.0 and OpenGL (Graphic Library); an object oriented programming was used, and its advantages are:

- **Productivity** — Build *software* is easier and cheaper;
- **Reliance** - *Software* is more reliable (reusing and new rules);
- **Maintenance** — Easier to improve and to find "bugs";
- **Extensibility** — Easier to accommodate new requirements ;
- **Modularity** — Abstraction and covering information;
- **Naturalist** — Object oriented programming by abstracting from the real world.

7. CONCLUSIONS:

The environment allows:

- Support the teacher in classroom;
- The creation of new problems and in them, a new set of situations, allowing the teacher to focus in specific subject trough examples built in the environment.
- Support students in classroom;
- Support the student in his study (at home) and encourage the discovery of new situations.
- Exercises, accompanied by an audio and written explication;
- The students to solve problems and to deliver them to the teacher;
- The teacher to visualization of the exercise's solution, or accompany the solution of the student;
- Check the student's time spent in solving a problem;
- An easy change of the solution obtained, without changing what's already done;
- Study followed with theoretical exposition, as well as the "teach yourself" process;

The environment developed and constantly updated has an award in the 4.th National Contest of Software – 2001 in the area of Education. At the moment is being promoted trough **APROGED** (Portuguese Association of Professors of Drawing and Descriptive Geometry), and the Secondary schools in Portugal. The environment must be considered as a help to the teaching/Learning process and not as a replacement of the teacher. Thus it is intended to be a complement to the teacher/student dialog and a tool that allows students to build their ratiocination and to prove them, trough the practice of exercises.

By programming in an object oriented language (C++), it encourages the possible extension of the system.

Future Work

- Possibility of saving all the steps given by the student when solving an exercise;
- Increase the number of exercises;
- Prove, using examples, the application of geometry to real life;
- Program a scratch module of drawing, where students can perform experiences, without using 3D representation;
- Improve the interface.

ACKNOWLEDGEMENTS

We thank APROGED (*http://www.aproged.pt*) for the strong motivation given to the project, and to Escola Superior de Tecnologia of Viseu for the support and motivation.

APPENDIX

Some images of the environment are presented.

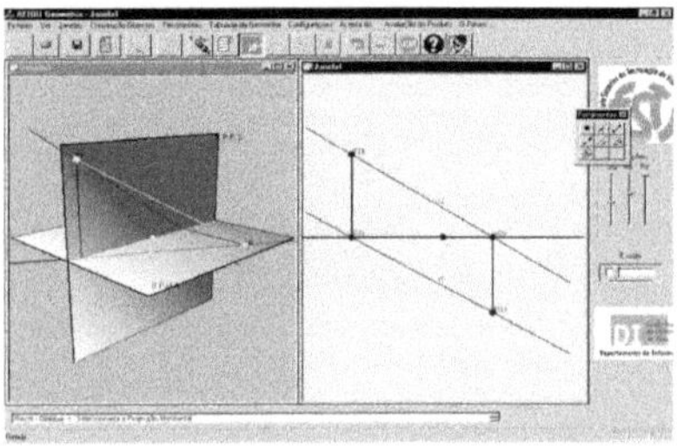

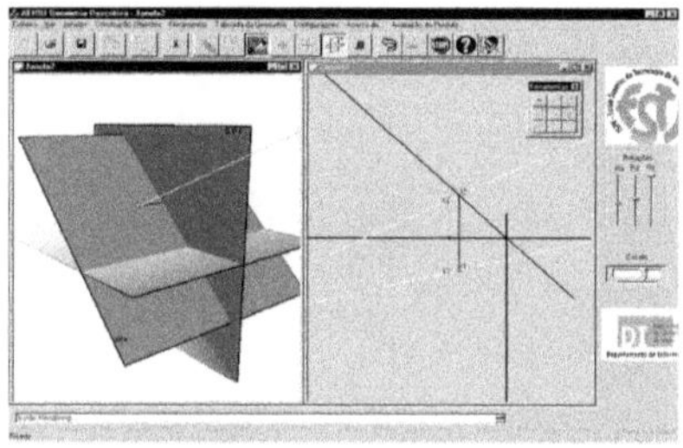

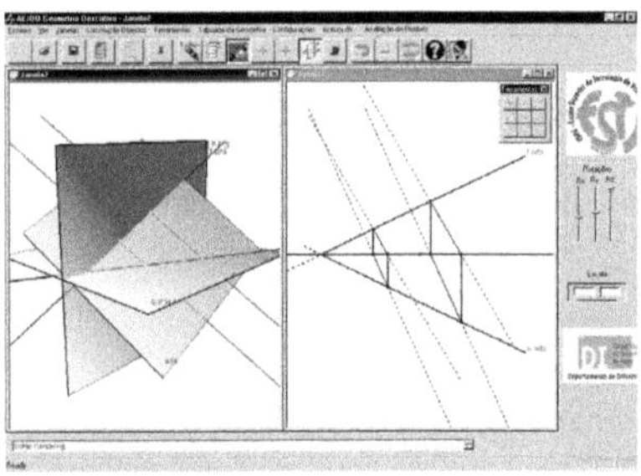

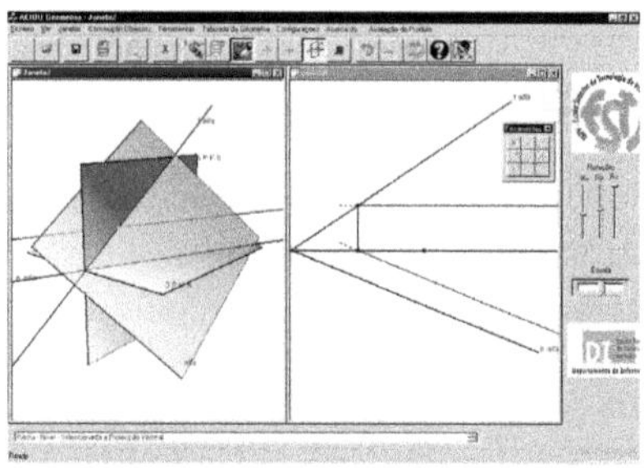

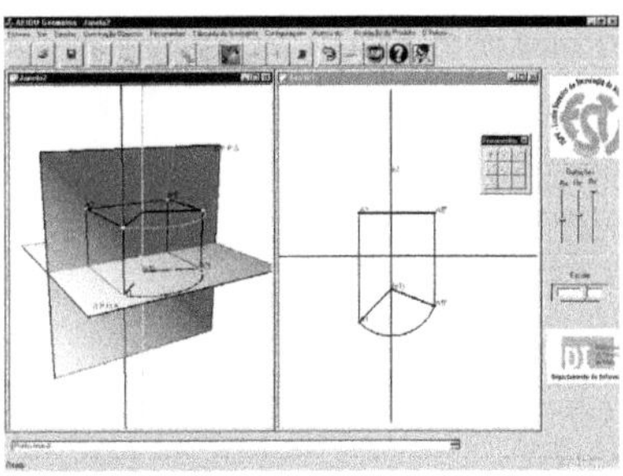

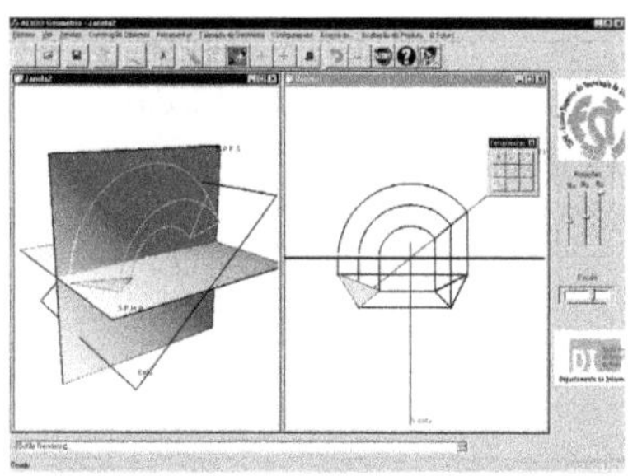

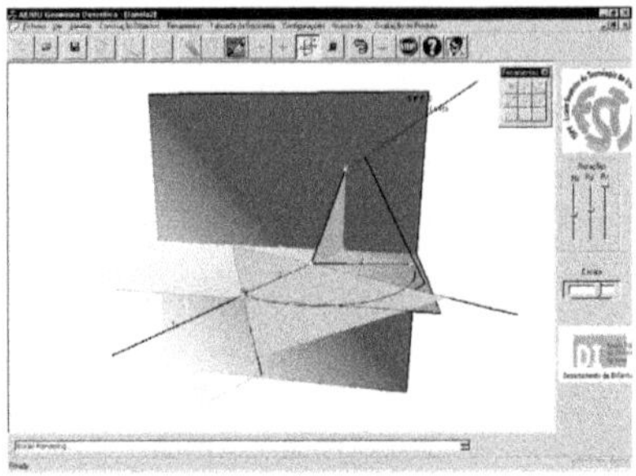

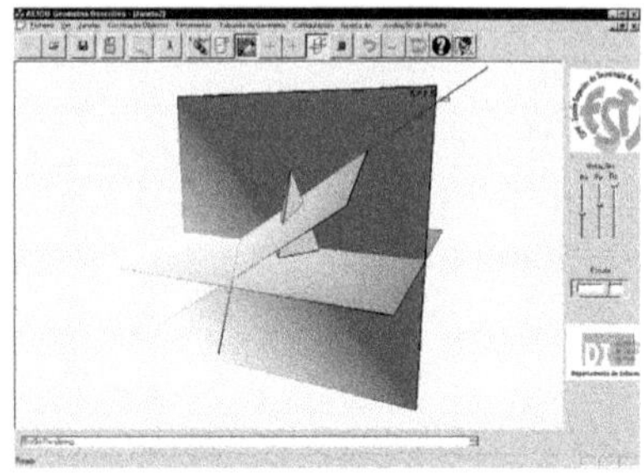

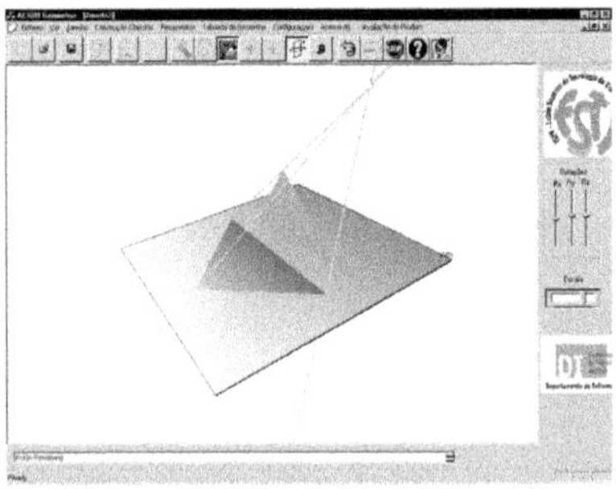

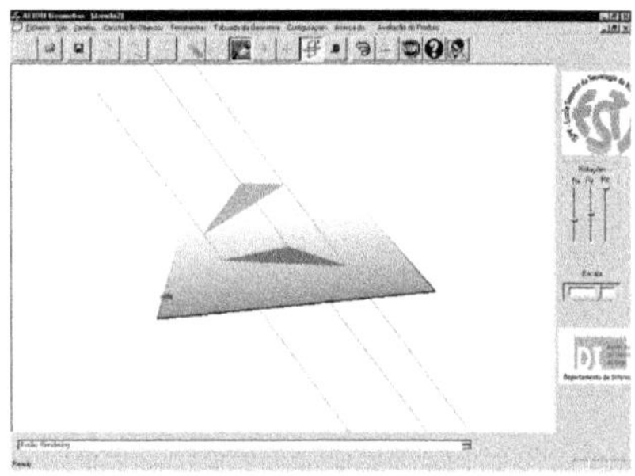

REFERENCES

1. F. Morgado, "Ambiente Interactivo para o Ensino da Geometria Descritiva", Dissertação de Mestrado, IST, Junho 1996.
2. Meyer, Bertrand, "Reusable Software: The Base Object-Oriented Component Libraries", The Object-Oriented Series, Prentice-Hall, 1994.
3. W. Alan, "Fundamentals os Three-Dimensional Computer Graphics", Addison-Wesley, 1989.
4. Associação de Professores de Matemática, Pinheiro, Alexandra, Canavarro, Ana Paula, Leal, Leonor Cunha, Abrantes, Paulo, "Dez anos de encontro", Évora, 1995.
5. Johnson, L. O. and I. Wladaver, "Elements of Geometry Descritive", Prentice-Hall, Englewood Cliffs,N.J.
6. http://www.estv.ipv.pt/PaginasPessoais/fmorgado/aeiou/default.htm

Chapter 22

E-CLUB: A UBIQUITOUS EDUCATION MODEL

Maximiliano Paredes[1], Pedro Pablo Sánchez-Villalón[2], Manuel Ortega[2] y J. Ángel Velázquez[1]
[1] Escuela Superior de Ciencias Experimentales y Tecnología,
Universidad Rey Juan Carlos
28933 Móstoles, Madrid
{m.paredes, a.velazquez}@escet.urjc.es
[2] Escuela Superior de Informática, Paseo de la Universidad s/n,
Universidad de Castilla La Mancha
13071 Ciudad Real
Manuel.Ortega@uclm.es

Abstract: With new wireless technologies, mobile devices with small displays (handhelds, PDAs, mobile phones...) are present in many environments such as offices, meeting rooms, classrooms, etc. We are interested in the effective use of such ubiquitous computing devices and traditional PCs for collaborative learning. In this chapter we present a platform (called e-CLUB) which integrates such technologies. We also show its application to a case study, the teaching of foreign languages by means of compositions. We identify the main problems of this approach to language education, describe the architecture and main applications of a prototype (called AULA) for language education, and show how it is used to overcome such problems.

Key words: Ubiquitous computing, CSCL, PDA, pervasive computing.

1. INTRODUCTION

The most recent works in ubiquitous and nomadic computing are focused on the integration of different devices (both in size and form), especially when the users are highly mobile [1]. These works assume that the PC disappears and is substituted by devices like Personal Digital Assistants (PDAs). We think that a heterogeneous computing environment, combining

M. Llamas-Nistal et al. (eds.), Computers and Education. Towards a Lifelong Learning Society, 263–274.

PCs and PDAs, would be a more effective and realistic approach. In effect, it could take advantage of the features of every kind of computer (the PDAs mobility and the PCs computing power).

In a ubiquitous computing environment, the user can interact with multiple devices by means of different user interfaces. Some works have given different solutions to multimachine user interfaces (called MMUI) [1-3]. In our proposal, the user interacts with one single interface on the mobile device in a collaborative learning environment. In this area, ubiquitous computing has a number of advantages [4,5]. The existent ubiquitous applications or systems [6-11] satisfy some of our domain needs, but not others (especially the discussion process).

In this work we describe a platform that improves the classical classroom environment thanks to the ubiquitous computing paradigm: e-CLUB (electronic UBiquitous CLassroom). In particular, we have implemented AULA (A Ubiquitous Learning Appliance), a prototype environment for language learning, in particular English like a Foreign Language (EFL). In this chapter we present the tools for the teacher and students. In section 2 we describe the traditional scenario of teaching by means of compositions, and identify its main problems. In section 3 we present the e-CLUB platform, its infrastructure and the AULA prototype. In fourth section we study one composition experience writing a text. To end up, we summarize the conclusions drawn and the work in progress.

2. LANGUAGE TEACHING THROUGH COMPOSITION

In this section we describe the stages of composition writing in foreign language learning, and we identify difficulties. We also show how AULA may contribute to provide solutions. In a traditional class, the teacher and the students make use of a whiteboard, notebooks, dictionaries and books as learning/teaching aids. When the class starts, the teacher gives instructions to the students (the subject to write about and the style to use, the final document title, the schedule for its accomplishment, the document type…). Afterwards, the teacher assigns tasks to the students, indicating the role of each student for the composition project. This is not an easy task for the teacher because he/she often does not have much information about the students.

At this moment, the students start to work collaboratively on the document elaboration. Every student writes individual notes about the suggested subject in his/her notebook. Once these ideas have been matured individually, the student shares them with the rest of the group. Therefore, the student has to write them again in the whiteboard. Later, a brainstorming process begins. Students discuss about the validity of their respective ideas, thus some are accepted and others are rejected. This procedure of setting individual ideas in common is a boring and tedious method because of the need of rewriting again.

In the following phase, the students complete the ideas they agreed upon by adding some language components. Now, the student needs to access to dictionaries or other information sources. These elements are typically sparse in the classroom; therefore the student has to stand up to the shelf, to fetch it, etc. As a consequence, the student stops paying attention to the composition. Once the students have finished the written composition, the teacher again plays an active role by evaluating the delivered works. This task is hard for the teacher because it is difficult to evaluate the individual effort within a group.

AULA facilitates the accomplishment of some of these tasks. Firstly, it supports work of the student out of the classroom (e.g. at home). When the student is out of the classroom, his work is persistently stored in the PDA's database. When the student enters to the classroom, automatically the system sends his work to the teacher's computer and to the student's device. Secondly, AULA assists the student in the procedure of setting individual ideas in common: the student writes down his/her ideas on the PDA and automatically the system sends them to his/her classmates' PDAs and projects them on the whiteboard. Thirdly, the system facilitates the process of discussing proposals through synchronous and asynchronous collaborative tools. Fourthly, AULA provides all the tools necessary for composition (e.g. a dictionary) in the student's PDA. In this way the student is fostered to maintain his concentration. Finally, AULA helps the teacher by recording the traces of the actions developed by the students. Thus, the teacher can consult these traces and assess the actions of students.

3. E-CLUB: A UBIQUITOUS COMPUTING ENVIRONMENT FOR DOCUMENTS COMPOSITION IN GROUP

3.1 Infrastructure

The ubiquitous classroom is composed of the following devices (see Figure 1): a Projection/Edition WhiteBoard, a server that manages the system database, a Location Manager that provides context-aware, the Session Coordinator that coordinates the classroom's devices, and the mobile devices (PDAs). Communications are supported by several communications networks: radio frequency wireless network (it connects PDAs and the Session Coordinator), infrared network (it connects PDAs and other devices such as printers) and a LAN network. The architecture of the

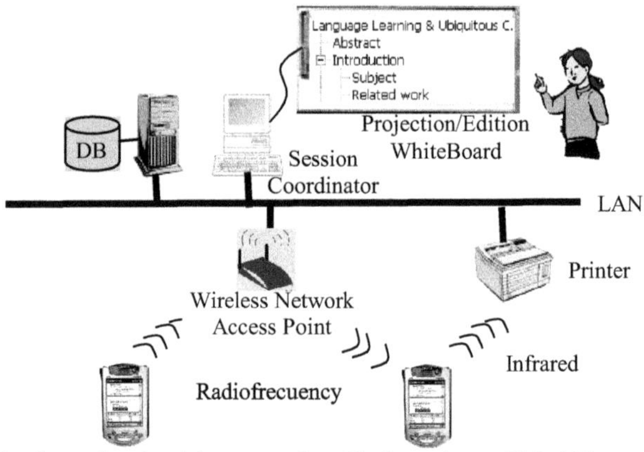

classroom is described with more detail elsewhere [12,13].

Figure 22-1. AULA infrastructure consisting of various networks and devices.

3.2 The Document Composition System

The *Composition Coordinator* is a subsystem of the Session Coordinator. This subsystem manages the students' work for the composition writing process (see Figure 2). We can identify three types of student actions during this composition process:

- Document actions: they modify the contents of the document, that is, the students' composition. For example, the student sends a proposal to the group. The result is visualized in the Collaborative Visualisation space.
- Attributes actions: they change some attributes of the composition. For example, the user votes a proposal. The result is visualized in the Collaborative Visualisation area.
- Personal actions: they modify the personal workspace. For example, the user creates a new aspect. The result is visualized in the Individual Edition space.

The Composition Coordinator subsystem interprets the actions invoked by the user and, depending on the action, performs different tasks. The tasks supported by this subsystem are:

- Packaging and unpacking messages. The messages between the *Composition Coordinator* and the PDAs are encoded to reduce the size of messages. The module Encoder manages packing and unpacking.
- Interpreting received messages. The Analyser interprets each message and deduces the type of action that must be executed. Afterwards, the analyser invokes an action to the appropriate module.
- Executing actions. Depending on the type of action, the system has to perform different tasks. The module *Document Attributes* modifies the attributes of the shared object and updates the users' PDAs. The *Collaborative Workspace Manager* updates the document and its new version is sent to all of the PDAs. The module Personal Workspace updates the user's individual work in the database.
- Recording traces. The actions invoked by the students are persistently recorded in the system's database. The data recorded are the following: user identification, actions and its attributes, context-aware information (date and time, inside or outside the classroom, etc.). The Trace Handler accomplishes this task.

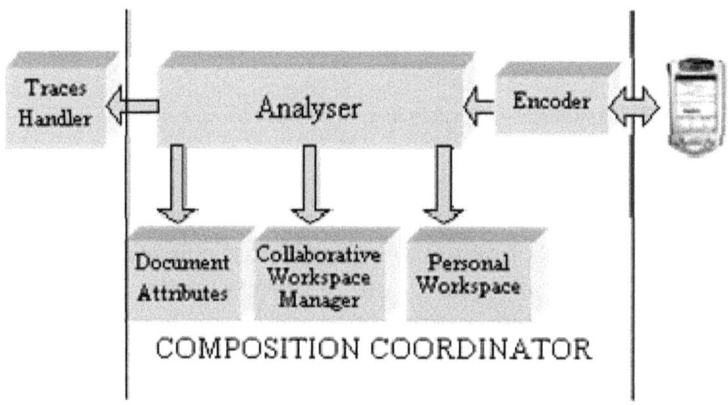

Figure 22-2. The subsystem Composition Coordinator.

We have implemented the system applications by means of Java and Visual C++ Embedded [13]. The architecture of e-CLUB can be supported in a classroom and has been used in other sites like smart homes [14,15].

3.3 AULA

The students access AULA tools through their PDAs. There are two tool types: collaborative tools (synchronous and asynchronous) and language tools. The collaborative tools are: a chat channel, a news board and the email facility. These tools are aimed at the communication process among the students and the teacher. The student uses this tool to make on-line requests of information to the teacher or to other colleagues, although the main utility of this tool is to support the discussion and debate process about the proposals at the brainstorming phase.

The system provides to student with three language tools: dictionaries (monolingual as well as bilingual), an electronic grammar book and a case database.

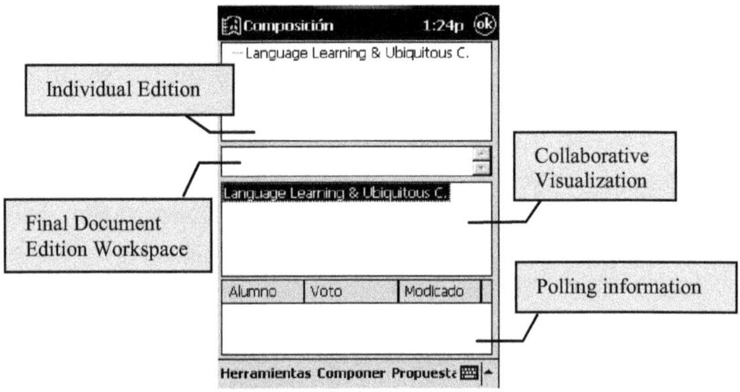

Figure 22-3. The application interface in a mobile device on beginning a composition.

The system structures all the resulting information from the composition process into so-called aspects, which are composed of ideas. Aspects and ideas are the blocks of partial information that constitute the framework that the students have to elaborate. Several aspects form a so-called topic. Figure 3 shows the application user interface of a mobile device when the composition process of a document is going to start. Notice that there are three well-defined working areas: the Individual Edition workspace (where the students write their individual contributions), the Collaborative Visualization workspace (where all the contributions of the group are displayed) and the Final Document Edition workspace (where the accepted proposals, which will be part of the document, are shown).

4. A COMPOSITION EXPERIENCE

At this section we introduce a typical session with the e-CLUB platform using the AULA prototype. In this session a small group of students must write a document in English about a given topic. The topic generates the title of the document. The accepted aspects will be the sections of the document and the ideas will be the paragraphs of these sections. We study in detail the students' work.

When the session begins, the teacher states the type of document that the students have to write. As an example, assume that it is a technical document: a paper on ubiquitous computing and education. Besides, the teacher gives the scheduled time and the title of the document. These matters are verbally explained by the teacher using the Projection/Edition WhiteBoard. Afterwards, the teacher proposes the following text as the topic of composition: "Language Learning and Ubiquitous C.". The topic proposed by the teacher is visualized in the display of the students' PDAs at the Individual Edition area and the Collaborative Visualisation area (see Fig. 3). At this moment, the students play an active role for the session: they propose his/her ideas and the brainstorming process begins.

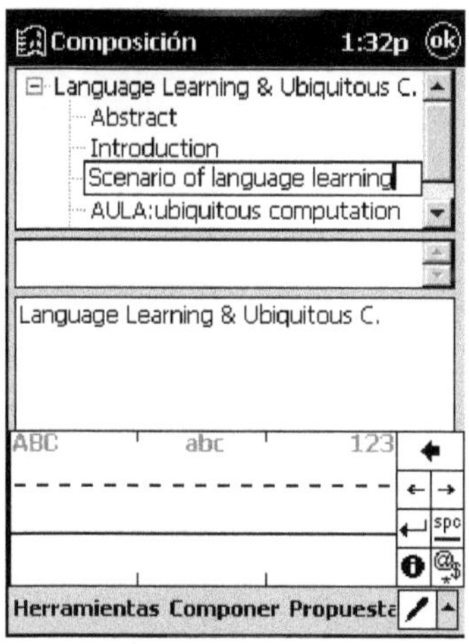

Figure 22-4. Inserting an aspect in Individual Edition workspace.

The student works by writing small sentences (items of information) in his/her mobile device (the student thinks that these sentences are important and they must be a part of the document). The student writes these items in the Individual Edition area, being each written item one aspect (see Fig. 4). The student later refines these aspects by writing several ideas for each aspect (see Fig. 5). In our example, a student thinks that the aspect Introduction must be composed of three blocks of information: an introduction to the subject, related works by other authors and a description of the paper structure. Therefore, the student creates in his/her PDA three ideas for the aspect Introduction: *subject, related work* and *paper presentation* (see Fig. 6).

When the student has written his/her aspects and ideas in his/her PDA's personal workspace, he/she delivers his/her work to the rest of the group. At this moment, those proposed aspects and ideas are visualized at the Collaborative Visualization area of all of their mobile devices (as well as any other proposed items).

This starts a discussion process among the students about the validity of the aspects and ideas proposed. In this way, the student argues and explains his/her ideas to the other students. The students can argue and explain their ideas verbally, using the Edition whiteboard. Besides, system provides some tools to support this process: polling of proposed works (see Figure7), chat, e-mail and news.

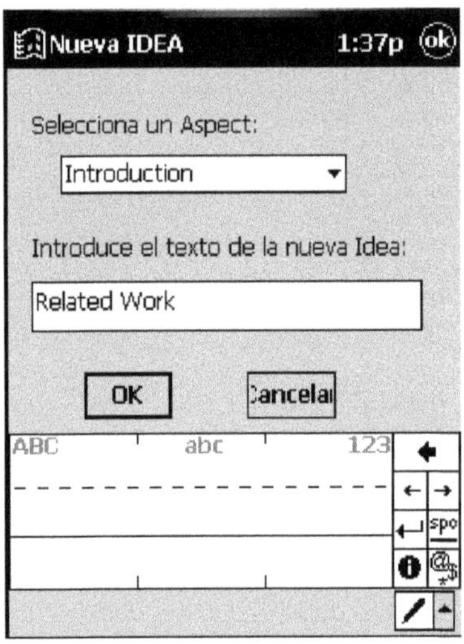

Figure 22-5. Introducing a new idea.

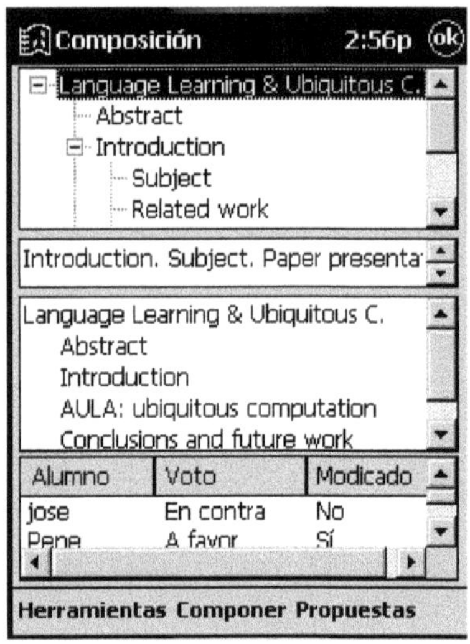

Figure 22-6. Proposals for the final document

As a consequence of this discussion process, some aspects and ideas are rejected. The student can modify his/her rejected aspects and ideas. Afterwards, these modified proposals may be sent to the group again. The accepted proposes are visualized in the Final Document Edition Workspace. The items in this space are basis for the sentences that will form the final document. The process of discussion finishes when the group of students achieve an agreement, accepting some suggested aspects and ideas and refusing others, through a polling process provided by the system. At this point, the students focus on adding small sentences to deliver the final document.

Notice that the information structure supported by the system (topic, aspect and idea) produces different parts of the document written by the students. In our example, the topic has generated a paper title ("Language Learning & Ubiquitous C."), the aspect *Introduction* has generated the section "Introduction" of the paper and the ideas of this aspect have generated the paragraphs of such a section (see Fig. 8).

When the document has been finished by the students, the teacher begins the evaluation process. In a typical class of English, the teacher evaluates in a postproduction process, where he/she assesses the activity by marking two issues: the resulting document delivered by the group of students and the performance of every student, based on the teacher's memory and ability to infer it. In general, this evaluation has two phases: firstly, the teacher dialogues with the students and secondly he/she examines their composition. This way of evaluating is very hard to the teacher due to the emotional implication it involves. Obviously, the teacher can make questions about the students' work (who suggested this particular idea?, did this student take an active role during discussion?, to what extent?...).

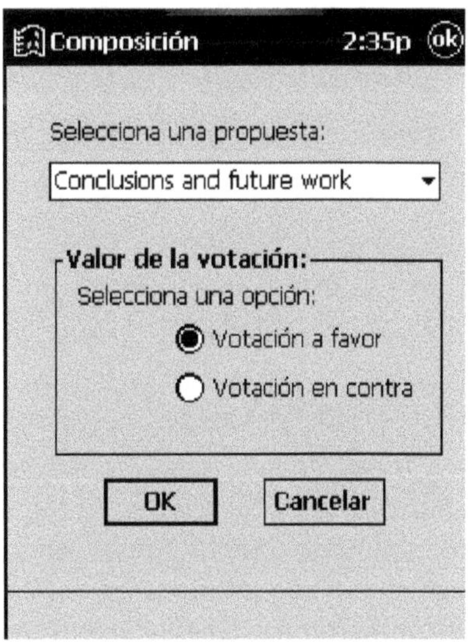

Figure 22-7. Polling a proposal.

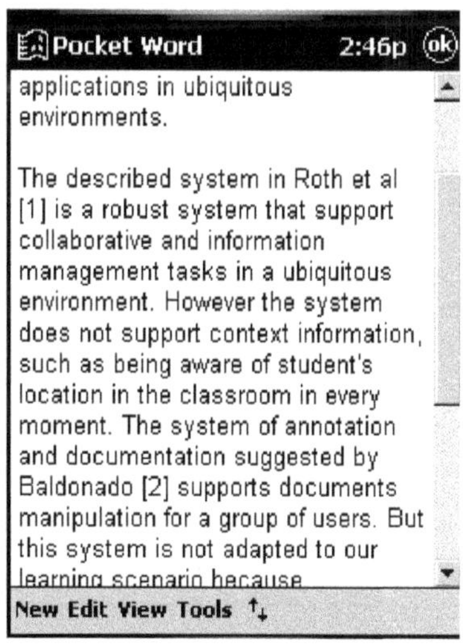

Figure 22-8. Solutions proposed

We have developed the AULA system considering indicators and analysis strategies of group work [16,17] to assist the teacher in evaluation. During the process of composition writing, the user's actions are structured as user's traces. Every action accomplished by a student is recorded by the system in its database as a trace. The teacher may later consult such traces to analyze more easily issues such as: the progress of each student in their language development (globally as well as in particular areas), the student's reaction to errors made by other members of the group or the participation history of a student in previous activities (see Figure 9).

Finally, the teacher chats with the group about the conclusions and possible corrections of the composition.

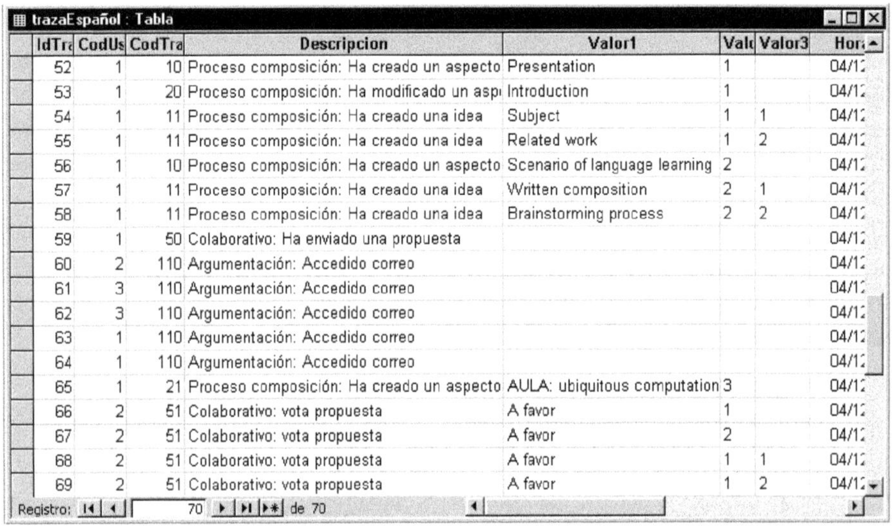

trazaEspañol : Tabla

IdTra	CodUs	CodTra	Descripcion	Valor1	Valo	Valor3	Hor
52	1	10	Proceso composición: Ha creado un aspecto	Presentation	1		04/1:
53	1	20	Proceso composición: Ha modificado un aspi	Introduction	1		04/1:
54	1	11	Proceso composición: Ha creado una idea	Subject	1	1	04/1:
55	1	11	Proceso composición: Ha creado una idea	Related work	1	2	04/1:
56	1	10	Proceso composición: Ha creado un aspecto	Scenario of language learning	2		04/1:
57	1	11	Proceso composición: Ha creado una idea	Written composition	2	1	04/1:
58	1	11	Proceso composición: Ha creado una idea	Brainstorming process	2	2	04/1:
59	1	50	Colaborativo: Ha enviado una propuesta				04/1:
60	2	110	Argumentación: Accedido correo				04/1:
61	3	110	Argumentación: Accedido correo				04/1:
62	3	110	Argumentación: Accedido correo				04/1:
63	1	110	Argumentación: Accedido correo				04/1:
64	1	110	Argumentación: Accedido correo				04/1:
65	1	21	Proceso composición: Ha creado un aspecto	AULA: ubiquitous computation	3		04/1:
66	2	51	Colaborativo: vota propuesta	A favor	1		04/1:
67	2	51	Colaborativo: vota propuesta	A favor	2		04/1:
68	2	51	Colaborativo: vota propuesta	A favor	1	1	04/1:
69	2	51	Colaborativo: vota propuesta	A favor	1	2	04/1:

Registro: 70 de 70

Figure 22-9. Traces stored in database system.

5. CONCLUSIONS AND FUTURE WORK

In this chapter we have presented a platform, called e-CLUB, to improve the traditional classroom environment with the collaborative and the ubiquitous computing paradigms. We have implemented a prototype, called AULA, developed for language education (in particular English as a Foreign Language, EFL) by means of composition writing in group.

Recent works on ubiquitous and mobile computing use a variety of different devices, like PDAs or telephones, and are based on wireless communications. In these works, the PC has been substituted by these new devices. The platform described in this chapter combines PC and PDAs, as well as other devices as printer, whiteboard, projector… In this way, we provide the user with two things: mobility (thanks to PDAs and wireless networks) and computing power (thanks to desktop PCs).

In a multimachine environment, the user must operate with several types of devices by means of different user interfaces. In our proposal, he/she interacts by means of one single user interface, that of the PDA. In this way, when the user makes a request to the system, he/she thinks that is using only one machine (his/her PDA). Actually, the requested function is performed by another machine (PC) transparently to the user.

During the composition writing process, a large amount of information is produced which is partly wasted. In particular, many of the student actions are not important at the beginning but they later play a relevant role for the teacher. A system such as ours is of great importance to the teacher because it records all these actions of the student (traces).

In addition, the teacher needs analysis tools to handle the recorded traces. We are researching on mechanisms of analysis of the composition process. We are working on analysis applications that may give conclusions about the working process and the final solution delivered by the students.

ACKNOWLEDGMENTS

This work was supported by projects TIC2002-01387 of the Ministerio de Educación y Cultura, PIGE-02-13 of the Universidad Rey Juan Carlos, and PBI-02-026 of the Junta de Comunidades de Castilla – La Mancha.

REFERENCES

1. Myers, B.A.; Using Hand-Helds and PCs Together., Communications of the ACM, 2001. 44(11), pp.34-41.
2. Myers, B.A.; Mobile Devices for Control., Conference of the 4th International Symposium Mobile HCI 2002, Pisa, Italy, Sept. 2002.
3. Abowd, G.D.; Classroom 2000: An experiment with the instrumentation of a living educational environment., IBM Systems Journal, Special issue on Pervasive Computing, 38 (4), pp. 508-530, 1999.
4. Soloway, E., Norris, C., Blumenfeld, P., Fishman, B., Krajcik, J., Marx, R.; Log on education: Handheld devices are ready-at-hand., Comm. ACM., Vol. 44- 6, pp 15-20, Jun 2001.
5. Weiser, M.; The future of Ubiquitous Computing on Campus., Comm. ACM., Vol. 41-1, pp. 41-42, Jan. 1998.
6. Roth, J., Unger, C.; Using Handheld Devices in Synchronous Collaborative Scenarios., Proceedings of the Second International Symposium on Handheld and Ubiquitous Computing, pp.187-199, Springer. Bristol, U.K., Sept. 2000.
7. Baldonado, M., Steve, C., Gwizdka, J., Paepcke, A.; Notable: At the Intersection of Annotations and Handheld Technology., Proceedings of the Second International Symposium on Handheld and Ubiquitous Computing, pp.100-113, Springer. Bristol, U.K., Sept. 2000.

8. Myres, B.A., Stiel, H., Gargiulo, R.; Collaboration Using Multiple PDAs Connected to a PC., Proceedings of the ACM 1998 Conference on Computer Supported Cooperative Work, pp. 285-294, Seattle, Washington, USA, 1998.
9. Danesh, A., Inkpen, K., Lau, F., Shu, K., Booth K.; GeneyTM: Designing a Collaborative Activity for the Palm TM Handheld Computer., Proceedings of the SIGCHI'01, pp. 388-395, Seattle, Washington, USA, 2001.
10. Zurita, G., Nussbaum, M.; Mobile CSCL Applications Supported by Mobile Computing., Pontificial Catholic University of Chile, Ret. Feb. 14, 2002 from http://julita.usask.ca/mable/Accepted.htm#Submission6
11. Ortega, M., Redondo, M.A, Paredes, M., Sánchez-Villalón, P.P., Bravo, C., Bravo, J.; Ubiquitous Computing and Collaboration: New paradigms in the classroom of the 21st Century., Computers and Education: Towards an Interconnected Society, M. Ortega and J. Bravo (Eds.), Kluwer Academic Publishers (2001), pp261-273.
12. Ortega M., Paredes M., Redondo M.A., Sánchez-Villalón P.P., Bravo C., Bravo J.; AULA: A Ubiquitous Language Teaching System, Upgrade Vol. II, Nº 5, pp.17-22. (2001).
13. Abowd, G.D., Mynatt, E.D.; Charting Past, Present, and Future Research in Ubiquitous Computing., ACM Transactions on Computer-Human Interaction, Vol 7, No 1, March 2000, pp 29-58.
14. Bravo, J., Ortega, M., Bravo, C., Redondo, M.A., Características ubicuas en los sistemas domóticos y su aprendizaje, III Congreso Internacional de Interacción Persona-Ordenador, pp 144-153, 2002.
15. Bravo, J., Ortega, M., Redondo, M.A., Bravo, C., Interacción abstracta en una clase ubicua, Revista Iberoamericana de Inteligencia Artificial, **16,** VI/02, 49-54 (2002).
16. Soller A.L.; Supporting Social Interaction in an Intelligent Collaborative Learning System, International Journal of Artificial Intelligence in Education, Vol. 12, pp. 40-62 (2001).
17. Barros, B., and Verdejo, M.F.; An approach to analyse collaboration when shared structured workspaces are used for carrying out group learning processes., Proceedings of Artificial Intelligence in Education. IOS Press, S. Lajoie and M. Vivet (Eds.), pp. 449-456. (1999).

Chapter 23

QUESTION GENERATOR SOFTWARE AGENTS VERSUS SHELLS FOR BUILDING HYPERTEXT

Effects on conceptual structure comprehension

Luis Facundo Maldonado Granados, Ph.D., Nerey Ortega del Castillo, M.Sc., Luis Bayardo Sanabria Rodríguez, M.Sc. , David Macías Mora M.Sc

Professors of Universidad Pedagógica Nacional, Bogotá TECNICE Group

Abstract: This paper summits the final results of the research project "Environment for Designing Meaningful Learning: an environment for designing hypertexts and learning assessment in social sciences"[5] The research purposes are: to compare a software based on constructivist strategy against another one based on a question generator software agent, focused on text comprehension, and to test the structuring effect on teaching performance of novel geography professors of an ontology based training process. The data analysis combines a statistical approach for the first objective with a qualitative analysis for the second one. The experimental conditions are organized around the two types of software. A question generator agent, in a hypertext, engages the student in a very intensive reading effort, and the student performance answering the questions formulated by the agent correlates positively with the scores in the evaluation test. The SIMAS constructive activity is more conceptually structuring than reading hypertexts elaborated by expert. Both types of software produce similar results in concept comprehension. Ontology based teacher training results in a positive effect on knowledge domain representation performance and the structures used are useful in the observation and description of knowledge representations made by the teachers.

Key words: Geography learning, teacher training, ontology, mental model, meaningful learning, percepts, perception, knowledge representation, conceptual structure, question generator software, frame systems, educational software, autonomous learning.

[5] Supported by Universidad Pedagógica Nacional and COLCIENCIAS, contract number 187/ 2000.

M. Llamas-Nistal et al. (eds.), Computers and Education. Towards a Lifelong Learning Society, 275–284.

5.1 Introduction

Pedagogical approaches focused on student developed constructions are becoming outstanding in the learning literature. Concept learning and conceptual structures are gaining research interest. Teacher's desire is that learners deal with conceptual structures as the experts do. A pedagogical challenge is how to accomplish this goal.

In a previous research we became aware of two reading hypertext related phenomena: in on hand, when reading hypertext, students seem less active than when playing computer games, and, on the other hand, when are presented with questions, search activity increases as well as the time allocated to read the hypertexts.

We are also motivated by readings which show representational activities as effective in assimilating conceptual structures accomplished by experts in the hypertexts.

As a consequence, this project compares one condition in which a question generator software agent behaves as a hypertext reader partner with one in which the reader is provided with a software tool for building a hypertext using a printed document as information source.

As an extension of this approach to teacher training, we evaluate learning transfer of novel teachers from the same experimental conditions to classroom activities.

5.2 Procedures

Frames or structured semantic networks are used as the fundamental basis to generate ontology structures applied to represent geography knowledge. Frame structures handle abstraction levels: a category and its own definition, a domain content associated with the category, and, finally an explanation linked to the category content. This quartet: category, definition, domain content, and explanation make a slot up. A node or frame is made of a set of slots and a frame network, of a set of nodes – frames -. As a consequence, a frame is an entity with slots as properties represented by category – identified by its name -, definition, domain content, and explanation. Figure 1 shows a frame example.

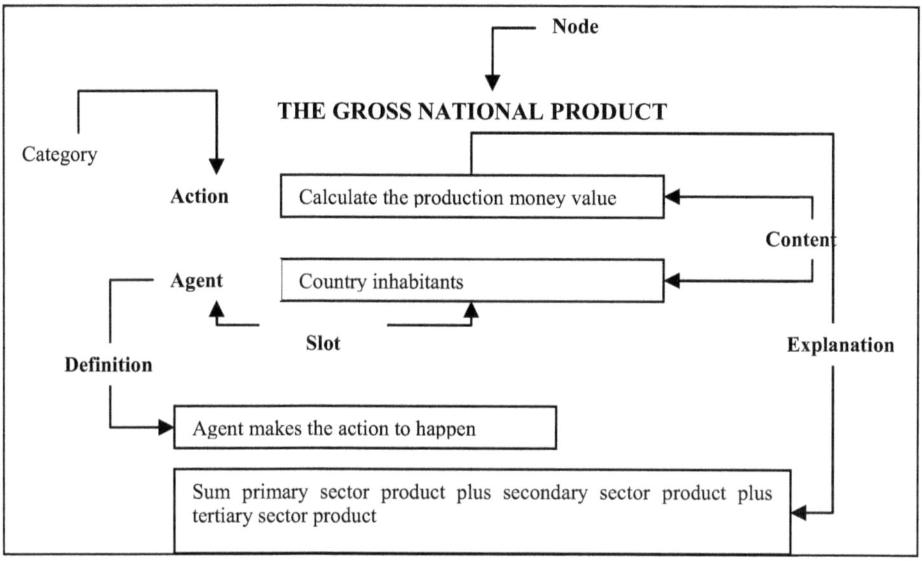

Figure 23-1: A framework example

Using the frame structure we developed a general model to represent content domain. Two types of software were originated in this model: hypertexts developed by experts in the knowledge domain of geography and a shell for the students to build their own hypertexts in the same domain.

Expert hypertexts include an additional software agent which identifies the hypertext structure, builds questions combining nodes and slots and fills a user model in. The user model allows following the student sequence of visited nodes.

To decide which slot to question about, the software agent pursues the next procedure:

a. Randomly select a node
b. Check if this is the node with less correct answers
c. Randomly select a slot of this node
d. Build a question about this slot
e. Keep the user answer and update the user model

According to this structure the software agent goes after these goals: make the user to read every hypertext node, identify the slot content and give the right answers.

When SIMAS is initialized it builds a map of the expert hypertext. It starts displaying a set of concept names – node candidates – and asks the student to link them with the appropriate relationship; once the link task is completed the system provides feedback on correct links and allows repeating this step. With the network of nodes the system builds the hypertext pages with navigation buttons. In the next step, it asks the student to build a set of slots for every node with the corresponding name, content, and explanation, provides feedback and asks if he or she wants to make changes. When every page slots are completed the hypertext is ready for navigation and the constructive process finishes.

In the hypertext condition, students study the expert hypertexts with the question generator included. In the SIMAS condition, the user takes a printed document on the domain of geography with the same content as the hypertext developed by experts and works his/her own hypertext in a step by step procedure.

In the hypertext condition the question generator assumes one of the next modalities: as an agent with or without initiative. When it behaves with initiative, it starts asking questions according to its own criteria, even if it accepts user's requests; as agent without initiative it waits to be activated by the user.

In the SIMAS condition it is organized in two variants: the student decides the network size to be configured or the system makes this choice.

Four students groups were organized as follows:

- Group 1. Builds own hypertext using SIMAS and decides the number of nodes for the network
- Group 2. Builds own hypertext using SIMAS and the network size is system controlled
- Group 3. Studies the expert hypertext with an autonomous question generator
- Group 4. Studies the expert hypertext with a question generator without initiative

The knowledge domain for the hypertext is geography and the knowledge level, ninth grade.

Two studies were conducted: the first one with ninth grade students evaluates concept learning; and the second with college education students tests the consequences of studying this type of materials on the teacher knowledge representation skills.

5.3 Part I: Effects on concept learning

In the ninth grade students the dependent variable is measured by means of a multiple choice test administered by a computer program. Using as framework the hypertext ontology, questions were classified according to the distance between nodes in the tree diagram, what we name "depth of inference".

121 ninth grade students from the same school participated in this study. They were organized in 5 courses, three of which studied in the morning and two in the afternoon. Each course was randomly distributed to form equal groups for each of the four experimental conditions.

Statistical results show, for the students which construct a framework system using SIMAS, a tendency to accomplish equal scores in concept comprehension and depth of inference than those who study the framework system elaborated by the experts.

GENERAL MANOVA		F(1,116)=,01; p<,9330	
TIPOSFTW	ACTVADOR	CALIFICA	Covar. JORNADA
HXT	AJ	4,513333	1,900000
HXT	SA	4,646667	1,966667
SIM	AJ	4,585714	1,928571
SIM	SA	4,678788	1,939394

Figure 23-2: Group means in the general test.

Figure 2 compares the four groups based on the student scores on a 30 question test. The means are statistically equal (F(1.116)=0.01 y p=0.9330).

The effect of study shift – morning or afternoon – calculated by means of the covariance is not statistically significant (t(116)=0.84, p=0.399, Figure 3).

Those who use SIMAS seem to score higher (average of 4.63) than those who use Hypertext and Question Generator (average of 4.58), however the differences are not statistically significant (F(1,1)=9.28; p=0.20).

In relation to the depth of inference as dependent variable, the same

GENERAL MANOVA	R: ,0783269 R-square: ,0061351 F(1,116) = ,7160648 p = ,39918				
variable	B-weight	Standard Error	beta	t(116)	p-level
JORNADA	,107434	,126960	,078327	,846206	,399180

Figure 23-3: Effects of study time as coverable.

groups are compared by means of a 20 items questionnaire. The average of hypertext group (4.24) is statistically equivalent to the SIMAS group's average (4.22) and consequently no significant differences are found (F(1,116)=0.007; p=0.92).

Concerning to the ontology, the same in both types of software, its effect seems to be strong for studying the instructional materials. In fact, it behaves as organizational tool in the information processing, and could help the long term memory to storage in a meaningful way. The results of this experiment are congruent with those of Jonassen (1993) in which the representation activities using production rules or semantic networks, supported by computer programs, do not generate significant differences of learning outcomes.

If we compare the two group comprehension of texts, the SIMAS group score a little bit higher than the one with hypertext and question generator agent, but these differences are not statistically different.

Those students who used hypertext with the question generator agent, as more correct answers they got, better scores they accomplished in a comprehension test after a few days of studying the instructional software. In a regression analysis the number of correct answers to the question generator agent correlates with the comprehension test scores (Beta=0.67; t(36)=2.07, p=0.04559). This relation does not hold for the number of questions answered (Beta=-0.41; t(36)=1.32, p=0.19). This means that there is a strong effect on comprehension of answering correctly the question formulated by the question generator agent, not just of using it. Indeed, this is a credit for this type of software as learning tool.

5.4 Part 2: Effects on the teacher knowledge representation skills

To analyze the consequences of studying the two types of materials on knowledge representation and teaching skills, a sample of 20 education college students was selected and randomly assigned to the hypertext and SIMAS condition to have two groups, each with 10 members. Three kinds of activities were scheduled for them to perform: hypertext study, teaching planning, and teaching performance.

The content domain belongs to geography and considers the following aspects: economic, physical and political ones. Table 1 summarizes the outcomes of the SIMAS group in the Physical Geography module. Similar tables were elaborated for every module, for the hypertext group as well as for the SIMAS group.

Tables are divided in two sections: The section on the left is a matrix that crosses comprehension levels with depth levels found for the group, and the section on the right shows the analysis of categories used by the students.

The **Connection Index** means the average number of links included in the student representation.

The **Comprehension Level** depends on the number of slots assigned to the nodes or entities. Based on this criterion, each node is assigned to a comprehension level by this way: Level I: entities with 1 to 3 slots; Level II: entities with 4 to 6 slots; and Level III: entities with more than 6 slots.

The **Depth Level** is the place on a sequence of nodes linked by the Instance Category or Relationship. The first level corresponds with the nodes at the higher level, the second at the next lower place, and so on.

Table 1. Summary of concepts and hierarchical levels. Module of physical Geography, SIMAS.

DEPTH LEVEL	COMPREHENSION LEVEL				CATEGORY REPORT					
	I	II	III	Average	**Software**	**Fr.**	**Index**	**Student**	**Fr.**	**Index**
I	4,43	3,29	0,43	2,71	Instance	75	0,362	Outcome	6	0,029
					Component	40	0,193	Production	5	0,024
II	0,71	0,57	0,14	0,48	Agent	3	0,014	Cause	5	0,024
					Action	9	0,043	Function	12	0,058
III	0,71	0,29	0,00	0,50	Time	2	0,010	Characterist.	10	0,048
					Consequen.	16	0,077	Purpose	1	0,005
Average	1,95	1,38	0,28		Beneficiary	1	0,005	Origin	4	0,019
					Territory	8	0,039	Factors	7	0,034
Connection Index				10				Environment	3	0,014
					Total	154	0,744		53	0,256

Inferences are supported on the average values of comprehension as well as depth levels. First of all we consider the times students apply each entity at a particular depth level of comprehension, next we calculate the sum of entities for the group at each cell, and then we divide this value by the number of students in the group to get the average at each cell. Finally we find the cell average of entities out.

On the right section of the table, each category is described by its name, frequency of use, and index. The category name is assigned by the researchers based on the student semantic structure; the frequency of use is the average of times that the group uses this category; and the index is the probability of using this category. This section provides information to compare the frequency of categories used by the software with those used by the students.

Based on the data tables we realized that the SIMAS Group in the first module represents concept with more links than the Hypertext and Question

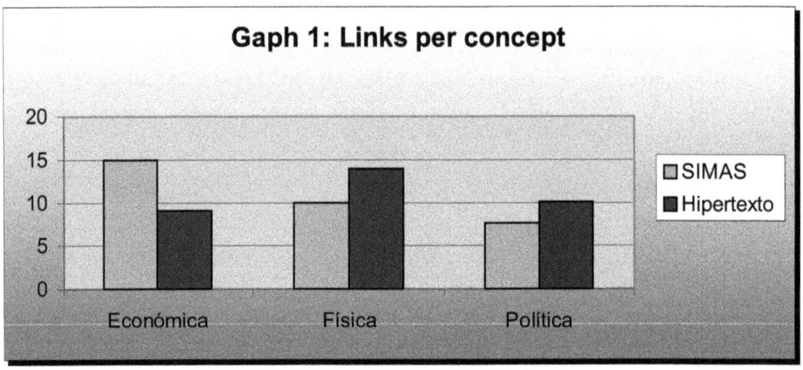

Generator group, but this difference was not held for the next modules in which the tendency changed, as it is illustrated by Graph 1.

On the other hand, category transfer is bigger for the SIMAS Group than for the Hypertext and Question Generator Group (Graph 2).

The overall student representations were those learned from the software but applied to different information of the knowledge domain. Those who studied the content domain by building framework systems using SIMAS, teach and assess concept learning similarly as those who studied using hypertext with the question generator agent.

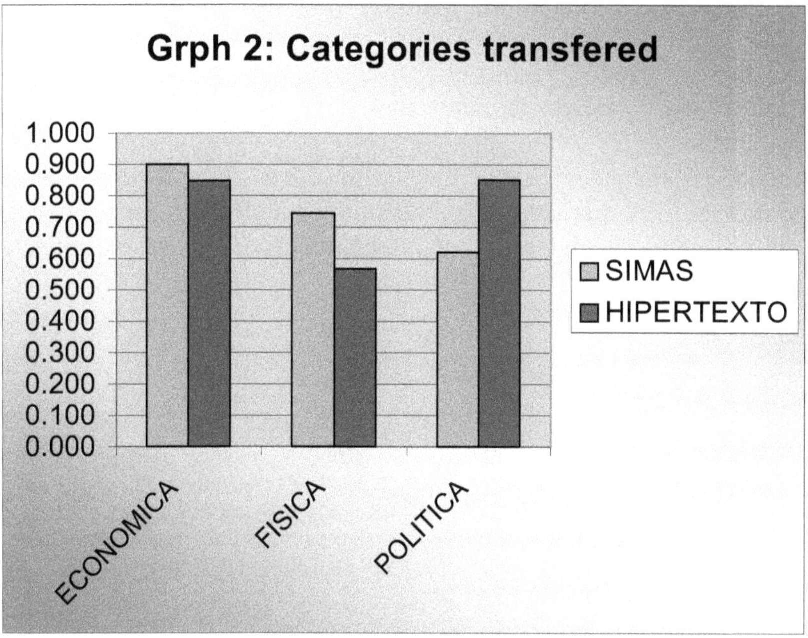

5.5 Conclusion

The data collected from this study support these conclusions: a question generator agent, in a hypertext, engages the student in a very intensive reading effort, and the SIMAS constructive activity is more conceptually structuring than reading hypertexts elaborated by experts.

On the other hand, education college students which studied the content domain using SIMAS taught more structured classes and with fewer ontology categories than their partners who studied the content domain from hypertexts elaborated by experts and with a question generator agent embodied. The differences grew as the class sessions went on.

The constructive activity privileged by the SIMAS learning environment makes the student transfer more categories from the instructional material to the teaching stage. On the contrary, activation of previous knowledge and concept contrast generated by the question generator agent is related to the introduction of categories not included in the learning material.

Novell teachers used nodes with fewer categories and lower levels of depth than the hypertexts elaborated by experts.

An important result drawn from the data analysis of the effects of the question generator agent on the student learning is that correct answers to the agent question predict good scores on the final evaluation test. This means that the agent behaves as mind tool helpful to increase the hypertext comprehension.

Finally, the characterization method for the teaching assessing process is a contribution of this research because the ontological perspective allows contrasting the actual teacher representations with those consolidated by experts.

REFERENCES

1. BIEMANS, H.J.A. and SIMONS, R.J. (1999). Computer – assisted instructional strategies for promoting coneptual change. In New perspectives on conceptual change, edited by SCHNOTZ, W. And CARRETERO, M. Amsterdam: Pergamon Edit.
2. BRACHMAN, R.J. (1979). On the epistemological status of semántic networks. In Brachman and Levesque (1985): Readings in Knowledge Representations. Los Altos CA: Morgan Kaufmann.
3. FLAMENT, C. (1972). Teoría de Grafos y Estructuras de Grupo. Madrid: Editorial Tecnos, S.A.
4. HALL, G. (1991). Perceptual and Associative Learning. Oxford: Clarendon Press.
5. HAYES-ROTH, B. (1996). An Architecture for Adaptive Intelligent Systems. Tomado de: Computational Theories of Interaction and Agency. Edit. Agre, P.E. & Rosenschein, S.J. Cambridge, Massachusetts. U.S.A., p. 334-338.
6. JONASSEN, D. H. (1995). Operationalizing mental models: strategies for assessing mental models to support meaningful learning and design – supportive learning environments. www-cscl95.indiana.edu/cscl95/jonassen.html.
7. JONASSEN, D. H.(1993). Changes in Knoledge Structures form Building Semantic Net versus Production Rule Representations of Subject Content. Journal of Computer Based Instruction, 20, 4, 86-106.
8. LUHMANN, N. (1984). System und Funktion. Frankfort: Edit. Verlag. Traducción: Sociedad y Sistema: la ambición de la teoría. Barcelona: Edit. Paidós, 1990.
9. MALDONADO, G.L.F., ORTEGA, N., SANABRIA, R.L.B., MACIAS, M.D. (2002). Ontologías y Aprendizaje de la Geografía: Software para Representar, Software para Comprender. Bogotá: Universidad Pedagógica Nacional y Colciencias.
10. MILLER, G. A. (1956). The magic number seven, plus or minus two: some limits on our capacity for processing information. Psychological Review, 63, 81-97
11. MINSKY, Marvin (1974). A framework for representing knowledge. In Haugeland, J. (1984), editor, Mind Design, pages 95-128, MIT Press, Cambridge MA. Reprinted in Brachman and Levesque (Eds).
12. MURDOCK, B. B. (1961): The retention of individual items. Journal of Experimental Psychology, 62, 618-625.
13. MURDOCK, B. B. (1965). A test of the limited capacity hypothesis. Journal of Experimental Psychology, 69, 237-240.
14. SOWA, J. F. (1986). Conceptual Structures: Information Processing in Mind and Machine. Reading MA: Addison Wesley Publishing Company.
15. SOWA, J. F. (1987). Semantics Networks. In Encyclopedia of Artificial Intelligence. New York, N.Y.: Edit. John Willey and Sons. Edited by Stuart C. Shapiro.

Index

M. Llamas-Nistal et al. (eds.), Computers and Education. Towards a Lifelong Learning Society, 285–287.

GPSR Compliance
The European Union's (EU) General Product Safety Regulation (GPSR) is a set of rules that requires consumer products to be safe and our obligations to ensure this.

If you have any concerns about our products, you can contact us on

ProductSafety@springernature.com

In case Publisher is established outside the EU, the EU authorized representative is:

Springer Nature Customer Service Center GmbH
Europaplatz 3
69115 Heidelberg, Germany

www.ingramcontent.com/pod-product-compliance
Ingram Content Group UK Ltd.
Pitfield, Milton Keynes, MK11 3LW, UK
UKHW020135160926
475607UK00003B/60
* 9 7 8 1 4 0 2 0 1 5 9 9 1 *